More Powerful Literacies

Edited by
Lyn Tett, Mary Hamilton and Jim Crowther

niace
promoting adult learning

Published by NIACE

© 2012 National Institute of Adult Continuing Education
(England and Wales)
21 De Montfort Street
Leicester
LE1 7GE

Company registration no. 2603322
Charity registration no. 1002775

NIACE has a broad remit to promote lifelong learning opportunities for
adults. NIACE works to develop increased participation in education and
training, particularly for those who do not have easy access because of class,
gender, age, race, language and culture, learning difficulties or disabilities,
or insufficient financial resources.

You can find NIACE online at www.niace.org.uk

Cataloguing in Publication Data

A CIP record for this title is available from the British Library

ISBN 978-1-86201-584-5 (print)
ISBN 978-1-86201-585-2 (PDF)
ISBN 978-1-86201-586-9 (ePub)
ISBN 978-1-86201-587-6 (online)
ISBN 978-1-86201-588-3 (Kindle)

Cover design by Book Production Services.

Designed and typeset by Cambridge Publishing Management, Cambridge, UK.
Printed and bound in the UK.

Contents

Foreword

I have been saying the title of this book over and over again to myself to work out what it means. Every time I say the words 'more powerful literacies', another meaning emerges, and I think I have now collected around half a dozen different possible interpretations. The emphasis can be on the first word: here are *more* powerful literacies – so the title is saying that earlier we had examples of those literacies that are powerful and here are some more of them. Or does it refer to the book of that name? Here is more of that book called *Powerful Literacies*. Then there are the first two words: 'more powerful'. Is the book about literacies that are even more powerful – more powerful than earlier powerful literacies? We could go on and look at the word 'literacies': how and why is it connected to the word 'powerful'? Is literacy the place to go to in order to examine and take hold of power? The possibilities seem endless with this short noun phrase of a book title.

Of course, the title has all of these meanings. This exciting and innovative book continues on from the earlier book *Powerful Literacies*. It has more examples and it goes into more depth about power and how literacies are powerful. It is also an unusual book in that it moves successfully back and forth between two strong meanings of the word 'literacies'. There is the meaning that starts out from everyday life and examines all the different ways of reading and writing, and the importance that they have for us. Jane Mace's detailed study of signatures is a good example of this, and what is more powerful than knowing when to sign something and when not to sign? This meaning of 'literacies' is fundamental to a social practice view of reading and writing. The other meaning of 'literacies' concerns the teaching and learning of reading and writing, whereby literacy programmes can empower through learning, and where teaching and learning can revolve around the sharing of power. Often these two meanings come together: in that understanding everyday practices can be a starting point for a way in to teaching and learning. This book's richness lies in how it puts studies of such everyday practices side by side with practical strategies for adult literacy education and work by new writers.

The chapters of the book have been written by people from all around the world. They sit well together, and even though there may be such very different contexts in India, Scotland, New Zealand and elsewhere, they all seem to be dealing with issues of mutual interest. Being based in England, what strikes me is that so much has happened in the world of literacy since the original *Powerful Literacies* book was published in 2001. When the original articles were being written, the Moser Report had only recently been published, Tony Blair was a popular prime minister and 'New Labour' was fashionable. The government focus on literacy had not yet been formalised and there was no Skills for Life Strategy. In the space of just a decade, this major strategy has come and gone. Those were heady years of constant media attention for literacy in England, with new programmes, new training, new forms of assessment, new funding and new research. Much of this has disappeared completely in a very short time. While it is still too early to understand the longer-term impact of this flurry of activity, part of the positive legacy of that period can be seen in this book, with a new generation of researchers and educators, with broader perspectives, and a sense of hope about the possibilities of establishing more powerful literacies.

David Barton, March 2012

More powerful literacies: An introduction

MARY HAMILTON, LYN TETT AND JIM CROWTHER

Background

We originally planned this book as an update to our edited volume *Powerful Literacies*, published more than a decade ago, but it has taken on a life of its own. The inspiration for the original book was a conference sponsored by the organisation Research and Practice in Adult Literacy and the University of Edinburgh. The aim of the conference was to bring together the insights of researchers and practitioners alike to enable new understandings of adult literacy informed by developments in their respective fields of work. This new book retains only two chapters from the original volume, which are as relevant now as when they were first written. The remainder of the chapters have been rewritten or are completely new contributions, reflecting the creative scholarship and practice emerging in adult literacies, as well as the changing social, cultural and political context.

At the turn of the twenty-first century, when *Powerful Literacies* was published, policy interest in literacy (in schools as well as in adult education) was high. This was in no small part due to the influence of international literacy league tables being created following initiatives such as the International Adult Literacy Surveys (OECD, 1997; 2000), which have shaped the literacy debate and our understanding of the issues involved in supporting literacy learning. In the policy agendas of both 'developing' as well as 'over-developed' countries, literacy has been linked with economic prosperity as part of the corporate model of human resource development that preoccupies many governments and international

1

organisations. This narrowly conceived model of literacy squeezes out opportunities for thinking more broadly about what literacy means in social worlds and the issues involved with developing alternative practices.

International pressures have intensified over recent years, and continue to exert a powerful influence on the field of adult literacy policy and practice. Combined with a culture of audit and accountability, and large fluctuations in funding, these pressures make for a challenging and often contradictory experience for practitioners and learners alike. A new 'space' needs to be created, where we can collectively imagine literacy differently (Gutierrez, 2008). Currently missing are the experiences of practitioners and researchers, as well as broader understandings of literacy and people's everyday use reading and writing.

The purpose of this book, like the previous one, is to contribute towards opening such a space for divergent critical voices to be heard; ones that are grounded in research and practice about the meanings of literacy and what it means to work with literacy learners.

Before we can speak about 'powerful literacies' we need to set the phrase against enduring assumptions made about adult literacy practice. The dominant model systematically fails to address issues of power relations in people's lives, including what they can do about them. The selection and distribution of literacy by and to different social groups is not something that happens neutrally, as it were, separate from the interests that pattern society. Instead, they are embedded in its infrastructure of power relationships. Literacy is deeply and inescapably bound up with producing, reproducing and maintaining unequal arrangements of power.

The literacy ladder

Definitions of what it means to be literate are always shifting. Literacy is socially constructed and cannot be seen outside of the powerful interests and forces that seek to fix it in particular ways. The common way to think about literacy at the moment is by seeing it as a ladder that people climb up. This begins in schooling, with adult literacy the extension of the process in post-school contexts. The emphasis is, therefore, on standardising literacy accomplishments: tests, core skills and uniform learning outcomes that are specified in advance of the learning process. People are ranked from bottom to top, with the emphasis placed on what they can't do rather than what they can. This leads to a deficit model whereby those on the bottom rungs are perceived as lacking skills that they need.

The frameworks used to define this ladder are top-down, constructed largely in terms of pre-vocational and vocationally relevant literacy requirements. Consequently, they do not recognise the validity of people's own definitions, uses and aspirations for literacy, so they are *disempowering* in the sense that they are neither negotiable nor learner-centred nor locally responsive. They define what counts as 'real literacy' and silence everything else. If, however, the emphasis is put on how adults can and want to use the many varieties of literacies, then the focus moves to what people have, rather than what they lack, and what motivates them, rather than what is foisted on them by others.

New research and practice has been at the forefront of undermining the conceptual adequacy of the discourse of deficit. It does so by grounding literacies in a social and ecological context. They are no longer disembodied skills, but aspects of real people's lives in everyday situations. What has become known as the 'New Literacy Studies' (NLS) (Barton 2007; Street and Lefstein, 2008) uses an approach that sets out from a different point – starting from the local, everyday experience of literacy in particular communities of practice. This approach is based upon a belief that literacy only has meaning within its particular context of social practice and does not transfer unproblematically across contexts. There are different literacy practices in different domains of social life, such as education, religion, workplaces, public services, families and community activities. These change over time, with different literacies supported and shaped by the different institutions and social relationships. Detailed studies of particular situations can be revealing about these differences and in turn help to identify the broader meanings, values and uses that literacy has for people in their day-to-day lives. We would argue that any research that purports to increase our understanding of literacies in society must take account of these meanings, values and uses; indeed they are the source of the ideas that statisticians use to interpret their findings. NLS, then, dispenses with the idea that there is a single literacy that can be unproblematically taken for granted. We have to begin to think in pluralistic terms about the variety of literacies that are used in different contexts in order to make meaning – and in order to make literacy practice meaningful to people. This is particularly significant in contexts of increased migration leading to the creation of new diversities and hybrid cultures (Cope and Kalantzis, 1999).

Another important strand of thinking about new literacies has developed from the rapid and radical changes in communication technologies that are also shaping literacy practices. The right of access to knowledge – including the infrastructure and use of communication technology – was discussed by Fiona Frank in the original *Powerful Literacies* book (Frank, 2001). In a world where electronically produced text carries meaning, exclusion from digital technologies can have disempowering consequences – especially for life in the home, community and workplace. New 'digital divides' have potentially important implications for power relations between tutors and students, perhaps, in some respects, helping to equalise them. New modes and conventions for communicating through information and communication technologies raise issues about what counts as 'real' literacy (Coiro *et al.*, 2008). The juxtaposition of icons, imagery and text is presenting new challenges for the process of communication and its associated literacies (Kress, 2009). In an information rich world, there is an increasing gap between those with access to information and those denied it. Redistributing information and making it accessible to the 'information poor' is an important educational and political task. Moreover, the demands of a 'knowledge economy' and the so-called 'information society' cannot simply be constrained within the traditional conventions of literacy understanding. Its development exposes the inadequacy of current thinking that constitutes literacy as externally defined rungs on a ladder that has been designed as an extension of initial schooling, rather than in terms of the real shape of literacy practices and goals in adult life. Rather than seeing literacy as a tool for organising our knowledge that is consistent with an economistic global vision, we need other ways of conceptualising literacy that can embody more democratic ideals.

Making power visible

Power that is recognisable is also negotiable (Melucci, 1988, p. 250)

Literacy that obscures the power relations inscribed in its construction ultimately disempowers. It treats as technical what is in fact socially and politically constructed, and is therefore misleading. In one sense, therefore, powerful literacies have to be oppositional. They have to open up, expose and counteract the institutional processes and professional mystique wherein dominant forms of literacy are placed beyond question. They have to challenge the way 'literacy' is socially distributed to different groups. They have to reconstruct the learning and teaching process in a way that positions students as politically and socially more equal. In another sense they should be propositional; that is they have to construct alternative ways of addressing literacy practices and interests grounded in real lives and literacy needs. They need to be critical and political too. The agenda for developing powerful literacies has to be informed by issues of social justice, equality and democracy in everyday life rather than be limited to a narrow, functional definition primarily addressed to the needs of the economy.

Researchers and practitioners have to construct alliances in order to develop their own agency to act back on the forces that seek to shackle them to a narrow and impoverished vision of literacy. Powerful literacies involve constructing a curriculum that enables workers to learn and share experience. This acts as a counter to the powerful forces that have dominated literacy discourse. Increasingly, the stage for these alliances has to be global as well as local. The forces that are impacting on literacy practice are – as many of the accounts here demonstrate – not restricted by national boundaries. Powerful literacies involve opening up the many voices that are silenced by the dominant definitions of literacy. It involves people deciding for themselves what is 'really useful literacy' and using it to act, individually and collectively, on their circumstances to take greater control over them. Literacy is a resource for people acting back against the forces that limit their lives. While literacy has to be understood broadly in that it involves social processes of making and communicating meanings, the importance of textual communication always figures prominently. It involves learning to be critical readers and writers in order to detect and handle the inherently ideological dimension of literacy, and the role of literacy in the enactment and production of power (Crowther and Tett, 2011).

Powerful literacies speak to an agenda informed by concerns to extend the autonomy of individuals and communities that have been marginalised and ignored. The emphasis is shifted from the idea of literacy as a deficit to an examination of people's literacy practices that recognises difference and diversity, and challenges how these differences are viewed by society. The deficit, if there is one to be located, is in a society that excludes, reduces and ridicules the rich means of communication that exist among its people. The policy discourse, both within the UK and in the wider world, is premised on a basic skills model that prioritises the surface features of literacy and language; we show, through a variety of contexts and practices, how inappropriate this is.

5

Structure of the book

In this book, voices are heard that subscribe to a variety of positions. The themes that they raise and the conceptual resources deployed reflect a range of perspectives that have a common aim of addressing questions of power, literacy and democratic life. The book is divided into three sections, each reflecting important themes that underpin an analysis of powerful literacies. The first section establishes the theoretical and policy frameworks upon which the book is predicated, and shows how literacies are situated in different geographical places, intellectual domains and cultural contexts. It also raises critical awareness of the policy discourses around literacy and how they construct the learner, the teacher, the institutional environment for literacy, and the goals and outcomes of literacies learning. In the second section, the concern is with making power visible, both in terms of the ideas that drive 'empowering initiatives' and in terms of the limitations on what has been achieved because of powerful forces in society. The third section focuses on the challenges faced by those learning, teaching and using literacy in contemporary societies, and the means used to resist these forces. It discusses how learners and teachers can be repositioned as active subjects and citizens rather than passive objects. It also examines the differential positions of tutors/students and how these can shift, and emphasises the importance of having a new vision – enabling choices that allow people to use literacy for their own purposes. The chapters in these three sections are described below.

Theoretical and policy frameworks
Systematic and sustained theoretical critique is needed to shift the literacy agenda away from its current preoccupations and limitations. At the forefront of this work is Brian Street, who sets out the conceptual framework for many of the contributions that follow by showing that there is a range of discourses that impact on both what we understand literacy to be and on our approaches to it. He shows that what are regarded as 'the basics' need to be broadened so that the view of literacy is shifted from a focus on rules towards a more creative and user-centred approach.

Mary Hamilton and Lyn Tett offer an overview and critique of the policy context within which many of the developments described in the rest of the book need to be understood. They focus on the four countries of the UK and Ireland, as well as considering the wider international scene. They suggest that some competing policy discourses offer possibilities for more open definitions of literacy than the dominant 'human resources development' model. With the ascendancy of the latter, the contestation of policy and the opportunity to inscribe in it more critical, creative and socially useful approaches to literacy practice require robustness, as the trajectories of the four countries studied affirm. The dominant policy discourse may set limits and constraints, but it also has to be engaged with dialectically to maximise the openings and spaces for more powerful literacies to emerge.

Making power visible

Literacy is, intrinsically, both personal and political, and this connection is evident in the most innocuous of acts of writing – the signature. Jane Mace, in her contribution reprinted from the original *Powerful Literacies*, explores the personal significance of being able to write your own name, especially in contexts where literacy is assumed and is therefore an embodiment of power. She suggests that to be unable to write one's own name in a society full of writing is equivalent to being unable to inscribe one's *self* in that society. She argues that the right to give or to withhold your name is an important civil right. A full-literacy life in a lettered world means a person being able to choose whether to write her or his name so that it can be read, or, when she or he so desires, in a way which is theirs and theirs alone.

The setting for Tannis Atkinson's chapter is Canada, but the theme addressed is universal. The author systematically and critically examines the political power of statistics by demonstrating the long-standing interest of governments in citizens' productivity, as indicated by their 'level of literacy'. She shows how literacy statistics have been increasingly refined in a way that draws on a troubled history of social engineering to establish criteria for distinguishing who should be the focus of policy attention, and how, in a neo-liberal era, international surveys such as the IALS have precisely articulated the literacy required of productive members of society. However, she ends with a message of hope about how practitioners might use statistics to construct compelling narratives showing that dominant literacy practices perpetuate inequities, and develops counter arguments to the dominant market-logic literacy.

Amy Burgess examines issues of power and authority in relation to writing, exploring the relationship between the discourses that adult literacy students draw on as they write and their developing identities as writers. Her data suggests that some of the most salient discourses on which the students drew positioned them as deficient or socially sub-ordinate, and that this negative positioning impeded their development as writers. Her study challenges the dominant view of literacy learners in the official policies of England and many other countries, which see adults' different ways of writing as stemming from deficiencies or 'problems'. She argues that difficulties with literacy often have social causes and are bound up with issues of identity, which need to be addressed before students can make real progress. Discourses that position learners as subordinate and/or deficient need to be recognised and actively challenged by teachers and learners.

Form-filling of various kinds now plays a very visible role in adult education as mandatory processes of accountability and recording have gained increasing weight within a more general culture of auditing. In their chapter in 2001's *Powerful Literacies*, Fawns and Ivanic raised issues of disempowerment and surveillance through considering the politics of official forms. They showed how form-filling is not just a matter of decoding and spelling, but a social practice imbued with issues of identity and power. Sandra Varey and Karin Tusting continue this exploration of the nature of paperwork and show that form-filling in an adult education setting is a complex, situated social practice; meanings are negotiated within the specific teaching practices and relationships that are built up in this setting. While many constraints and tensions emerge, it is never-theless possible for tutors and learners to work with these constraints in creative ways that promote the autonomy of the learner and the pedagogical practices the tutor is committed to developing.

While the hegemony of literacy for 'human resources development' is structurally powerful and ubiquitous, the final chapter in this section continues the theme of the uses of literacy in opposition to established practices and ideas by arguing that literacy can contribute to democracy as a *way of life*. Literacy, access to information and effective communication skills, Jim Crowther and Lyn Tett suggest, must be considered as part of the way in which inequalities of power are systematically reproduced. Literacy education should contribute towards enabling people to interrogate the claims made on their behalf and, in turn, encourage them to develop the skills, confidence and powers of analysis to make their own voices heard. Adult literacy workers with an interest in social purpose have to contest the meaning of citizenship, since democracy is too important to be left to the policy-makers and politicians. Tutors need to become resources that enable individuals and collectives to take some control over their lives by building a broad and rich curriculum that firmly embraces literacy education for democracy.

Resistance and challenges

Working back against powerful forces involves, among other things, a repositioning of the 'teacher' and the 'learner'. In contrast to a good deal of literacy work, which starts from individual need and personal development, the pieces in this section locate adult literacies in processes of collective struggles against inequality and injustice. If literacy is to be powerful, it has to be a resource enabling less powerful 'communities of interest' to regain some measure of control over their lives. It will involve, in one way or another, inserting literacy into a process of social action and collective organisation. The obstacles to this are often formidable. Narrow definitions of literacy can serve to shackle individuals and groups to a 'deficit view' of themselves, limiting their ability to assert, communicate and act on their own interests with a more positive sense of their identities. The accounts in this section document work to develop strategies for enabling people to acquire a voice and to organise effectively in order to make these voices heard.

Maggie Feeley looks at the connection between literacy, care and equality through a four-year ethnographic study of childhood and adult literacy practices with survivors of institutional abuses in Irish industrial schools. She shows that care is a pivotal factor in all literacy work – formal and informal. Across the contexts of home, community and adult learning, evidence of love, care and solidarity were cited as the antithesis to the oppression, violence and abuses of the institutional schooling experience. The concept of state care also emerged from the research as a determining foundation upon which other aspects of care are constructed. Feeley proposes a model of learning care that foregrounds the affective dimension of literacy as a social practice, and goes on to discuss the practical implications for adopting a care-full approach to literacy education.

Malini Ghose and Disha Mullick reflect on the work of Nirantar, a feminist-inspired agency working in India with the aim of empowering women through addressing their subordinate economic, social and political position. In a context where women's lives are routinely subject to both physical and mental violence, this kind of work is both difficult and urgent. In their first example, the authors discuss how the curriculum and the development of literacy skills are grounded in thematic material, such as land and water, which also brings to the fore structures of power, such as caste, class and gender relations. In their second example, they describe their work in promoting women as journalists, using both traditional and digital media, in the production of a local newspaper. This provides opportunities for developing the skills of literacy in a setting allied to the public sphere of information and politics. By drawing on their own experiences, both the process and results of these projects/interventions are candidly analysed in terms of their impact on women's lives.

The next chapter moves us into the powerful world of global corporate practice and its intersection with language and literacies. Judy Hunter argues that the issue of transnational migration and employment has become a political and social flashpoint in an era of globalisation wherein migrant populations are frequently marginalised. She draws on a study of communication demands among skilled employees in Aotearoa (New Zealand) to examine how workplaces both enable and constrain migrants' agency, participation and learning. Although national policies serve the dominant business and government views that high scores on standardised language and literacy skills are the key to employment, Hunter challenges these views. Her case studies show that situated practices, purposes and relationships around texts actually have more influence on the way they are received than the language itself.

The role of sport in motivating adult learners is addressed through the work of the Glory and Dismay Football Literacy Programme, which is discussed by John Player. His work with the Freirean-inspired Adult Learning Project in Edinburgh shows how everyday interests, particularly among adult males traditionally seen as 'hard-to-reach' learners, can be a resource for a rich curriculum of study that simultaneously aims to 'conscientise' and develop literacy skills. The status of football in contemporary culture makes it an ideal lens for studying globalisation, inequality, racism and other systematic processes of exploitation and marginalisation – as students 'read the world' of football they also develop the skills of 'writing the word'.

The implications of using social media for literacy and language learning are taken up by James Simpson and Richard Gresswell. Their chapter examines how young adult refugees learning English can challenge the limited identity positions offered to them by the discourses and policies that govern their lives and learning. They argue that when students are enabled – through the use of new technology – to claim a broader range of identity positions, their scope for language development and identity making (and remaking) also extends. They show that there is a space for an ESOL pedagogy corresponding to the everyday lives of young people outside the classroom that would enable literacy practices to emerge at the intersection of new technology, language learning and global culture.

Finally, the cultural politics of language and literacy is the focus of Alan Addison's contribution, which is reprinted from *Powerful Literacies* (2001). Although Scots is an official language in Scotland it has, historically, been marginalised in the curriculum of schooling and in adult literacy. This has begun to change, particularly in schools, although in adult literacy such work is still marginal and under-exploited. This fact should concern policy-makers subscribing to a social practice perspective focused on sensitivity to the context of learners' lives. Addison shows that using the language of the community can be a powerful resource for adult learning and a locus for intergenerational family learning.

References

Barton, D. (2007) *Literacy: An Introduction to the Ecology of Written Language.* Blackwell.

Coiro, J., Lankshear, C., Knobel, M. and Leu, D. (eds) (2008) *Handbook of Research on New Literacies.* Mahwah, NJ: Lawrence Erlbaum Associates.

Cope, B. and Kalantzis, M. (eds) (1999) *Multiliteracies: Literacy Learning and the Design of Social Futures.* Routledge.

Crowther, J. and Tett, L. (2011) 'Critical and social literacy practices from the Scottish adult literacy experience: resisting deficit approaches to learning', *Literacy*, Vol. 45 No 3, pp. 126–31.

Frank, F. (2001) 'Empowering literacy learners and teachers: the challenge of ICT', in Crowther, J., Hamilton, M. and Tett, L. (eds) *Powerful Literacies.* NIACE, pp. 144–54.

Gutierrez, K. (2008) 'Developing a Socio-critical Literacy in the Third Space', *Reading Research Quarterly*, Vol. 43 No 2, pp. 148–64.

Kress, G. (2009) *Multimodality: Exploring Contemporary Methods of Communication.* Routledge.

Melucci, A. (1988) 'Social movements and democratisation of everyday life', in Keane, J. (ed.) *Civil Society and the State.* Verso, pp. 245–60.

Organization of Economic Co-operation and Development (1997) *Literacy Skills for the Knowledge Society.* Paris: OECD.

Organization of Economic Co-operation and Development (2000) *Literacy in the Information Age: Final Report of the International Adult Literacy Survey*. Paris: OECD.

Street, B. (1996) 'Literacy, economy and society', *Literacy Across the Curriculum*, Vol. 12 No 3, pp. 8–15.

Street, B. and Lefstein, A. (2008) *Literacy: An Advanced Resource For Students*. Routledge.

SECTION ONE

THEORETICAL AND POLICY FRAMEWORKS

CHAPTER ONE

Contexts for literacy work: New Literacy Studies, multimodality, and the 'local and the global'

BRIAN STREET

Introduction

In this chapter I will take account of developments and debates in the literacy field, notably the concern with the 'local' and 'global' that has been raised by a number of researchers (Brandt and Clinton, 2002; Collins, 1995; Reder and Davila, 2005). I will also consider the link between literacy and what some have termed the 'new work order' (Gee et al., 1996) and the relationship between literacy and other modes of communication in the field known as 'multimodality' (Kress and van Leeuwen, 1996; Jewitt, 2006). I will propose that approaches to literacy work be based on new and broader understandings of both literacy and language, and multimodality, that take into account the contexts of 'local' and 'global', and of the 'new work order' within which contemporary work in literacy must be sited.

New Literacy Studies

New Literacy Studies (NLS) have proposed theoretical perspectives rooted in critical ethnography and culturally sensitive research, leading to programmes that are negotiated and participatory (Gee, 1991; Heath, 1983; Heath and Mangiola, 1991; Villegas, 1991). NLS (Barton and Hamilton, 1998; Barton, 1994; Gee, 1991; Street, 1984) consists of a series of writings, about both research and practice, that treat language and literacy as social practices rather than technical skills to be learned in formal education. The research requires language and literacy to be studied as they occur naturally in social life, taking account of their different meanings for different cultural groups and in different contexts. The practice requires curriculum designers, teachers and evaluators to take account of the variation in meanings and uses that students bring from their home backgrounds to formal learning contexts such as the classroom. NLS emphasises the importance of 'culturally sensitive teaching' (Villegas, 1991) in building upon students' own knowledge and skills (Heath, 1983; Heath and Mangiola, 1991). Research and practice are based upon new ideas about the nature of language and literacy, and have in turn reinforced and developed these ideas. There are two major tenets of this new thinking:

a) the notion of 'social literacies';
b) that language is 'dialogic'.

Social literacies

This phrase (Street, 1995) refers to the nature of literacy as a social practice and to the plurality of literacies that this enables us to observe. That literacy is a social practice is an insight both banal and profound. It is banal in the sense that once we think about it, it is obvious that literacy is always practised in social contexts; even the school, however 'artificial' it may be accused of being in its reading and writing teaching methods, is also a social construction. The site of learning (whether at school or within adult literacy programmes) has, like other contexts, its own social beliefs and behaviours into which its particular literacy practices are inserted. The notion is also profound in that it leads to new ways of understanding and defining what counts as literacy, and has important implications for how we learn and teach reading and writing. If literacy is a social practice, then it varies with social context and is not the same, uniform concept in each case.

I have described the view that literacy in itself has consequences irrespective of context (Street, 1984) as an 'autonomous' model of literacy. In contrast with this view, I have posed an 'ideological' model of literacy, which argues that literacy not only varies with social context and with cultural norms and discourses (regarding, for instance, identity, gender and belief), but that its uses and meanings are always embedded in relations of power. It is in this sense that literacy is always 'ideological' – it always involves contests over meanings, definitions and boundaries, and struggles for control of the literacy agenda. For these reasons, it becomes harder to justify teaching only one particular form of literacy, whether in schools or in adult programmes, when the learners will already have been exposed to a variety of everyday literacy practices (Street, 2011). If literacy is seen simply as a universal technical skill, the same everywhere, then the particular form being taught in school comes to be treated as the only kind, the universal standard that naturalises its socially specific features and disguises their real history and ideological justifications. If literacy is seen as a social practice, then that history and those features and justifications need to be spelled out, and students need to be able to discuss the basis for the choices being made in the kind of literacy they are learning.

Dialogic language

New theories of language that are closely associated with those regarding social literacies focus upon the nature of language as a continually negotiated process of 'meaning-making' as well as 'meaning-taking'. In this research tradition, language is viewed as always a social process, as interactive and dynamic (Volosinov, 1973; Hymes, 1977; Halliday, 1978). For Bakhtin (1981), language is both centrifugal and centripetal. By this he means that users are always struggling to extend its boundaries and meanings (the centrifugal perspective), while working within prescribed limits (the centripetal view). It is dialogic in the sense that it is always part of a dialogue – language, even when employed silently by single individuals, is always part of a social interaction, whether with imagined others or with the meanings and uses of words that others have employed at other times and places. As Bakhtin states, 'words come saturated with the meanings of others'. Again, this view of language might appear commonsensical at one level – we all know that languages vary, whether that means the differences between French and English, or at a more local level between different dialects such as Creoles and Patois. But the implications of this stance, like that of social literacies, are at the same time profound. If language is always contested, negotiated and employed in social interaction, then the appropriateness of particular uses and interpretations have likewise to be opened to debate. It becomes impossible to lay down strict and formal rules for all time, and the authority of particular users – whether teachers, grammarians or politicians – becomes

17

problematised. We all, as it were, take possession of language again, rather than being passive victims of its entailments.

Theorists in the NLS have tended to root their ideas about reading and writing as aspects of language within these broader linguistic theories of a dialogic and constructivist kind. Gee (1991), one of the leading exponents of NLS, poses a view of language that corresponds more closely to the ideological model of literacy. From this perspective, language is dynamic in the sense expressed by writers like Bakhtin, Kress and so on.

> *In fact, language is always something that is actively constructed in a context, physically present or imagined, by both speaker/writer/and hearer/reader through a complex process of inferencing that is guided by, but never fully determined by, the structural properties of the language.* (Kress and van Leeuwen, 1996, p. 28)

Critiques of NLS: The 'local' and the 'global'

Brandt and Clinton (2002) have challenged some of the tenets of NLS outlined above by expressing concern that it appears to focus too much on the 'local' at the expense of wider, 'global' concerns. They argue that NLS ought to be more prepared to take account of the relatively autonomous features of literacy without succumbing to the autonomous model with its well-documented flaws. This would involve, for instance, recognising the extent to which literacy does often come in to 'local' situations from outside, and brings with it both skills and meanings that are larger than the local perspective favoured by NLS can detect. While acknowledging the value of the social practice approach, they:

> ... *wonder if the new paradigm sometimes veers too far in a reactive direction, exaggerating the power of local contexts to set or reveal the forms and meanings that literacy takes. Literacy practices are not typically invented by their practitioners. Nor are they independently chosen or sustained by them. Literacy in use more often than not serves multiple interests, incorporating individual agents and their locales into larger enterprises that play out away from the immediate scene.* (Brandt and Clinton, 2002, p. 1)

They also point out the important and powerful role of consolidating technologies that can destabilise the functions, uses, values and meanings of literacy anywhere. These technologies generally originate outside of the local context; they cannot be understood simply in terms of local practices. While the field has learned much from the recent turn to 'local literacies', they fear that 'something [might] be lost when we ascribe to local contexts responses to pressures that originate in distant decisions, especially when seemingly local appropriations of literacy may in fact be culminations of literate designs originating elsewhere' (p. 2).

I would agree with most of Brandt and Clinton's characterisation here of the relationship between the local and the 'distant', and indeed it is the focus on this relationship, rather than on one or other of the sites, that characterises the best of NLS. Brandt and Clinton's account here provides a helpful way of characterising the local versus global debate in which literacy practices play a central role. But, I would want to distinguish between agreeing with their caveat about overemphasising the 'local', and labelling the 'distant' as more autonomous. The distant literacies to which Brandt and Clinton refer are also always ideological, and to term them autonomous might be to concede too much to their neutralist claims: their distant nature, their relative power over local literacies and their 'non-invented' character as far as local users are concerned, do not make them autonomous, only distant, new or hegemonic. To study such processes we need a framework and conceptual tools that can characterise the relationship between local and distant. The question raised in the early NLS work concerning how we can characterise the shift from observing literacy events to conceptualising literacy practices (Street, 2000) does, I think, provide both a methodological and empirical way of dealing with this relationship and thereby takes account of Brandt and Clinton's concern with the 'limits of the local'.

NLS practitioners might also take issue with the apparent suggestion that distant literacies come to local contexts with their force and meaning intact. As Kulick and Stroud (1993) indicated a decade ago in their study of new literacy practices brought by missionaries to New Guinea, local peoples more often 'take hold' of these new practices and adapt them to local circumstances. The result of local–global encounters involving literacy is always a new hybrid of the two, rather than a single essentialised version of either. It is these hybrid literacy practices that NLS focuses on, rather than romanticising the local or conceding the dominant privileging of the supposed global. It is the recognition of this hybridity that lies at the heart of an NLS approach to literacy acquisition with regard to the relationship between local literacy practices and those of the school.

Collins and Blot (2002) are similarly concerned that, while NLS has generated a powerful series of ethnographies of literacy, there is a danger of simply piling up more descriptions of local literacies without addressing general questions of both theory and practice. In exploring why dominant stereotypes regarding literacy are so flawed, such as the notion of a great divide between oral and literate, and the now challenged assumptions of the autonomous model, they invoke NLS, but then want to take account of its limitations and to extend beyond them:

> *Such understanding also has a more general intellectual value for it forces us to explore why historical and ethnographic cases are necessary but insufficient for rethinking inherited viewpoints... although ethnographic scholarship has demonstrated the pluralities of literacies, their context-boundness, it still has also to account for general tendencies that hold across diverse case studies.* (pp. 7–8)

They argue, then, for 'a way out of the universalist/particularist impasse' which had troubled Brandt and Clinton as we saw above, 'by attending closely to issues of text, power and identity'. These are issues that are at the heart of current developments in NLS, some of which I summarise briefly below.

Janks (2000), located in South Africa, links literacy studies to broader social theory, invoking the concepts of 'Domination, Access, Diversity and Design' as a means of synthesising the various strands of critical literacy education. Freebody, writing from Australia, but like Janks taking a broad theoretical and international view, writes of the relationship between NLS and critical literacy, an approach to the acquisition and use of reading and writing in educational contexts that takes account of relations of power and domination (Freebody, 2006). Bartlett and Holland (2002) also link NLS to broader social theory. They propose an expanded conception of the space of literacy practices, drawing upon innovations in the cultural school of psychology, sociocultural history and social practice theory. In locating literacy theory within these broader debates in social theory, they build on the concern of Bourdieu in characterising the relationship between social structures (history brought to the present in institutions) and 'habitus' (history brought to the present in person), and suggest ways in which NLS can adapt this approach:

> *Bourdieu's theory suggests that we can analyze literacy events with*
> *an eye to the ways in which historical and social forces have shaped a*
> *person's linguistic habitus and thus impinges upon that person's actions*
> *in the moment* (Bartlett and Holland, 2002, p. 6).

However, they argue that Bourdieu's theory is itself 'limited by his tendency to underplay the importance of culturally produced narratives,
images and other artefacts in modifying habitus' (p. 6). It is here that they
suggest ways of extending both Bourdieu and literacy studies by putting
them together with other key concepts in their work:

> *We propose to strengthen a practice theoretical approach to literacy*
> *studies by specifying the space of literacy practice, examining in*
> *particular the locally operant figured world of literacy, identities in*
> *practice, and artefacts.* (p. 6)

Applying their concept of 'figured worlds' – 'a socially produced and
culturally constructed realm of interpretation' – to literacy practices, they
suggest that 'a figured world of literacy might include "functional illiterates", "good readers" and "illiterates", any of which might be "invoked,
animated, contested and enacted through artefacts, activities and identities in practice"' (p. 6). In the world of schooled literacy in particular,
scholars have noted the tendency to invoke and deploy such figurings
and identities to characterise children and their attainment – Holland
and Bartlett enable us to see such characterisations as part of what we
should be taking into account when we try to understand literacy practices in context. We should be wary of taking them at face value, a scepti-
cism that will prove useful as we move towards applying social literacy
theory to education in general and to schooling in particular (see also
Grenfell *et al.*'s forthcoming book for further analysis of the relationship
between NLS and Bourdieu's approach).

The 'new work order'

Another way of describing the macro social changes that have taken
place in recent years (and that provide the new context within which we
have to understand the uses and meanings of literacy) is what Gee and
others (Gee *et al.*, 1996; Holland *et al.*, 1998), drawing upon the writings
of economists, business theorists and critical sociologists, have attempted

to characterise as the 'new work order' associated with globalisation of production and distribution. They consider the implications of these changes for the kinds of language needed in work and in educational contexts. These changes represent the context within which contemporary literacy work is taking place, and force us to question the theoretical underpinnings of literacy itself. Work, they suggest, is no longer defined and organised along Fordist lines, with mass production on assembly lines and its Taylorist principles of work organisation and discipline.

There is now a shift towards forms of production that employ new ways of making goods and commodities, serving more differentiated markets, or niches, through segmented retailing strategies. A great deal more attention is paid to the selling environment at every level of production, from design to distribution. So while the old work order stressed issues of costs and revenue, the new work order emphasises asset building and market share (Gee *et al.*, 1996, pp. vii–viii).

Associated with these defining concepts are ideas about proper organisational behaviour, including attention to flexibility and adaptation to change. Procedures are put into place to ensure both flexibility on the one hand, and also uniformity and guarantee of standards on the other. If consumers are perceived, through market research and company predictions, to demand the same jackets or the same tomatoes in shops across their travelling experience, then mechanisms need to be put into place to ensure that wherever these items are produced, they conform to those standards. This Total Quality Management (TQM) has been a particular feature of the new work order that has impinged directly on the educational setting. TQM has provided models for quality control there too, imposing reductionist and unitised notions of measurement and quality on educational outputs and 'products'.

A further organisational change in the new work order that has been of special significance for language and literacy is the notion of teams working on projects rather than hierarchical organisations that simply pass orders down a chain of command. In the new, project-focused work order, all members of a team combine to design, negotiate and develop 'products' for sale and distribution. In order to accomplish this, all members of a team have to be equipped with the discursive skills that such negotiation and development involve, such as the ability to present and hear arguments, and to develop material for presentation on communicative devices such as overhead projectors, slide projectors, computer displays and so on. Radical researchers confronted with these changes have focused particularly on the claims often associated with them that suggest a commitment to democracy. Words like 'collaboration', 'participation', 'devolution' and 'empowerment' – all cherished terms of oppositional groups, such as those working in Freirean literacy campaigns – are now used to indicate a partnership between managers and workers. Gee and his colleagues are highly suspicious of these claims and would have us examine them critically, while acknowledging that changes are indeed taking place in both the work order and the communicative demands associated with it. Literacy programmes, then, now need to take account of such shifts and critiques if they are to handle the complex communicative needs of the new work order.

Multimodality and New Literacy Studies

Another theoretical perspective that we now need to take account of, but which was less developed at the time of the first *Powerful Literacies* volume, is multimodality. Kress and others (Kress and van Leeuwen, 1996) have attempted to redress the emphasis on language as the salient mode of communication in favour of a recognition of how other modes – visual, gestural, kinaesthetic – are key communicative practices: they are developing a language of description for such modes that enables us to see their characteristic forms, their affordances and their distinctive links with each other. According to Kress (2010):

> Multimodality *assumes that the field of meaning is defined by many means for making meaning, speech and writing being but two – and not necessarily the central two of such means. In itself, that assumption has profound ontological impact for those societies whose cultures have rested on a taken-for-granted assumption that it is 'language' which is central, which provides a comprehensive means for communicating, which guarantees 'rationality' and, in that, defines what it is to be human. Yet by itself, multimodality is not a theory: it maps a field for attention for those who have an interest in* meaning *in some way: for the archeologist who uncovers the traces of a past layered in the ground; for a psychologist interested in means whereby attention maybe gained and recall of 'information' enhanced; for the historically oriented sociologist who uncovers a history of the social practices of surgery as much in the changes in the* naming *of the instruments of surgery as in their shape. In other words, a theoretical framing,*

> *something that can and does pose a question, is needed: a theory in which questions around effects of difference in mode becomes significant. For me, that question is "How do I make meaning in that which I take to be my world?"* (p. 2)

Kress argues that the approach that best answers this question is social semiotics. Its central entity is the sign. In a social account of sign-*making* – in contrast to sign-*use* – the semiotic work of the sign-makers, their agency, is at the centre. In this approach, sign-makers choose a form (a signifier) which, in its material characteristics and as the result of shaping in often long histories of social and semiotic 'work' in different social places, bears the potential to express most aptly that which I wish 'to mean' at this moment here, right now.

Reading and writing practices of literacy, then, are only one part of what people are going to have to learn in order to be 'literate' in the future (Kress and van Leeuwen, 1996; Heller and Pomeroy, 1997; Lankshear, 2007). They are going to have to learn to handle both the teamwork literacies associated with the new work order, and the iconic systems evident in many communicative practices. These include the kinds of icon and the signs evident in computer displays like the Microsoft® Word package, with all its signs, symbols, boundaries, pictures, words, texts, images and so on. The extreme version of this position is the notion of 'the end of language' – that we are no longer talking about language in its rather traditional notion of grammar, lexicon and semantics, but rather as a wider range of 'semiotic systems' that cut across reading, writing and speech. Kress and van Leeuwen subtitle their book *Reading Images: the Grammar of Visual Design* in order to suggest that this new approach to the semiotic order can apply similar 'grammatical' analyses to those applied to language in its more traditional sense. By this they want to indicate not so much a traditional focus on rules, knowledge of which sets the professional apart from the amateur, but rather grammar as meaning the way in which the people, places and things depicted in images 'are combined into a meaningful whole' (Kress and van Leeuwen, 1996, p. 1). Grammar in this sense is more than a system of rules, it is also a set of possibilities and an active engagement with meaning in which every language user participates. This provides a broader framework for handling questions of literacy and language in both education and the workplace that, again, new literacy programmes are going to have to take into account.

Kress and Street (2010) attempt to work out what is similar and different in their respective fields – NLS and MM – that is how these approaches can 'speak to each other', in attempts to find similarities and differences. All the authors cited here resist moves to polarise, looking instead for complementarities in theoretical aims and approach. For instance, in both approaches there is a worry about the stretching of the term 'literacy' well beyond the NLS conception of 'social practices of representation' to become a metaphor (and often much less than that) for any kind of skill or competence. One needs to ask whose interests are advanced and how by the use of labels such as 'palpatory literacy' (skills in body massage), 'emotional literacy' (skills in affective massage?), 'cultural literacy' (skills in social massage?), and so on. Of course, one clear effect of such moves is that where a 'literacy' is identified, those with an interest in finding the corresponding illiterates are never far behind with their remedies. But even such uses where some aspects of literacy practices are involved – computer literacy, visual literacy – bring their own problems, not least of them the blunting of analytic and theoretical sharpness and power. Where there is a label, there is already an answer; and where there is an answer, any need for questions has stopped. More significantly perhaps, there is the question of 'complementarity'. This poses, quite simply, a thorny question: where does the 'reach' of one theory stop – or, maybe better, begin to attenuate or 'fizzle out'.

A social semiotic theory of multimodality, then, can attempt to expand its domain to include the features of the sign-maker and of the environment of sign-making; it would do so by treating all of the world as signs – the practices, the characteristics of social organisation, and so on. A theory of literacy as social practice addresses similar questions but, perhaps, focuses on a narrower range of semiosis – the uses of reading and writing, although always in association with other modes such as speech or visual representation. What NLS has added to both traditional approaches to literacy and to new approaches to multimodality has been the recognition that reading and writing and their associated signs vary across cultural time and space – the meanings associated with them vary for participants and are rooted in social relationships including, crucially, relationships of power. Indeed, the very definitions of what counts as literacy already frame social relationships of literacy and what people can do with it, as we see in increasingly narrow government demands on curriculum and assessment. How these schooled literacies relate to those of everyday social life, with its multiple literacies across different cultural and institutional contexts, is a key question raised by NLS and for which, at present, schooled literacy advocates are not providing answers.

I conclude, then, with a brief comment on how such broader conceptions of literacy and multimodality, located in the wider contexts of local and global and of the new work order discussed above, can be applied to education – both policy and practice.

Applications to education

The implications of the view of language, literacy and multimodality outlined above are only just being felt in applied studies. With respect to education, these perspectives have been partly conveyed through the notion of critical language awareness (Fairclough, 1995), which argues that learners should be facilitated to engage in debates about the nature and meaning of language, rather than be treated as passive victims of its 'structural properties'. This includes learning some metalinguistic terms, but a more inclusive set of such terms, learned for a different purpose than those often put forward by state institutions. NLS and multimodality have, I suggest, extended this approach and I would like to briefly indicate how they might be linked with policy development in the UK regarding literacy.

In a recent paper (2011) I argued that the approaches adopted by governments during the 1990s and early 2000s were flawed from an NLS perspective, which I label NLS1. The English National Literacy Strategy I label as NLS2, since it arrived somewhat later on the scene and its views are secondary to those we have been reviewing here.

The English National Literacy Strategy as it was originally conceived was rooted in 'the basics', which it saw as surface features of language and literacy, such as rules of grammar in the traditional sense, and rules for phoneme/grapheme relations (Sealey, 1999). NLS on the other hand, as we have seen, views 'the basics' as generative, deep structures that facilitate learning and activity, of the dialogic and ideological kind outlined above. Bernstein (1997, pp. 75–6) refers to 'the heart of discourse' as the recognition of ambiguity, creativity and provisionality, recognition of how the rules work, not simply learning the rules themselves. It is this that lies at the heart of learning and development. In the context of literacy, teaching students to read and write as a set of rules to be learned – rules about sign/sound relationships and about 'phonics' – rather than as a set of possibilities – the ways in which language is always changing and the potential for 'meaning-making' of varieties, across regions and registers – keeps education 'safe'. But this approach undermines its own claims to either equality or access, in that it denies students the 'power' to question the rules and procedures and to develop their own uses of language and literacy. Ironically, the rhetoric of equality and access is currently at its most intense with respect to the communicative requirements of the new work order: here it is precisely the ability of new workers entering the workforce to handle change, ambiguity and variation that employers are asking for. The definition of 'basics' being applied to schooling and to the new adult literacy curriculum, then, contradicts the very possibility of achieving these ends. While those of us working in NLS might agree with politicians and educators that there have to be 'basics' – structures on which learning and activity can be built – we would disagree on content, what counts as basic. Rather than opposing the National Literacy Strategy outright, many researchers and activists have come to challenge it at this conceptual level. This involves working in particular to broaden the concept of 'basics' being employed in both child and adult programmes, and to shift the view of language from a focus on rules towards a more creative and user-focused approach. This has implications for curriculum, pedagogy and assessment, which many authors in this volume are addressing.

Andrew Goodwyn (2011), in a recent overview of the current position, has suggested that 'the signs are that the era of NLS[2] is over and the strategies are being revised'. Although this may be true, it does not appear at present that the revisions at government level are moving far enough in the direction that research suggests is needed. Indeed, recent public claims from UK Government ministers that the curriculum should return to 'basics' and the need to maintain 'standards' indicate more of the same that we have seen in the past decade. On the other hand, the complexity of the arguments put forward by researchers, such as in *The Cambridge Primary Review* (Alexander, 2009), the largest review of the field for 50 years, suggests that research might be hard to ignore. However, borrowing insights from colleagues in the USA, where a similar struggle has been evident over this period, we are probably not yet in a position to see any significant shift from NLS2 to NLS1.

I have considered elsewhere these implications with respect to Development (Street, 2000), the National Literacy Strategy (Street, 1999), English in Education (Street, 1997) and Adult Literacy (Street, 1996). The purpose of this paper has been to put these considerations of practical work in literacy into the broader perspective of multimodality on the one hand, and the 'new work order' and local and global on the other, with respect to how NLS approaches can take these new perspectives into account. I hope thereby to have engaged both practitioners and researchers in reflexive debate about these issues, and I look forward to continuing the conversation beyond the pages of this book.

References

Alexander, R. (ed.) (2009) *The Cambridge Primary Review* (CPR). Routledge.

Bakhtin, M. (1981) *The Dialogic Imagination*. Austin: University of Texas Press.

Bartlett, L. and Holland, D. (2002) 'Theorising the space of literacy practices', *Ways of Knowing Journal*, Vol. 2 No 1, pp. 10–22.

Barton, D. (1994) *Literacy: An Introduction to the Ecology of Written Language*. Blackwell.

Barton, D. and Hamilton, M. (1998) *Local Literacies*. Routledge.

Bernstein, B. (1997) 'Social class and pedagogic practice', in *The Structuring of Pedagogic Discourse: Vol. IV Class, Codes and Control*. Routledge, pp. 63–93.

Brandt, D. and Clinton, K. (2002) 'Limits of the local: expanding perspectives on literacy as a social practice', *Journal of Literacy Research*, Vol. 34 No 3, pp. 337–56.

Collins, J. (1995) 'Literacy and literacies', *Annual Review of Anthropology*, Vol. 24, pp. 75–93.

Collins, J. and Blot, J. (2002) *Texts, Power and Identity*. Routledge.

Fairclough, N., (ed.) (1995) *Critical Language Awareness*. Longman.

Freebody, P. (2006) 'Critical Literacy', in Beach, R. *et al.* (eds) *Multidisciplinary Perspectives on Literacy Research*. Cresskills: Hampton Press.

Gee, J. (1991) *Social Linguistics: Ideology in Discourses*. Falmer Press.

Gee, J., Hull, G. and Lankshear, C. (1996) *The New Work Order: Behind the Language of the New Capitalism*. Allen & Unwin.

Goodwyn, A. (ed.) (2011) *The Literacy Project: A Critical Response to the Literacy Strategy and the Framework for English*. Routledge.

Grenfell, M., Bloome, D., Pahl, K., Rowsell, J. and Street, B. (forthcoming) *Language and Classroom Ethnography: Bridging New Literacy Studies and Bourdieu*. Routledge.

Halliday, M. (1978) *Language as Social Semiotic*. Edward Arnold.

Heath, S.B. (1983) *Ways with Words: Language, Life and Work in Communities and Classrooms*. Cambridge University Press.

Heath, S.B. and Mangiola, L. (1991) *Children of Promise: Literate Activity in Linguistically and Culturally Diverse Classrooms*. Washington DC: NEA/AERA.

Heller, S. and Pomeroy, K. (1997) *Design Literacy: Understanding Graphic Design*. New York: Allworth Press.

Holland, C., with Cooke, T. and Frank, F. (1998) *Literacy and the New Work Order: an International Literature Review*. NIACE.

Hymes, D. (1964) 'Introduction: towards ethnographies of communication', *American Anthropologist*, Vol. 66 No 6, pp. 1–34.

Hymes, D. (1977) *Foundations in Sociolinguistics*. Tavistock.

Janks, H. (2000) 'Domination, Access, Diversity and Design: a synthesis for critical literacy education', *Educational Review*, Vol. 52 No 2, pp. 175–86.

Jewitt, C. (2006) *Technology, Literacy and Learning; a Multimodal Approach*. Routledge.

Kress, G. (2010) *Multimodality: a social semiotic approach to contemporary communication*. Routledge.

Kress G. and Street, B. (2006) 'Multi-Modality and Literacy Practices', foreword to *Travel Notes from the New Literacy Studies: Case Studies of Practice*, Pahl, K. and Rowsell, J. (eds). Multilingual Matters Ltd.

Kress, G. and van Leeuwen, T. (1996) *Reading Images: the Grammar of Visual Design*. Routledge.

Kulick, D. and Stroud, C. (1993) 'Conceptions and Uses of Literacy in a Papua New Guinean Village', in Street, B. (ed.) *Cross-Cultural Approaches to Literacy*. Cambridge University Press.

Lankshear, C. (1997) *Changing Literacies*. Buckingham and Philadelphia: Open University Press.

Lemke, J. (ed.) (1998), 'Language and semiotics in education', special issue of *Linguistics & Education*, Vol. 10 No 3.

Pahl, J. and Rowsell, J. (2010) *Artifactual Literacies: Every Object Tells a Story*. New York: Teachers College Press.

Prinsloo, M. and Breier, M. (eds) (1996) *The Social Uses of Literacy: Case Studies from S. Africa*. Amsterdam: John Benjamins.

Reder, S. and Davila, E. (2005) 'Context And Literacy Practices', *Annual Review of Applied Linguistics*, Vol. 25, pp. 170–87.

Rowsell, J., Kress, G. and Street, B. (in press) 'Visual optics: Interpreting Body Art, Three Ways', *Visual Communication*. Sage.

Sealey, A. (1999) *Theories about Language in the National Literacy Strategy*. Centre for Elementary and Primary Education, University of Warwick.

Street, B. (1984) *Literacy in Theory and Practice*. Cambridge University Press.

Street, B. (1995) *Social Literacies: Critical Approaches to Literacy in Development, Ethnography and Education*. Longman.

Street, B. (1996), *Adult Literacy in the UK: a History of Research and Practice*, NCAL Technical Report TR95–05. Philadelphia: University of Pennsylvania.

Street, B. (1997) 'The implications of the new literacy studies for literacy education', *English in Education*, NATE, Vol. 31 No 3 (Autumn), pp. 26–39.

Street, B. (1999), 'New literacies in theory and practice: what are the implications for language in education?', *Linguistics & Education*, Vol. 10 No 1, pp. 1–24.

Street, B (2000) 'Literacy Events and Literacy Practices', in Martin-Jones, M. and Jones, K. (eds), *Multilingual Literacies: Comparative Perspectives on Research and Practice*. Amsterdam: John Benjamin, pp. 17–29.

Street, B. (ed.) (2000) *Literacy and Development: Ethnographic Perspectives*. Routledge.

Street, B. (2011) 'NLS1 and NLS2: Implications of a social literacies perspective for policies and practices of literacy education', in Goodwyn, A. (ed.), *The Great Literacy Debate: A Critical Response to the Literacy Strategy and the Framework for English*. Routledge.

Villegas, A.M. (1991) *Culturally Responsive Teaching*. Princeton: ETS.

Volosinov, V.N. (1973) *Marxism and the Philosophy of Language*. Orlando: Academic Press.

CHAPTER TWO

More powerful literacies: The policy context

MARY HAMILTON AND LYN TETT

Introduction

This chapter offers an overview of the policy context within which many of the developments described in the rest of this book need to be understood. It focuses on the four countries that make up the United Kingdom and Ireland, but also comments on the wider international scene. It aims to describe briefly the recent history of adult literacies in the UK, to compare and contrast developments in the different countries, and to identify the main influences that are shaping the field. In the first edition of *Powerful Literacies* we identified how policies regarding lifelong learning, the knowledge economy and the knowledge society were defining and promoting particular literacies. These policies are still there, but the impact of the globalisation of the world economy on individual economies, and the influence of international bodies such as the Organisation for Economic Co-operation and Development (OECD), are becoming more powerful.

We begin by sketching this international context, and then offer brief overviews of the history and current situation in each country. The second part is more critical and evaluative. In organising the information about variations in policy, we have been guided by four main questions with the aim of getting to the values embodied by a set of practices in adult literacies that for the most part are only implicitly stated in government documents. These questions are:

- What concept of literacy underpins recent policies?
- How are learners and teachers positioned by the policies?

- What kinds of learning activity or process are programmes or initiatives expected to engage in?
- What outcomes are literacy programmes and learners expected to achieve?

Adult literacies, the international context, and policies in the countries of the UK and Ireland

International influences

UK national governments currently operate within layers of international policy (Henry *et al.*, 2001). The most influential of these are the OECD and its regional partners in the European Union (EU). The OECD and the EU broadly share a view of countries, and their citizens, as competitors in a global marketplace. They concur on the importance of developing policy indicators that can measure performance across nations. The EU promotes the harmonisation of educational and training qualifications to facilitate the movement of labour between member countries. This entails developing common benchmarks of achievement, and since the late 1980s there have been continuing efforts in the UK to produce a standardised national framework for adult literacy and numeracy qualifications that can be calibrated against national frameworks for vocational qualifications, school measures of achievement and the levels of the International Adult Literacy Survey (Lawn and Grek, 2009; Hamilton and Hillier, 2007).

External pressures such as these constrain the outline of national policy, but local factors complicate their effects as they play out in the countries of the UK. A challenge for literacy policy analysis is to identify these effects, teasing out specific, local characteristics from the broader layers of international interventions. What causes change to local practice is not always clear on the ground, particularly in situations where practitioners feel they are excluded from the processes of consultation and decision-making, so that policy simply 'arrives' without explanation (Hodgson *et al.*, 2007). The origins and development of international policy agendas are not generally visible to practitioners in the UK, who often become aware of them through funding changes or through the changing discourses of policy-related documents and the demands to implement these.

An example of this from recent literacy policy is the adoption from the EU of the notion of 'social exclusion'. This concept originated in

France and was integrated into UK policy with the human resource model of literacy development that prevailed during the 1980s and early 1990s, to produce a specifically 'New Labour' version of neo-liberalism (Newman, 2002; Welshman, 2006; Levitas, 2005). This can be clearly traced, for example, in the unfolding of the English Skills for Life Strategy over the last ten years (for a more detailed discussion, see Hamilton and Pitt, 2011). A belief in the importance of the cultural and behavioural dimensions of social exclusion led New Labour to place a high value on education. Education is then seen as a key area for policy action – a central vehicle for changing attitudes, skills and knowledge, and life opportunities. The move to make literacy (as a foundational element of education) one of the key indicators of social exclusion had profound effects on the visibility and energy with which the Skills for Life Strategy was pursued. It accounts for the relentless attention to measurement and targets, since progress on this indicator was monitored directly by the Cabinet Office and had to be reported back annually to both the EU and the OECD. The first National Action Plan for Social Inclusion (Department for Work and Pensions, 2001), for example, contained 24 mentions of literacy.

As in a number of other OECD countries, the publication in 1997 of the first results of the International Adult Literacy Survey findings renewed policy attention on adult literacies in the UK (OECD, 1997). The countries of the UK and Ireland were found to score low in the tables of findings (Carey, 1997, 2000; Moser, 1999; Government of Ireland, 2000; Scottish Executive, 2001), and this was used as a key rationale for committing major new funding to the area over the following ten years. In addition, the survey results from 1997 are still referred to in current policy documents (for example, Government of Ireland, 2006; Scottish Government, 2011) as a justification for the need to focus on adult literacy. While it is not clear how long this policy commitment will remain, given the new conditions of economic austerity now being imposed on governments across Europe, international testing frameworks for adult competencies are still being enthusiastically developed. The most recent of these, the Programme for the International Assessment of Adult Competencies (PIAAC) is a collaboration between the OECD and the EU that draws on both the Programme for International Student Assessment (PISA) and the International Adult Literacy Survey (IALS) (see Schleicher, 2008; Gal et al., 2009; Brookes, 2011). Currently in its pilot phase, the PIAAC will focus on what are considered to be the key cognitive and workplace skills required for successful participation in the economy and society of the twenty-first century.

Adult literacy policies in the UK and Ireland

We use the term UK here as the generic name for the union of England, Scotland, Wales and Northern Ireland. Each of these countries now has greater autonomy, and this means that there are more distinctive differences between them in the recent history and organisation of their educational provision.

England

The Right to Read literacy campaign in the early 1970s was the first time that adult literacy was identified as a national policy issue in the UK. A public awareness campaign was initiated by volunteer activists and supported by politicians and the broadcasting services, especially the BBC. The campaign mobilised many volunteer teachers, motivated by the social justice concerns of the time. Community, adult and further education throughout the country began to offer one-to-one and small group tuition. A national agency for England and Wales was set up which became a focal point for the new field. The agency produced materials for students and tutors, organised training events, supported new developments and disseminated good practice. During the subsequent 30 years, the name and scope of the field constantly changed, with numeracy, English for Speakers of Other Languages (ESOL) and Information and Communications Technology (ICT) skills being added at different times (Hamilton and Hillier, 2006).

The Further and Higher Education Act of 1992 was crucial to the shape of adult literacy in England and Wales, because it made basic skills part of the statutory system of further education that is mainly concerned with providing accredited vocational qualifications for the 16–19 year age group. As a result of these developments, adult literacy and numeracy provision became more firmly established, increasingly formalised and less rooted in the interests and experiences of adults in local communities. By 1998, about two-thirds of the approximately 320,000 basic skills students in England and Wales (Further Education Funding Council, 1998) were studying within further education colleges, and less than a quarter were in local authority adult and community-based programmes. This reversed the proportions at the start of the 1990s. This reorganisation of practice also served policy efforts to link education more closely with initial education and the economy, and to provide clearer measures for evaluation and achievement.

In 2001 the national government in England funded the first ever national policy for adult literacy, the Skills for Life Strategy (DfES, 2001), setting ambitious targets for improvement. Skills for Life built on the National Literacy Strategy in schools. It responded to the publication of the OECD's IALS findings (OECD, 2000) and a review of adult literacy, language and numeracy carried out by Sir Claus Moser in 1999 (Moser, 1999). Driven by a vision of a much tighter, quality-controlled system of provision, the strategy created what was called a new 'infrastructure' designed to rebalance supply and demand in basic skills education and training. The infrastructure consisted of core curricula in ESOL, numeracy and literacy that were aligned with performance in school-based subjects. A variety of assessments were developed: diagnostic, formative and summative, including a national multiple-choice test of Level 2 achievement (one of five levels in the national framework, equivalent to a minimum pass in the English GCSE school examination). A specialised qualification structure and a set of professional standards were developed for practitioners, together with short training courses to induct teachers into the new curriculum and assessments. A high profile publicity campaign targeted specific priority groups of adults. New emphasis was put on computer-based learning technologies for both teacher training and learner provision, and local partnerships were developed between agencies.

Better quality and inspection systems were also introduced, along with a new funding agency, the Learning and Skills Council. A well-resourced national research and development agency was created and produced many reports between 2003 and 2010 to support and evaluate the strategy (for example, Carpintieri, 2007).

These were big changes for a field that had previously existed precariously in the margins of adult education and training, and that valued informality and creativity in assessment, curriculum and teacher–learner relationships. The volunteerist origins of the adult literacy movement in the 1970s and 1980s left a long-lasting legacy, and even today the majority of those working in literacies do so in part-time or voluntary posts. There has been, however, growth in the number of full-time paid staff and an increasing emphasis on professionalism that has accelerated in recent years through the Skills for Life Strategy (Cara et al., 2008).

In the early days of its administration the New Labour government strongly supported the concept of lifelong learning, and in a series of important reports it expressed concerns about the effects of social exclusion (Tight, 1998). A language of entitlement was used in Skills for Life policy documents alongside 'functional illiteracy' (DfES, 2001). After the publication of the Leitch report (2006), however, the achievement of literacy became ever more closely identified with functional skills for employment. The main flow of funding was directed through employer-led rather than learner-responsive provision, and the literacy curriculum was revised to enable it to be embedded in vocational training courses (DIUS, 2009). Further efforts were made to merge Skills for Life qualifications with the key skills qualifications offered in schools, in order to tidy up the field and avoid duplication. However, the very different forms of assessment used for these two previously different fields and client groups have so far proved difficult to reconcile: key skills assessments are much more detailed and comprehensive than the multiple choice test used in Skills for Life.

In 2004 the Skills for Life Strategy met its aim of 750,000 adults gaining an appropriate qualification, a significant increase on the numbers from the 1990s (see above). Despite controversy about how these participation targets have been defined and met (Bathmaker, 2007), further targets were set such that by 2010, it is claimed that a total of 2.25 million adults had improved their basic skills. The strategy was particularly successful in mobilising ESOL learners, but this led to a major controversy about the funding of ESOL in 2006 and the entitlement to free courses was removed, except for those on welfare benefits (Cooke and Simpson, 2009). This marginalised ESOL once again from the broader field of basic skills.

While Skills for Life was successful in terms of increasing participation, the evidence about actual skills gained from the courses was less impressive. Enthusiasm for Skills for Life was dampened by research findings suggesting that the costly model delivered learning opportunities that were too short to be effective, especially in terms of employability (Wolf and Evans, 2010; Vorhaus *et al.*, 2011).

So far the coalition government that replaced the Labour administration in 2010 has allowed the existing structures and initiatives to take their course, while reducing funding for Skills for Life learners as part of the across-the-board cuts in public funding. Functional skills are now replacing other types of assessment in England, and there is no longer a national focus on adult literacy, numeracy and ESOL. A distinct remit for all-age basic skills remains within NIACE, which recently carried out a national review of literacy (NIACE, 2011). This recommended that the focus on professional development, multi-agency partnerships and intergenerational learning programmes should be maintained as a matter of urgency.

Wales

Wales is a bilingual country that includes the extremes of remote rural regions and areas formerly home to mining and heavy industry. Survey results show that in 2004, 25 per cent of the working-age population in Wales lacked basic literacy skills, a higher proportion than in any of the English regions.

The lack of basic skills varies between areas, with the former industrial 'Valleys' (Blaenau Gwent, Merthyr Tydfil, Caerphilly, Torfaen and Neath Port Talbot) having the highest proportions of people lacking basic literacy and numeracy skills. (See The Poverty Site, 2011.)

Until devolution in 1999, adult literacy policy and practice in Wales was closely linked to England, since it was included in the remit of the London-based Basic Skills Agency (BSA). The main difference from English provision was the inclusion of Welsh as an official language for educational provision, resulting in bilingual materials and tuition. After devolution, the BSA continued to guide a new, all-age National Strategy for Basic Skills in Wales (BSA, 2000), in partnership with the newly developing Welsh agencies responsible for education and training, and with local education authorities, schools, colleges and private training providers. In some ways this strategy paralleled the English Skills for Life, but there were significant differences, too, due to the development of a distinctively Welsh model of education (National Assembly for Wales and the Basic Skills Agency, 2001).

Following devolution, control of education passed to the Welsh Assembly. A separate Welsh Inspectorate (now Estyn) was introduced, run on the same lines as the English Ofsted, and a separate curriculum accommodated Welsh language teaching in secondary schools. More flexibility and local discretion has been allowed in school-based literacy teaching strategies in Wales and, unlike England, there are no primary school league tables or compulsory literacy hour. Different forms of assessment and qualifications have also been developed for adult literacy learners that reflect the value placed on informality and flexibility in the wider Welsh approach to education. The National Literacy Test used in England had no particular status in Wales, where learners were able to work towards a variety of qualifications including, for example, those of the National Open College Network, that were compatible with other accreditation systems in the UK.

The first phase of the national literacy strategy for Wales lasted until 2005. It had a publicity strategy and policies that addressed learners of all ages and stages of literacy, and did not define priority target groups. It linked basic skills needs explicitly with patterns of poverty in the Welsh population. It emphasised the value of lifelong learning and intergenerational family literacy initiatives, and it introduced an employer pledge to encourage workplace provision. Every college in Wales received public funds for post-16 basic skills teaching, and literacy and numeracy screening assessment was introduced for all students enrolling on college courses. A new body, Education and Learning Wales (ELWa), was formed to oversee post-16 and adult education.

A further five-year strategy was announced in 2005 with increased funding, and this time priority groups were identified (National Assembly for Wales, 2005). It aimed to get 80 per cent of adults to Level 1 in English and Welsh language – a less ambitious target than in England, which set targets for Level 2.

In 2007 the BSA ceased to exist and was replaced in Wales by Basic Skills Cymru, a division inside the Welsh education department, and since then the personnel associated with the strategy have been gradually reduced and dispersed within the department, to be embedded in other aspects of its work. The four-year literacy plan announced in 2010 (National Assembly for Wales, 2010) focuses on literacy in primary schools, and a recent review of adult literacy in Wales (Furlong, 2011) concludes that the policy focus on adult literacy in Wales is now minimal, with most post-16 provision supported through European funding and supplemented by a very small budget for adult and community learning.

Essential Skills Wales (2010) introduced a new suite of qualifications to replace the former key skills and basic skills qualifications. As in England, this results in a unified qualifications framework for school-based and adult learners to which other qualifications can be mapped.

After a decade of action around adult literacies that kept a consistent focus on intergenerational and lifelong learning, adult literacy now appears to be eclipsed by a shift of attention towards primary school children. Wales has developed a distinctive approach to adult literacy that showed evidence of some success. Recent surveys of adult skills in Wales (Welsh Statistics Directorate, 2010) show improvements in literacy but little significant change in numeracy, and still a high level of need among further education college students for teaching at Level 1 and above (Furlong, 2011).

Scotland

As in the other countries of the UK, adult literacy emerged as a field of work in Scotland in the early 1970s and provision was mainly provided in the community through community education services rather than further education. Unlike England, however, this community focus on adult literacy and numeracy continued after the 1992 Further and Higher Education (Scotland) Act, although this legislation gave colleges a new duty to provide ESOL.

There was a low priority placed on adult literacies in Scotland until the late 1990s, but this began to be addressed particularly through the task group Literacy 2000, which comprised practitioners as well as government and local authority policy-makers. This group was established to provide a focus for the development of national policy and strategy on adult literacy and numeracy. In 2000 the group commissioned a number of research reports that outlined the contextual factors associated with low literacy and numeracy, as well as the views of employers. The reports showed that low literacy or numeracy skills had wide-reaching effects on the lives of individuals, which impacted on their families, communities, working lives and aspirations. In addition, the consequences for employers and the economy as a whole, for health and support services, and for social cohesion were identified (Slwika and Tett, 2008).

In 2001, following the findings of this research, the Scottish Government published its policy document *Adult Literacy and Numeracy in Scotland*, known as ALNIS (Scottish Executive, 2001). ALNIS defined adult literacy and numeracy as 'the ability to read, write and use numeracy, to handle information, to express ideas and opinions, to make decisions and solve problems' (Scottish Executive, 2001, p. 7). This definition frames literacies as being influenced by the contexts in which they occur, and as a very broad concept that reflects the realities of learners' lives. The strategy document also led to the establishment of a national organisation called Learning Connections in 2003, which included a specific Adult Literacies Team.

As a result of their activities the quality of adult literacies provision increased, especially in relation to the training and development of tutors

(Slwika and Tett, 2008) that had been rather neglected up to this point. One of the team's first tasks was to commission a group of researchers and practitioners to develop a curriculum for adult literacy and numeracy. *An Adult Literacy and Numeracy Curriculum Framework for Scotland* (Scottish Executive, 2005) advocated the use of a social practices account of adult literacy and numeracy. It was suggested that rather than seeing literacy and numeracy as the decontextualised, mechanical manipulation of letters, words and figures, literacy and numeracy should be regarded as being located within social, emotional and linguistic contexts.

From 2003 additional funding for adult literacies was routed through local authorities to Community Learning Strategy Partnerships, who decided how the resources could be used most effectively to meet local needs. This was the first significant investment in adult literacies provision in over 25 years, and it continued until 2008 when a change of government resulted in new ways of allocating local authority expenditure. The additional funding led to a considerable increase in the number of learners participating in programmes and this has meant that since 2001, over 200,000 adults have accessed literacies learning opportunities. These opportunities have been spread throughout Scotland and across a range of settings – local authority, voluntary, college, prison and workplace (Scottish Government, 2011).

In 2007 a Scottish National Party-led minority government was elected, and it brought in different policies for the funding of local authorities and new ways of ensuring that its policies were implemented. These changes were continued when it was re-elected in 2010, this time as a majority government. The new approach was established through a *Concordat* with the Convention of Scottish Local Authorities (COSLA) that was expected to deliver the government's overarching strategy by setting key strategic approaches, priorities and outcomes, and indicators that assessed these outcomes that were agreed with each local authority (Scottish Government, 2007a, part 8). This meant that funding was no longer 'ring fenced' and was simply part of the overall financial allocation to local authorities. So, because there is no legal requirement to provide literacies education for adults, the funding allocated to it declined significantly. Another impact was that a National Indicator was adopted to 'reduce the number of working age people with severe literacy and numeracy problems' (Scottish Government, 2007b, p. 10). This meant that local authorities, further education colleges and the voluntary sector had to show how the provision they were making was impacting on literacy and numeracy. Although the indicator was couched in deficit terms and left out the retired population, it at least meant that local authorities in particular gave more attention to adult literacies than they would have without this indicator.

Following a long period of consultation, a new strategy for adult literacies was published called *Adult Literacy and Numeracy in Scotland 2020* (Scottish Government, 2011). The new vision for adult literacies in Scotland was:

> *By 2020 Scotland's society and economy will be stronger because more of its adults are able to read, write and use numbers effectively in order to handle information, communicate with others, express ideas and opinions, make decisions and solve problems, as family members, workers, citizens and lifelong learners.* (Scottish Government, 2011, p. 2)

There is much continuity between this strategy document and ALNIS 2001, in the overall emphasis on a learner-centred approach and a curriculum that starts from the goals of the individual participant. One clear change, however, is the much stronger emphasis on the economy.

In Scotland over the last ten years there has been considerable development of provision for learners, a growing infrastructure of training and support for tutors, and policy developments that have prioritised adult literacies developments. However, these positive changes are in danger of being reversed as funding is reduced in the public sector, especially as there is no statutory requirement to provide adult literacies education.

Northern Ireland

In Northern Ireland provision is mainly located in further education colleges, and responsibility for its promotion and development is located in the Department for Employment and Learning (DEL). The first and only separate strategy paper on adult literacies was published in 2002 by DEL, with a foreword from the Minister for Employment and Learning. The document defined literacy and numeracy as:

> *Essential Skills, which require: the ability to communicate by talking and listening, reading and writing; to use numeracy; and the ability to handle information* (DEL, 2002, p. 6).

The reference to 'essential skills' reflects the economic and skills focus of policy that was evident in previous government documents in relation to their Lifelong Learning Strategy (DENI, 1998). However, there was also reference to assisting adults in improving 'their overall quality of life [and] their personal development' (DEL, 2002, p. 6).

The strategy aimed to develop a structured and coherent framework for essential skills and to increase the quality of provision. To this end it focused on three key initiatives: the introduction of core curricula for adult literacy and adult numeracy; the development of essential skills qualifications in literacy and numeracy; and the development of qualifications for tutors. The first of these was addressed by adopting the 'Adult Literacy and Numeracy Core Curriculum used in England' (*ibid.*, p. 10), but the other two areas were specifically developed for Northern Ireland. The strategy had two phases, with the first devoted to improving the provision framework and the second aimed at building capacity.

By 2004 most of the framework was in place. Essential Skills qualifications in Adult Literacy and Numeracy at Entry Level and in Communication and Number at Levels 1 and 2 within the National Qualifications Framework were available, and so were the qualification requirements for tutors. In addition, tutors based in further education colleges were supported and informed of developments in delivering Essential Skills provision by the Learning and Skills Development Agency for Northern Ireland as part of the strategy's commitment to delivering 'quality in all aspects of provision' (*ibid.*, p. 7).

The criteria for establishing what could be funded from the specific Essential Skills Fund, however, has been rather narrow, with the initial emphasis on attendance (for at least 40 hours of tuition) and the gaining of recognised Essential Skills accreditation (DEL, 2005). In 2008 DEL introduced a new funding mechanism for further education, and Essential Skills was brought within the new methodology of Funded Learning Units (FLUs). In this methodology, further education received maximum funding for delivering Essential Skills courses of 55 hours.

There has always been an emphasis on initial assessment but, as a result of weaknesses identified through inspections, guidance issued in 2009 emphasised 'rigorous initial and diagnostic assessment that includes a screening of each learner's prior academic achievement in English, mathematics and ICT' (DEL, 2009, p. 3), in order to ensure that learners progressed to the correct courses. This emphasis on delivering a pre-set curriculum focused on 'skills' requirements determined mainly by the providers seems to be a long way from the strategy's original aim of 'widen[ing] access, in particular to those in greatest need' (DEL, 2002, p. 7).

Until 2004 a number of community development projects had been supported by the EU 'Special Programme for Peace and Reconciliation' (EGSA), but this funding is no longer available. This means that much of the innovative community development work carried out by organisations within communities is no longer funded, and any courses are now expected to be provided through further education colleges and delivered in the community.

Overall then, Northern Ireland has considerably increased the number of learners participating in provision and developed better quality provision through a range of structures, but this provision is more narrowly focused on the kinds of learning that are funded by the Department of Employment and Learning.

Ireland

In Ireland the vast majority of literacy tuition takes place in the locally based Vocational Education Committees' (VEC) schemes. It is also an integrated component of other adult education and training programmes. The National Adult Literacy Agency (NALA) is the national body that is involved in tutor training, developing teaching materials, distance education services, policy making, research and campaigns to raise awareness of the causes, extent and responses to adult literacy difficulties in Ireland. It is an independent charity that receives a grant towards its work from the Department of Education and Skills. NALA defines literacy as:

> ...the skills needed by individuals to participate fully in society. It involves listening, speaking, reading, writing, numeracy and using everyday technology to communicate and handle information (www. nala.ie/literacy–ireland).

This definition reflects the wide variety of contexts in which learning and teaching take place, and the concern with starting from the needs and interests of individuals. In terms of policy, the only document that has specifically referred to adult literacy in Ireland was the report of a committee, the *Joint Oireachtas Committee on Education and Science Report into Adult Literacy* (Government of Ireland, 2006). However, a number of policy documents in a range of areas have advocated the importance of adult literacy to achieving the government's overall goals (Government of Ireland, 2002; 2007) including basic workplace education, social inclusion and the National Skills Strategy (Expert Group on Future Skills Needs, 2007; 2010) that sets targets for the achievement of higher qualifications among the working population.

Until 2008 Ireland had a booming economy, but it is now experiencing high unemployment and much reduced public expenditure, and these factors are having a strong impact on its policies. The focus is now very much on the role of literacy and numeracy in improving people's skills and helping unemployed people get back into the labour market. In a climate of budget reductions and organisational mergers, NALA has worked to try to ensure that adult literacy provision was not reduced, and reported in 2010 (NALA, 2010) that adult literacy budgets, including those for family and workplace projects, had survived the Budget relatively intact. NALA also drew on the finding from the National Skills Strategy (Expert Group on Future Skills Needs, 2010) that stated that the most significant challenge facing the country was to up-skill those at Levels 1–3 in order to advocate for the integration of literacy and numeracy across the curriculum in vocational education and training (NALA, 2010).

In 2001 Ireland had low participation rates, but this has changed considerably with 50,000 adults attending courses in 2011 compared with 13,000 in 2000. This change has occurred because of the way in which adult literacy and numeracy has been seen as a priority by all government departments as a result of OECD and EU influences. This means that in the period when funding was available, it did attract increased resources, albeit from a low base. NALA has played an important role in keeping the area on the agenda of ministers through discussions, policy briefing papers and guidelines that are designed to lead to the improvement of the quality of provision.

More work is needed, however, to develop the literacy workforce, as only the adult literacy organiser in the VEC is employed on a permanent basis (while literacy tutors are mostly employed on a temporary basis). One-to-one support, usually through volunteer tutors, is still an essential element of provision, and work is still needed to make sure that they follow a clearly defined structure (Dorgan, 2009). However, one-to-one work is only 10 per cent of the provision, and all the growth has been in group tuition delivered by paid tutors.

It appears then that adult literacy in Ireland has developed considerably over the last ten years. Despite the recession it still has a place in the country's policies, and the intervention of NALA has managed to keep it firmly on policy-makers' agendas. More work is needed, however, to improve the opportunities available for both the paid and the unpaid staff.

A comparison of policies addressing four key questions

What concept of literacy underpins recent policies?

In England, Northern Ireland and Wales, an earlier discourse of individual rights and welfare in educational and social policy coexisted for many years with a narrow functional definition of literacy. However, the discourse of human resource development now dominates the literacy agenda with managerial, technicist and corporate notions (Crowther and Tett, 2011; Hamilton and Pitt, 2011). This has resulted in an increasingly standardised definition of literacies that is linked to formal educational structures and methods of assessment, at both initial and post-school levels. The New Labour government overlaid this approach with a rhetoric that drew on concepts of lifelong learning and social exclusion, reflecting an increased sensitivity to European and other international thinking in the field. Vocational and functional rationales are still powerful, however, and continue to be reinforced by the coalition government in the UK.

In Scotland, policy and practice has been largely influenced by the same forces as above. However, the concept underpinning literacies is more open. One reason for this is that much of the provision of literacies is through community-based providers that are part of the strong tradition of community education in Scotland. This tradition validates the breadth and depth of knowledge that adults acquire in a variety of contexts and particularly through their lived experience (Tett, 2010). The approach means that the learner is seen as being at the centre of provision, and both individual and collective gains are recognised. Wales, too, has maintained a strongly holistic approach, emphasising lifelong and intergenerational aspects of literacy.

In Ireland, as in Scotland, literacies learning is viewed as being not only the acquisition of a technical competence, but also includes the social, cultural and emotional development of the learner; it goes far beyond the mere technical skills of communication. Government documents also recognise the importance of diversity, and view literacies learning as having an important role to play in promoting social inclusion. This means that it is somewhat distanced from the market-driven rhetoric that is otherwise dominant.

How are learners and teachers positioned by the policies?

The influence of the IALS can be seen in how adult learners are constructed by policy in the different countries. In the IALS, adults are treated as one undifferentiated mass of people whose basic skill needs have been defined by experts, and who may or may not recognise the difficulties that they face. The assumption made is that people with literacies difficulties have a deficit that needs to be rectified – primarily because of the needs of the economy. There is a strong tendency for this approach to be reflected in the policy statements that draw upon the IALS findings. The emphasis is on the huge scale of the 'problem', rather than a fine appreciation of its many dimensions in terms of diverse cultural groups and more nuanced understandings of literacies (see the introduction to this book). Despite reference to particular target groups and some specific commitment to cultural diversity, the overall impact is a homogenising one that projects an inadequate mass in need of help.

The English documents most strongly follow the IALS in characterising learners as reluctant and deficient recipients who must be persuaded into programmes designed to address needs they may not yet be aware of. The Moser report (1999, paragraph 1.8) states that 'people with difficulties are often understandably reluctant to acknowledge, or are unaware, that they have a problem', and suggests that 'persuasive publicity' will be needed to encourage people into ABE programmes (see also Sticht, 2003). This discourse is less evident in Wales, Ireland and Scotland, where the approach is more inclusive and evokes a more student-centred model.

Ireland has a particularly distinctive approach that emphasises individual student input and negotiation. Students are construed as willing, voluntary participants with the right to determine what they get within an adult literacy programme, and views about what they need. In Scotland, too, the Curriculum Framework for Adult Literacy and Numeracy (Scottish Executive, 2005) is underpinned by a principle of learner participation.

Teachers are unevenly present in the policy documents. Their role is defined very much in terms of how the learners are seen (joint partners in the learning process or receivers of knowledge). In the English policy documents, the teacher is positioned as a technician, rather than as a professional, who is to be 'upskilled' through short, prescriptive training programmes; there is sporadic consultation, but no right to be involved in the process or representative bodies able to put forward the perspectives of practitioners.

In Scotland, by contrast, there was extensive consultation about the Curriculum Framework, and practitioners met regularly to discuss different aspects of provision under the auspices of the literacies team at Education Scotland.

A working group comprising practitioners, researchers and policy-makers was set up in Scotland in 2011 to report on how to improve the competencies and skills of adult literacies practitioners; it will also be developing a Continuing Professional Development framework in 2012. In Ireland, too, tutors' needs for professional development and accreditation are given top priority. In Wales, quality standards for providers of adult programmes specify a minimum level of qualifications for practitioners (Level 3 of the national framework), but training has never been mandatory and is therefore vulnerable to shifts in funding and policy priorities to other groups. England has seen the greatest formalisation of practitioner qualifications, though these have not drawn strongly on traditions of adult teaching and are aligned with the school-based curriculum.

Overall, tutors rarely appear as powerful actors shaping literacies provision. The dominant assumption is that a strong, preformed framework for delivery is needed to ensure systematic and effective learning, rather than relying on the judgements of securely funded, high level professional staff.

What kinds of learning activities/processes are programmes or initiatives expected to engage in?

There are big differences between the institutional frameworks of the different countries reviewed here. The institutional possibilities are very wide for literacies. This is unlike almost any other kind of education or training, where there are usually clear-cut institutional affiliations and bases (for example, school is the only widespread institutional setting available for children's initial education). This is extremely important for understanding the shape of literacies provision and its development (Hamilton, 2012) and is one of the focal points for policy debate and strategy. The constraints and possibilities for literacies situated within a formal further education college are different from those in a prison setting, a workplace or a community project.

The relationships of cooperation and competition between these different agencies are also crucial. In England, Wales and Northern Ireland, provision is mainly in the formal further education college sector. In Scotland it is mainly in the Local Authority-run community education sector staffed by paid tutors and volunteers, while in Ireland provision in the VECs is the norm. However, despite these different starting points, there is rhetoric common to all the policy documents referring to partnerships between institutions, with local learning plans being formulated by consortia of organisations.

Institutional structures also affect the learning processes that are possible or easy to support. In England, Wales and Northern Ireland, most learners are taught in a college setting, either in groups or in open learning centres. In Scotland, tuition in the community is currently in small groups, although some one-to-one provision still takes place in rural areas, and support for vocational learning mainly takes place in colleges. Formal accreditation in both settings is available through the Core Skills Units introduced by the Scottish Qualifications Authority.

In Ireland, tuition is one-to-one and in small groups, supported mainly by volunteer tutors, and control of programmes is fairly decentred. Tutors are seen as being in partnership with students and are encouraged to carry out self-assessments, and there is a concern to develop robust consultation processes. A learner-centred approach is advocated, with built-in progression opportunities including accreditation. Participation for learners is voluntary and there is an emphasis on the importance of guidance and flexibility of learning opportunities.

What outcomes are literacy programmes and learners expected to achieve?

In all countries, the IALS is used to justify the need for increased participation rates in education and training, with the ultimate aim of achieving increased levels of literacy/numeracy in the population. In England, Wales and Northern Ireland, these aims are realised with target numbers to be met by specific dates.

In England and Northern Ireland there is a very strong emphasis on standardised tests and learner qualifications that fit with the National Vocational Qualification system, and will follow seamlessly from the Key Skills now embedded within initial education. Since the first national accreditation framework (Wordpower and Numberpower) was developed in the late 1980s, the development of assessment has been a central thread in the organisation of adult literacies in England. This effort continued throughout the period of the Skills for Life Strategy, and can most recently be seen in further changes to functional skills assessment. In Wales there is a wider choice of qualifications available, but all are now aligned through the Essential Skills framework with other assessment systems across the UK.

Within programmes in England and Northern Ireland funding has been tied to learning outcomes linked to the national test, and through this accountability to funders has become central to the day-to-day practice of adult literacies. One result of this has been to skew the field towards learners with less complex needs who are easier to move over the threshold test levels (Bathmaker, 2007).

In Scotland a number of different outcomes are important, including targets for increased participation rates, increased levels of literacy/numeracy in the population, and changes in self-esteem and confidence.

This latter issue is also of importance in Ireland, where empowerment and critical reflection and the fulfilment of individual needs are at the forefront of NALA's strategic vision. There is also a concern for progression through flexible learning and accreditation opportunities.

Discussion

It is possible from the detail offered above to draw out some main themes that will determine the shape of the adult literacies of the future.

A renewed policy interest in literacies prompted by international influences

As a service mandated by legislation, literacies now has a secure funding and institutional base in England, Northern Ireland and Wales. Scotland and Ireland have yet to achieve this security, but in all of the countries there has been a renewed policy interest in, and commitment to, literacies. Priority has been given to improving the quality, extent and coherence of provision. An integrated approach to delivering courses through multiagency partnerships, and the inclusion of English, Maths, ESOL and ICT under the umbrella of basic or essential competences was designed to avoid the marginalisation of adult literacies that has limited it so much in the past. Moving into the mainstream, however, risks losing some of the creativity, accessibility and responsiveness that has characterised the best literacies work.

Things are changing swiftly in all four countries, and it is important to understand where the impetus for this change is coming from and who is involved in shaping the future of literacies in these countries. The publication of the IALS 'league tables' for international literacy and numeracy rates has played a major role in the drive to increase participation rates in the adult population, with a corresponding deficit view of people's existing capabilities. The IALS survey, and its successor, the PIAAC, has to be seen as part of broader OECD and EU influences that are also reshaping the larger schooling and training system as part of an agenda of human resource development (Hamilton and Pitt, 2011). This agenda emphasises both literacy and lifelong learning for their assumed contribution to economic prosperity, and aims to integrate basic skills provision across all educational and training sectors. The result is to give prominence to formal, standardised provision, and an associated tendency to develop strongly controlled and narrowly focused approaches to literacies, evident in all the countries reviewed here.

The marketisation of literacies: Standardising frameworks

As described above, one consequence of the renewed interest in literacy is a common concern with the quality, consistency and coherence of provision and accountability to public funders. In England a substantial part of the funding released over the last ten years has been used to put in place a standardised infrastructure consisting of a national curriculum and tests for adult literacy, underpinned by a tightly drawn standards framework. Despite a rhetorical commitment to social inclusion and citizen participation, this system is driven by a market ideology and a vision of the needs of global economic competitiveness. The imperative is to create a skilled workforce and an active consumer, rather than a critically informed citizen. It is based on a top-down definition of literacy, where need is defined for learners rather than negotiated with them on the basis of their perceived needs. However subtle and flexibly designed the curriculum is, it is difficult to transcend this fundamental feature because curricula are designed *for* learners, rather than *with* them or *by* them. To this extent, the more open and humanistic possibilities of a lifelong (and life-wide) system of learning opportunities for literacy are weakened and obscured.

The pressures towards an imposed system of literacy learning increase in times of economic recession and high unemployment, when government funding is typically reduced and refocused on young jobseekers (Tusting and Barton, 2007). These changes have already arrived in Ireland, one of the first countries to experience the impact of the 2008 financial crisis, and they are likely to reverberate across all the countries of the UK into the foreseeable future.

The role of the literacies professional

In none of the settings we have reviewed here does there appear to be a strong professional voice moderating the official policy agendas. This is in contrast to what has happened in school-based reforms, where teachers were able to exert some influence over the development of new assessments and curricula. The reasons for this are clear: a fragmented and low status workforce, including many volunteers and part-time workers; and a lack of training and no representative professional associations or stable networks that could develop such bodies. Despite the progress made in England in introducing a framework for professional qualification, there has been little change in these working conditions.

This means that literacies practitioners are ill-equipped to move into more powerful positions in the expanded provision that has developed. They are used to working creatively 'in the cracks', with inadequate funding or formal structures that do not support the understandings that they have gained from their experience about what good practice entails. However, they are not used to being involved in the wider processes of policy formation or designing structures that can work, arguing their case in public or systematically documenting their achievements. Some spaces for this have been available, especially through practitioner-led research initiatives funded in Scotland and England, and through individual pieces of continuing professional development (Hamilton and Appleby, 2009).

The role of research

While the educational and linguistic research base for adult literacies has developed considerably over the last 20 years, it has proved difficult for research to challenge the economic arguments advanced by both national and international bodies to underpin policy rationales in the field. Evidence-based policy activity has led to a step change in government-funded research. However, the debates and pressures described above for practitioners are also felt within the research community. It has been hard to keep open the spaces for more participatory or qualitative research evidence to be accepted, which could offer alternative perspectives that acknowledge the complexity of the everyday practice of literacy learning and teaching. For alternative arguments to have persuasive force in policy circles, they need to be well articulated and based on a coherent model of literacy, such as that advanced by the research work of the New Literacy Studies (see Chapter 1).

Conclusion

In Scotland and Ireland especially, and in community-based literacy in all countries, there is evidence of attempts to build in respect for some of the core values of adult literacies work within transparent, consistent frameworks, for improving access and quality in the context of a consultative and empowering policy process. How powerfully these values will be represented in the literacies of the future depends on the larger social policy context in each country, and the possibilities for democratic control of the policy process. As always, there are competing policy discourses that may pull adult literacies in different directions. In this case, the lifelong learning, active citizenship and social inclusion agendas, if they are creatively and critically understood, offer possibilities for more open definitions of literacies than the human resources development model still dominant within initial education.

Policy waves rise and fall over time (Hodgson *et al.*, 2007) and we can learn from other countries' experiences of literacy and language policy, especially from Australia, Canada and other European and Scandinavian countries with contexts close to our own (see, for example, Lo Bianco, 2003).

The last decade was a particular moment of opportunity for literacies in the UK and in Ireland, in which the field expanded and was integrated within the landscape of lifelong learning in new ways. In the changed political and economic climate that has followed, it will be instructive to see what is sustainable from the developments introduced during this time. These were mainly the result of top-down policy initiatives that did not build strongly on the history of participatory approaches to adult learning, traditions of voluntary and popular associations.

A great deal of new research has been produced that can underpin and justify a broad-based and sustainable approach to practice (Crowther *et al.*, 2010; Crowther and Tett, 2011). In the longer term it remains to be seen how the different perspectives of potential learners, students, providers and policy-makers will be heard about what adult literacies are, where they stand in relation to other aspects of lifelong learning, and in what ways they will contribute to the vision of the countries of the UK and Ireland as dynamic learning societies. Arguably, the Skills for Life Strategy will leave its mark through the discourses and the infrastructure it set up, as will the Adult Literacies Policy in Scotland. Pressures from the international policy community will continue through new waves of survey activity including the PIAAC, which is likely to be very influential in the way that policy is developed and in shaping our definitions of adult literacy and numeracy in the future.

In developing the field of adult literacies, individual countries can exert a strong national steer, but this will inevitably be within a wider framework of interconnected social polices and international agendas. As practitioners and researchers, we need to understand this complexity and how it shapes day-to-day practice and funding opportunities. We need to be clear about where our commitments and underpinning values and assumptions about literacy lie, and skilful in articulating these within the policy arena.

Acknowledgements

We are grateful to the following individuals and organisations who provided us with information for this chapter: Inez Bailey, NALA; Marie Thompson, LSDA Northern Ireland; Rachel Stubley, Newport College.

References

BSA (Basic Skills Agency) (2001) *Improving Standards of Literacy and Numeracy in Wales: a National Strategy*. BSA.

Bathmaker, A.-M. (2007) 'The impact of Skills for Life on adult basic skills in England: how should we interpret trends in participation and achievement?'. *International Journal of Lifelong Education*, Vol. 26 No 3, pp. 295–313.

Brookes, G. (2011) *A Tale of IALS's Influence (or not) in the UK*. Paper presented at the Centre for Literacy Studies Fall Institute IALS (International Adult Literacy Survey) Its Meaning And Impact For Policy And Practice, October 23–25, 2011.

Cara, O., Litster, J., Swain, J., Vorhaus, J. (2008) *The Teacher Study: The Impact of the Skills for Life Strategy on Teachers – Summary Report: a Study of 1027 Teachers of Literacy, Numeracy and ESOL in England from 2004 to 2007*. NRDC.

Carey, S. (1997) *Adult Literacy in Britain.* Office for National Statistics.

Carey, S. (ed.) (2000) *Measuring Adult Literacy: The International Adult Literacy Survey in the European Context.* Office for National Statistics.

Carpentieri, J. (2007) *Five Years On: Research, Development and Changing Practice. NRDC 2006–7.* National Research and Development Centre for Adult Literacy, Numeracy.

Cooke, M. and Simpson, J. (2009) 'Challenging agendas in ESOL: Skills, employability and social cohesion'. *Language Issues,* Vol. 20 No 1, pp. 19–31.

Crowther, J., Maclachlan, K. and Tett, L. (2010) 'Adult literacy, learning identities and pedagogic practice'. *International Journal of Lifelong Education,* Vol. 29 No 6, pp. 651–64.

Crowther, J. and Tett, L. (2011) 'Critical and social literacy practices from the Scottish adult literacy experience: resisting deficit approaches to learning'. *Literacy,* pp. 126–31.

DEL (Department for Employment and Learning) (2002) *Essential Skills for Living. Equipped for the Future: Building for Tomorrow.* DEL.

DEL (Department for Employment and Learning) (2005) *Essential Skills Fund 2005/06 FE 05/05.* DEL.

DEL (Department for Employment and Learning) (2009) *Operational Guidelines For Essential Skills in Application of Number, Communication and ICT 2009/2010, FE 06/09.* DEL.

DENI (Department of Education for Northern Ireland) (1998) *The Learning Age.* DENI.

DfES (Department for Employment and Skills) (2001) *Skills for Life Strategy.* The Stationery Office.

DIUS (2009) *Skills for Life: Changing Lives.* Available at www.talent. ac.uk/news_details.asp?newsid=1920 [accessed 2 July 2012].

Department for Work and Pensions (2001) *National Action Plan for Social Inclusion.* The Stationery Office.

Dorgan, J. (2009) *A Review for the National Adult Literacy Agency.* Dublin: NALA.

Expert Group on Future Skills Needs (2007) *National Skills Strategy.* Dublin: Government of Ireland. Available at www.skillsstrategy.ie/ [accessed 2 July 2012].

Expert Group on Future Skills Needs (2010) *National Skills Strategy Implementation Statement.* Dublin: Government of Ireland. Available at *www.forfas.ie/media/egfsn2110504-Statement_of_Activity_2010.pdf* [accessed 2 July 2012].

Freire, P. (1976) *Pedagogy of the Oppressed*. Penguin.

Furlong, C. (2011) 'We need a joined-up approach to basic skills'. *Adults Learning*, Vol. 23 No 1, pp. 38–9.

FEFC (Further Education Funding Council) (1998) *Curriculum Area Survey Report: Basic Education*. FEFC.

Gal, I., Alatorre, S., Close, S., Evans, J., Johansen, L., Maguire, T., Manly, M. and Tout, D. (2009) *PIAAC Numeracy: a Conceptual Framework*. Paris: OECD.

Government of Ireland (2000) *Learning for Life: White Paper on Adult Education*. Dublin: Government of Ireland.

Government of Ireland (2002) *Report of the Taskforce on Lifelong Learning*. Dublin: Government of Ireland.

Government of Ireland (2006) *Joint Oireachtas Committee on Education and Science Report into Adult Literacy*. Dublin: Government of Ireland. Available at www.oireachtas.ie/documents/committees29thdail/committeereport2006/Adult-lit.pdf [accessed 30 October 2011].

Government of Ireland (2007) *National Action Plan for Social Inclusion 2007–2016*. Dublin: Government of Ireland. Available at www.social inclusion.ie/documents/NAPinclusionReportPDF.pdf [accessed 30 October 2011].

Hamilton (2012) 'The effects of the literacy policy environment on local sites of learning', in Special Issue of *Language and Education* on 'Literacies and Sites of Learning'. Vol. 26 No 2, pp. 166–182.

Hamilton, M. and Appleby, Y. (2009) 'Critical perspectives on practitioner research: introduction to the special edition'. *Studies in the Education of Adults*, Vol. 41 No 2, pp. 107–17.

Hamilton, M. and Hillier, Y. (2006) *Changing Faces of Adult Literacy, Language and Numeracy: a Critical History*. Trentham Books.

Hamilton, M. and Hillier, Y. (2007) 'Deliberative policy analysis: adult literacy assessment and the politics of change'. *Journal of Educational Policy*, Vol. 22 No 5, pp. 573–94.

Hamilton, M. and Pitt, K. (2011) 'Changing policy discourses: constructing literacy inequalities'. *International Journal of Educational Development*, Vol. 31 No 6, pp. 596–605.

Henry, M., Lingard, B., Rizvi, F. and Taylor, S. (2001) *The OECD, Globalisation and Education Policy*. Amsterdam: International Association of Universities Press, Pergamon.

Hodgson, A., Edward, S. and Gregson, M. (2007) 'Riding the waves of policy? The case of basic skills in adult and community learning in

England'. *Journal of Vocational Education and Training,* Vol. 59 No 2, pp. 13–229.

Lawn, M. and Grek. S. (2009) 'A short history of Europeanizing education: the new political work of calculating the future'. *European Education Issues and Studies* Vol. 41 No 1, pp. 32–54.

Leitch, S. (2006) *Prosperity for All in the Global Economy: World Class Skills, Final Report of the Leitch Review of Skills.* The Treasury.

Levitas, R. (2005). *The Inclusive Society? Social Exclusion and New Labour.* Palgrave Macmillan.

Lo Bianco, J. (2003) *A Site for Debate, Contestation and Negotiation of National Identity: Language Policy in Australia.* Strasbourg: Council of Europe.

Moser, C. (1999) *Improving Literacy and Numeracy. A Fresh Start: the Report of the Working Group Chaired by Sir Claus Moser.* Department for Education and Employment.

NALA (2010) *A Literature Review of International Adult Literacy Policies.* Prepared for NALA by the NRDC. Institute Of Education.

National Assembly for Wales and BSA (Basic Skills Agency) (2001) *Improving Standards of Literacy and Numeracy in Wales: A National Strategy.* BSA.

National Assembly for Wales (2005) *Words Talk – Numbers Count: the Welsh Assembly Government's Strategy to Improve Basic Literacy and Numeracy in Wales.* National Assembly for Wales Circular No: 15/2005, April 2005.

National Assembly for Wales (2010) *National Literacy Plan – Basic Skills Budgets 2010–2011 Statement of Information.* Welsh Government.

Newman, J. (2002) 'Changing governance, changing equality? New Labour and the modernisation of public services'. *Public Money and Management,* Vol. 22 No 1, pp. 7–14.

NIACE (2011) *Work, Society and Lifelong Literacy Report of the Inquiry into Adult Literacy in England.* NIACE.

OECD (Organization of Economic Co-operation and Development) (2000), *Literacy in the Information Age: Final Report of the International Adult Literacy Survey.* Paris: OECD.

Schleicher, A. (2008) 'PIAAC: A New Strategy For Assessing Adult Competencies'. *International Review of Education.* DOI 10.1007/s11159-008-9105-0. Springer.

Scottish Executive (2001) *Adult Literacy and Numeracy in Scotland.* Stationery Office.

Scottish Executive (2005) *An Adult Literacy and Numeracy Curriculum Framework for Scotland*. Stationery Office.

Scottish Government (2007a) *Scottish Budget Spending Review 2007*. Scottish Government.

Scottish Government (2007b) *Scotland Performs, National Indicators*. Scottish Government.

Scottish Government (2011) *Adult Literacies in Scotland 2020: Strategic Guidance*. Scottish Government. Available at www.scotland.gov.uk/ Publications/2011/01/25121451/0 [accessed 13 June 2012].

Sliwka, A. and Tett, L. (2008) 'Case Study: Scotland', in *Teaching, learning and assessment for adults: improving foundation skills*. Paris: OECD. Available at http://dx.doi.org/10.1787/172212187274 [accessed 26 November 2011].

Sticht, T. (2003) *Have the literacy skills of adults in England improved since 1997? A critique of the Skills for Life literacy survey of 2003*. New Zealand Literacy Portal. Available at www.nzliteracyportal.org.nz/ download/20040210010214Critique%20of%20the%20UK%20 Skills%20for%20Life%20Literacy%20Survey1.txt [accessed 19 June 2012].

Tett, L. (2010) *Community Education, Learning and Development*. Dunedin Press.

The Poverty Site (2011) *Welsh Indicators*. Available at www.poverty.org. uk/summary/wales.htm [accessed 2 July 2012].

Tight, M. (1998) 'Education, Education, Education! The vision of lifelong learning in the Kennedy, Dearing and Fryer reports'. *Oxford Review of Education*, Vol. 24 No 4, pp. 473–85.

Tusting, K. and Barton, D. (2007) *Programmes for Unemployed People since the 1970s: the Changing Place of Literacy, Language and Numeracy*. NRDC.

Vorhaus, J., Litster, J., Frearson, M. and Johnson, S. (2011) *A Review of Research on Improving Adult Skills*. Department for Business, Innovation and Skills research paper number 61. Available at www.bis.gov.uk/ assets/biscore/further-education-skills/docs/r/11-1418-review-research-on-improving-adult-skills.pdf [accessed 2 July 2012].

Welsh Statistics Directorate (2010) *National Survey of Adult Skills in Wales First Statistical Release*, SDR 119/2011. Welsh Government. Available at http://wales.gov.uk/docs/statistics/2011/110713sdr1192011en.pdf [accessed 2 July 2012].

Welshman, J. (2006). *Underclass: a History of the Excluded 1880–2000*. Continuum Books.

Wolf, A. and Evans, K. (2010) *Improving skills at work*. Routledge.

SECTION TWO

MAKING POWER VISIBLE

CHAPTER THREE

Signatures and the lettered world

JANE MACE

To be able to write your own name is the first literacy ambition. To begin with, you copy it, forming the letters. Later, when it comes easily, you doodle a little, play with a different way of crossing the 't' or looping the 'g'. You are writing your name independently. You may even be able to do it in front of witnesses. This written version of your name, at another time, might have appeared in a public register and formed the basis of a calculation as to how many people in your village could read and write. It is evidence that yours is a hand capable of manipulating pen or pencil and therefore of writing other signs and symbols, such as a tick on a voting slip. It signifies that you are a person who can scribe your self on a page other than with your thumb.

When I stop to think about it, I seem to have been puzzling over the meaning of signatures for some time. In 1994, when I was invited to give a keynote speech at a national conference on adult literacy in Australia, this was the topic that I worked on. I wanted to have another look at the ways in which literacy achievement is measured, and the strange concept of using marriage register signatures as a measurement tool for literacy would not leave me alone (Mace, 1995). In the course of thinking about those things, I was reminded of the many ways in which the signature features in public and private settings – often, in fact, signalling an overlap between the two. During that time, too, I had begun my own kind of historical research, seeking out accounts from living memory of the literacy lives of mothers bringing up children in the late nineteenth and early twentieth century (later published in Mace, 1998), and among many stories came pictures of women who kept autograph books. Reading about and visiting literacy programmes in African countries for the first time, a couple of years later, helped me to think about *franchise* and literacy – the difference between the print of a thumb and the mark of a pen. So it is that, in this chapter, I have chosen to bring together some of these lines of thought and invite you to consider with me the different meanings that signatures and name writing hold in the lettered world of the early twenty-first century. At a time when the technologies of writing allow us to transmit texts in all kinds of fonts and formats across great distances in a matter of seconds, the signature continues to be (I suggest) a literacy practice that has a deeply symbolic importance as a tool for empowerment.

I begin with some examples of how the signature has featured in the work of historians. I then consider what it means as a form of writing that is different from simply writing a name, and what that means for the owner of the name. By the end, I want to have shown you that the act of writing a signature remains a donation: the gift of our consent, agreement and commitment.

The historian

From the mid-1800s until the early twentieth century, one source above others was used as an indicator of literacy: the marriage register. Throughout Europe, the practice of recording a marriage in a register had been prevalent since the sixteenth century, but only from the early nineteenth century did it become common to require that both bride and groom should write their names on it (Houston, 1988, p. 123). The first national report on literacy in England, made in 1840, was based on statistics of signatures in marriage registers. On this evidence, it concluded that 67 per cent of males and 51 per cent of females were literate (Altick, 1983, p.170). Today we have serious misgivings about a signature being an indicator of literacy. But it is worth considering today what attractions it had then.

To discover the extent of literacy in a past beyond living memory, historians have had to rely on what has been written: school attendance figures, sales of published writing, autobiographies, and so on. They may also, in the case of some European countries, turn to data provided by self-assessments – a source which can only ever tell part of the story. If you or I opened our door to a stranger asking if we could read and write, our answer would be a chosen version of a very relative matter, coloured by the mood we happened to be in, what we were in the middle of doing, when the questioner arrived, and so on. The likelihood of the answer being anything near an objectively measurable 'truth' seems to be fairly remote. No wonder that historians read statistics based on these statements with caution. How much more straightforward must the signature on a register appear. It is, surely, authentic evidence of at least the writer's ability to write their own name. But of course it will say no more than that and, in fact, as a measure of literacy, it says almost nothing. Even if it can suggest the ability to read and write, the signature cannot tell the reader whether the writer actually *did* either of these things. Similarly, being able to write your name on one occasion does not mean you could write it again. In addition, in the absence of any witnesses who could confirm this either way, it's impossible to know how many people *copied* their name. (In seventeenth- and eighteenth-century France, it was apparently common for the writing teacher to write out the pupil's name on a slip of paper so that it could be copied when the need arose: a *modèle* (Houston, 1988, p. 126.)

'The task of signing the marriage register', writes David Vincent:

> *was the only examination the great majority of the population would ever face. Those who signed displayed both their identity and their independence; those who did not remained anonymous until the register was completed by another hand.* (Vincent, 1993, p. 21)

'Anonymous'? Well, not to those who were there, of course. To the witnesses, family, friends and spouse, the groom or bride who picked up the pen and made a cross on the page was very much a person with an identity, a history and a future. It is to the rest of us, those not present, examining the records, that this person lacks existence.

In unlettered company, the question of whether you could write your name may have little importance compared with other abilities. For researchers reading such signatures from within another time and place, there is a deceptive simplicity about them. But what of the cross, or mark? Is that always the sign of someone who cannot write their name or might it be possible, just occasionally, to think that a person who *could* write their name actually chose not to? In a culture that prizes literacy, we might find that surprising. Yet here is a story in which, apparently, a woman did just that.

On the one hand, there are the 'facts'. In 1852, the parish of St Albans in Hertfordshire had a population of 18,000 men, women and children.

Of the couples who were married that year, apparently just over half signed their names, and just under half signified their names with a mark or cross (Stephens, 1987, p. 324). Now for the 'fiction'. It is the description of a scene set in a village church not far from St Albans, just a year or two before 1852. The scene is observed through the eyes of someone called Esther:

> *The bridegroom, to whom the pen was handed first, made a rude cross for his mark; the bride, who came next, did the same. Now, I had known the bride when I was last there, not only as the prettiest girl in the place, but as having quite distinguished herself in the school; and I could not help looking at her with some surprise. She came aside and whispered to me, while tears of honest love and admiration stood in her bright eyes. 'He's a dear good fellow, miss; but he can't write, yet − he's going to learn of me − and I wouldn't shame him for the world!' Why, what had I to fear, I thought, when there was this nobility in the soul of a labouring man's daughter!*

This episode occurs in *Bleak House*, the novel that Charles Dickens published between 1852 and 1853 in 19 monthly parts. For Dickens (through the character of Esther), its dramatic interest lies not so much with the groom's 'rude cross' but with that of his bride. Here is a woman who is able to write her name but chooses to pretend that she cannot. Here, as he put it, is the 'nobility in the soul' of a labourer's daughter who avoids shaming her husband by drawing attention to her own literacy. Here, too, however, is a marriage register mark which has to be read as that of a literate pretending illiteracy. And if one person might have done that, what are we to think of the rest of the writing in that register?

Another story adds possibilities to this one. Among the Mass Observation Archive writers who contributed to my own research on the literacy lives of mothers rearing children in the late nineteenth and early twentieth century, one recalled contrasting uses of signature and mark by the same woman. Her grandmother, she recalled, married in 1896 and signed the marriage register. A year later (in 1897), the same woman registered the death of her mother. This time she did not give her signature, but made the mark of a cross on the register. The woman, who had been born in 1874 of an 'extremely poor' family, had grown up in Lancaster, later moving to Manchester. The question that intrigued her granddaughter was: why did she write her name one year, and the next resort to a mark? These were her speculations on the matter. Either:

1 *she hadn't learned to write her married name, or*
2 *she was too shocked and upset to write, or*
3 *she did not want to put her name to what was on the death certificate (it was not all correct information).*
(J931 quoted in Mace, 1998, p. 114)

As for the *Bleak House* scene, it appears that Dickens was (as so often) echoing a prevailing concern of his time. Victorian researchers had their own doubts about the validity of signatures:

There was some concern that the pressures surrounding the marriage ceremony might cause a literate bride or groom to make a mark out of nervousness, or out of fear of embarrassing an illiterate spouse. (Vincent, 1993, p. 17)

In reporting this, David Vincent goes on to say why he does not share this concern – and would presumably read the actions of Dickens' 'noble soul' as a fiction in the full sense of the word. In a closely argued chapter on family literacy in the early nineteenth century, he rejects the association of shame with illiteracy, largely on the grounds that illiteracy was too ordinary to carry any stigma –

In households, in the informal relationships in the neighbourhood, literate and illiterate were everywhere in each other's company. (Vincent, 1993, p. 23)

– and evidently marriage ceremonies were no exception. From an analysis of signatures and marks in marriage registers between 1839 and 1854, Vincent found that only three out of ten newly-weds could sign their name, yet as many as three in four weddings managed to include at least one literate individual in the ceremony. Witnesses to marriages, Vincent argues, are as important to the literacy historian as the bride and groom themselves. Using a study of witness marks and signatures, he looked to see if there was evidence that literate spouses felt they should avoid illiterate witnesses. Instead, he found literate couples accepting illiterate witnesses as often as he found illiterates seeking out literates (1993, p. 31–2). 'The issue of embarrassment', he concluded, 'was not as acute as observers sometimes assumed' (1993, p. 17).

We cannot be sure either way. To confuse the picture still further, here is a story cited by Richard Altick. He writes of W. I. Sargant, a Victorian commentator who was concerned at the high number of marks in marriage registers as a valid measure of literacy. Like Dickens, Sargant suggested sentimental reasons for a person who could write to disguise their literacy – this time with the opposite gender slant. In the 1867 *Journal of the Statistical Society*, Sargant suggested that when a literate man took an illiterate bride 'he chivalrously wrote his X instead of his name to save her embarrassment' (Altick, 1983, p. 170).

The owner of the name

So far I have been exploring a little of the mystery behind the apparent simplicity of signatures as a measure of literacy. Far more mysterious than this, I believe, is the personal significance of being able to write our own name. Given the opportunity, we learn young to make marks and draw. Later, with help, we turn these into the shapes and lines that might, later still, correspond to our own names. Once we can do this, many of us repeat the experience over and over again in idle moments during lessons or meetings – copying, recopying, trying out styles and shapes until we find the one that pleases us. But what if we find ourselves unable to do it, while others can? What then might be our sense of loss? Ursula Howard has a suggestive answer. In her study of self-educated working-class women and men in the nineteenth century, she writes of the evident loneliness of some of these individuals and their determination to teach themselves, in the absence of any other teachers. Reflecting on their autobiographical writing, she concludes:

> *The self who lived without a signature and without a voice in a lettered world was a different self than one who could write.* (Howard, 1991, p. 107)

For any one of us who happens to have grown up in a society full of writing, she suggests that being unable to write our own name is equivalent to being unable to inscribe our selves in that society; to write our names is to write ourselves into the world.

If, on the other hand, we can write our names, and write them in public places, readers may have very different reactions to this, according to context. Sometimes we read these names as romantic inscriptions; at other times, we see them as defacements. Debbie Pounds, in her poem *Same as it ever was*, captures something of this contrast in the reactions of the reader:

We carved our names on trees of oak
Scratched true love on legs of desks
Whittled away the world's wood.
> *Romantics.*
They spray paint initials on corrugated iron
Scribble dirty jokes on plastic tables
Deface flats with felt tip pens.
> *Vandals.*

> (Pounds, 1989)

The petty vandalism of lovers is innocent, part of a nostalgic past; their writing material is of the oldest kind. The inscriptions of those who 'scribble' and 'deface', by contrast, are shown as offensive; their initials and dirty jokes are alive and present – the spray paint may be barely dry. Mary Wolfe's analysis of the challenges posed by urban graffiti sees these as a private dialogue in public spaces: a deliberate contradiction. The 'tagging' by the graffiti artist is his or her personal signature, intelligible only to those in the know. In this sense, she argues, the graffiti artist is challenging conventions, maintaining a secret identity to all but the initiates:

> *This is writing as counter culture; in a prohibited public space, it is the personal made public.* (Wolfe, 1998, p. 19)

Whether seen as romantics or vandals, these writers are writing in secret: whittling away their names or scrawling defiant jokes in private for others to read later in public. Not for them the twentieth century 'conceit of cultivated illegibility' (Vincent, 1993, p. 21). Each letter in the words 'Gary loves Sharon' (for instance) is etched so that it can be read. 'Vandals' who have purposes other than romantic ones may indeed choose to write anonymously, but (unlike the person who can only represent themselves in the register by writing a mark) this anonymity is a choice.

Our signature is the way we write our name, which is distinctive to us and us alone. In writing it, we ask ourselves to do two things at once: to produce a version that no one else can, and to write it so that we ourselves will be able to repeat it in exactly the same way every time. In contrast to the secret name writing of lovers, formal name writing is a very public matter to which there are, very often, witnesses who are there to ensure that the signature is authentic. At its most extreme, the publicly witnessed signature is part of a very public ceremony where signatories are representatives of whole peoples. In her study of media images of literacy, Mary Hamilton refers to the 'legal power' of this kind of signature writing in which the writing of the signature not only confers authority to the document but is a performance for public purposes 'within political and business deals'. She chooses the useful term 'literacy as ritual public gesture' to sum up this kind of literacy (Hamilton, 2000, p. 21). These gestures carry the burden of history with them, as this example suggests. The story is of two public signature rituals, more than a century apart, deep in the cultural history of Aotearoa (New Zealand). The first and most recent is that of the British monarch. In 1995, the Queen signed a document formally recording the apology of her government to the Maori people for the historic damage by its predecessors to Maori lands and ancestors. In doing so, she was acting out the same symbolic literacy event that her antecedents had imposed on the Maori leaders more than a century before.

The second, nearly two centuries ago, is that of 240 Maori chiefs, who, on 6 February 1840, signed the document at Waitangi transferring ownership of Maori lands to the British crown. The Maori leaders felt a mark of particular significance was necessary for this transaction. With customs that transcended documentary promises and silent writing, the chiefs were agreeing to pledge their allegiance to a queen who lived on the other side of the world. In choosing how to mark their consent, a few chose European-style signatures for the benefit of the Governor General's men standing beside them. Many, however, preferred the authority of their own marks: those that derived from each chief's particular moko or facial tattoo. This facial signature had a depth of meaning that those of us who are illiterate in Maori symbolic and cultural life can only guess at (Hailstone, 1993).

In the years between these two historical moments, the newspaper image of heads of state grasping fountain pens and signing peace treaties has become commonplace. Caught up in the bureaucracies of industrial society, it is easy to forget the significance of such pictures. Whether written by a queen in apology for her people's historic crimes, or by a single parent claiming the benefit to which she is entitled, the signature is a symbol. It stands as the writer's agreement to all that has gone before, as if the writer is saying: all this is true, and my own name written here by me shows that I am not lying in what this says, and that I give my consent to it. Only with a signature is the legal document made valid. Globalisation may run on the Internet but the handmade inscription is still necessary for transactions to be complete. For transactions between the individual and the state, a kind of public ceremony is called for: the beneficiary of pension or income support must queue up in person to sign at a counter in front of others. The person as well as their signature must be present.

To be unable to write your name, to sign it in your own idiosyncratic way, is to be deprived of the choice *not* to give your name to something. One adult literacy learner, looking back on a time before he had achieved 'nominal literacy', expressed it like this:

> *If I don't agree with the contents of the document ... I just don't sign. Whereas before, one could never refuse to sign.* (Nelson, 1981, p. 87)

To have the right to give or to withhold your name is an important civil right. For a democracy to function, it may not be absolutely essential that a population can write their own name because we do not write when we vote. However, the ability to hold a pen and make a mark may make the difference between a wasted ballot paper and a vote. The print of a thumb may blur the line between one box and the next. Naigaga Irene Ouma, a local councillor in the county of Bugiri, Uganda, told me recently:

> *The Council has supported adult literacy because they want votes in the future. In the last elections in '96, many votes were spoilt with so many people using the thumbprint.* (Mace and Keihangwe, 2000)

She and others with whom I spoke during a short visit to her country spoke of rural people increasingly feeling 'disgusted' at being forced to use their thumbs to signify their choice or their agreement. I visited women in villages who were participants in literacy classes and, with the

69

help of an interpreter, asked them to tell me something of what they had learned. At each interview, I asked first if the woman would write her name for me in my notebook, so that I would be sure not to mistake the spelling of it. Each time, I witnessed the writing of the speaker's name. I was a witness, she the signator, slowly scribing her name to help me know her. These were women who until recently had had to rely on thumbs. In the course of learning the act of writing, they had also been learning much else, building on what they already knew about their communities and their lives to make new possibilities happen – for water supplies, for food production, for their own health.

In the United Nations Educational, Scientific and Cultural Organization (UNESCO) catalogue of posters, published to celebrate International Literacy Year, there is a particularly striking image on this theme. Produced by the Directorate of Education in Jaipur, India, it shows a large thumb planted firmly on a page of script. Beneath the poster is a translation of the text, half-concealed beneath the thumb:

> *We borrowed one hundred rupees. We gave our thumbprint on a paper. For many years we have been paying interest. But the debt still remains unpaid.* (Giere, 1992, p. 47)

This is an image of betrayal. Literate people stand accused. If we had been able to read the small print of your paperwork (say the thumb owners), we would never have given our agreement to it. You claim we owe you money, but you owe us your literacy: you, the world's rich, are using yours to cheat us. Here, the thumbprint is not the mark that risks spoiling a ballot paper. It is a humiliation.

So?

I began this essay by noting that writing your name is not the same as signing your name. For myself, I write my *name* (Jane Mace) clearly, so that it can be read. When I write my *signature* (Jane S. Mace), however, the curve and push of the lines are almost entirely out of alignment with the shape of the letters they purport to represent. The 'J' swoops up from bottom to top, across the upright and back, making a lasso of the 'a'. This doubles back to push a track in which neither of the letters ('n' and 'e') due to follow can be discerned. Then comes the forward snake of an 'S' (my middle initial). Up rushes the great wave of the 'M', a breaker tumbling down into the ripple that ends it all (and could not possibly be taken for the three letters that spell out the rest of the name).

I have been writing my signature like this for years, although I could not be sure when it got fixed in that shape. Some days I have reason to write it several times. I sign letters, I write cheques, I fill in forms and sign my name at the bottom. And each time my hand (more or less) reproduces the same combination of loops and ripples. It is my signature, the graphic me, as near-impossible as possible to reproduce. Accept no substitute: only I can write my name like that. Woe betide me if I suddenly take it into my head to loop the 'J' differently. The clerk in front of me, if she is doing her job, would compare it with the scrawl on my card and see an unacceptable difference. Worse still is the moment when, on a form designed to be machine read, I write my signature so that some part of it trespasses outside the designated box – as I recently did, not once, but three times on the form for renewing my passport. But I can also write my name so that it is clear and legible, in carefully joined–up writing, keeping to a straight line. The reason I do not have to write the legible version very often is either that there is a typed name already there, or that I have written the printed version alongside the signature.

Literacy classrooms across the world are full of stories about name writing. Day after day in this 'lettered world', decisions have to be made about where and how to sign a name. Literacy learners know they may be able to get help to fill in the form, but only they can sign it – and in signing it, they have committed themselves. Let me offer a couple of possibilities we might use, any of us, among a group of people interested in literacy:

- Let each person write their name, putting down all the names they have, whether or not they use them every day. Invite each person to tell the group about these names – about who chose them, and which ones they like or dislike – and get them to teach the rest of the group the proper spelling. Write the preferred names of the group on a whiteboard or flipchart sheet of paper. Consider them.
- Give everyone in the group two cards of two different colours. Ask them to write their name on one in their best handwriting. Then ask them to write on the other in the way they feel is most personal to them. Exchange cards. Spend some time wondering about handwriting style. Invite people to try out the style of their neighbour's signature. Reflect on this.

We expect signatures to be unique to their owner and we expect the signer to reproduce the same version of the signature every time they write it. These two expectations have not always been there: they are the creature of our times. To be able to inscribe your name in full is indeed a primary literacy ambition – to write it in a way that no one else could reproduce is about showing that the name is yours and yours alone. Here, from among the stories offered by Mass Observation Archive writers for my research on mothers in the 1890s, is a picture that captures the special activity this represents:

> *Although she was a great reader, her writing skills were almost non-existent. I always took this for granted, but can clearly remember how, whenever she had to write her name, anyone who was around was called in to assist; and the only picture in my mind that I have of her writing is of her surrounded by a small crowd holding their breaths.* (R446 quoted in Mace, 1998, p. 113)

This is the writing of the name as a performance, complete with audience, breathless with anticipation. It is a good moment to end this collection of thoughts about signatures and name writing. It seems to me to portray something of the fundamental importance that the ability to write our own name represents: an ability which is, or should be, a human right. Each one of us should have the right to write our names in at least two ways – legibly and illegibly – and to have the choice not only about *how* we write it but also *whether* we do so. A full literacy life in a lettered world means a person having the choice of being able to write her or his name so that it can be read, but also, when she or he so desires, to write it in the way that is theirs and theirs alone.

References

Altick, R. (1983) *The English Common Reader: A Social History of the Mass Reading Public.* Chicago: University of Chicago Press.

Giere, U. (1992) *Worlds of Words: An International Exhibition of Literacy Posters.* Stuttgart: UNESCO.

Hailstone, M. (1993) 'Te tiriti' (The treaty), *Visible Language,* Vol. 27 No 3, Summer, pp. 302–19.

Hamilton, M. (2000) 'Exploring literacy as social practice through media photographs' in *Situated Literacies,* (eds) Barton, D., Hamilton, M. and Ivanic, R., pp. 16–34. Routledge.

Houston, R. A. (1988) *Literacy in Early Modern Europe: Culture and Education 1500–1800.* Longman.

Howard, U. (1991) 'Self, education and writing in nineteenth-century English communities' in *Writing in the Community,* Barton, D. and Ivanic, R., pp. 78–109. Sage.

Mace, J. (1995) 'The politics of measurement: from signatures to significance' in *Critical Issues, Essential Priorities: Conference papers – 18th National Conference,* (ed.) Palfreeman, A., pp. 35–43. Melbourne: Australian Council for Adult Literacy.

Mace, J. (1998) *Playing with Time: Mothers and the Meaning of Literacy.* UCL Press.

Mace, J. and Keihangwe, S. (2000) *'We are Together, We are Many': Adult Literacy in Rural Uganda.* World University Service (UK).

Nelson, A. J. (1981) *On the Importance of Being Literate.* Melbourne: Australian Council for Adult Literacy.

Pounds, D. (1989) *Same as it ever was* in *Once I was a Washing Machine: The Working Class Experience in Poetry and Prose,* p. 44. Federation of Worker Writers and Community Publishers (reproduced with permission of the author).

Stephens, W. B. (1987) *Education, Literacy and Society, 1830–1870: The Geography of Diversity in Provincial England.* Manchester University Press.

Vincent, D. (1993) *Literacy and Popular Culture: England, 1750–1914.* Cambridge University Press.

Wolfe, M. (1998) 'Shake, rattle and write', *RaPAL Bulletin,* No 35, Spring, pp. 17–20.

CHAPTER FOUR

Beyond disempowering counts: Mapping a fruitful future for adult literacies

TANNIS ATKINSON

Over the past few decades, adult literacy advocates in many parts of the Global North have found it increasingly difficult to campaign for programmes that address the ways that 'low literacy' affects the lives of adult learners. It has become ever more challenging to deal with – or even to discuss – the complex of exclusions such as poverty, poor health, lack of employment and high rates of incarceration that correlate to lack of fluency in dominant literacies.

Perhaps advocates' and practitioners' frustration results largely from the fact that current policies do not build on the substantial knowledge about adult literacy practice developed over the past century. The policies ignore the fact that successful mass literacy campaigns in the twentieth century required 'national (political) commitment and the participation of the people', conditions that were only met in campaigns 'conducted by socialist or revolutionary regimes such as the Soviet Union, China, Cuba, Tanzania, and more recently, Nicaragua' (Thomas, 1983, p. 35). The policies also overlook what could be learned from countries that set access and equity as core aims of adult education (Rubenson, 2006; Tuijnman, 2003). The complex connections between low literacy and social inequality are irrelevant for what currently passes as 'adult literacy' policy in many English-speaking countries in the Global North. Instead, Organisation for Economic Co-operation and Development (OECD) definitions of literacy have become dominant transnationally as the International Adult Literacy Survey (IALS), the Adult Literacy and Life Skills Survey (ALL), the Programme for International Student

Assessment (PISA) and the Programme for the International Assessment of Adult Competencies (PIAAC) have constructed a global policy consensus (Grek, 2009; Rubenson, 2008). This has had disconcerting effects on the ground.

This chapter begins from my curiosity about two effects of the OECD statistical surveys and reports, and the policies influenced by them. Firstly, these policies have intensified accountability requirements that leave practitioners feeling they are less educators than technicians (Hamilton, 2009) and that reporting is more important than education (Crooks *et al.*, 2008). Secondly, there is the fact that policies lead to programmes for those who can most easily show improvement rather than programmes that would address the systemic barriers faced by people who have the greatest struggles with dominant literacies (Bathmaker, 2007; Veeman *et al.*, 2006).

Historicising the role of statistics reveals that numerical accounts have played significant roles in governance for a long time, and that linking adult literacy to economic competitiveness is not new. This is not to say that statistical accounts in the current era are exactly the same as earlier 'counts', nor that the economic interests are identical. However, examining the history in which the OECD surveys are located could offer fresh insights about the political power of statistics. In this chapter I draw attention to a long-standing interest by governments in citizens' productivity, as indicated by their level of 'literacy'. I note an increasing refinement of literacy statistics over the twentieth century, and argue that this shift draws on a troubling history of social engineering to define 'fit' citizens and to establish criteria for distinguishing who should be the focus of policy attention. I consider how statistics operate in the era of neo-liberalism, or 'advanced liberal' rule (Rose, cited in Larner, 2000, p. 13) and close with a call to develop alternative ways of representing the power of literacy: as engagement with print that either enables people to exert power in their lives, their communities and our collective future, or limits their possibilities for doing so.

State power and the rise of statistics

The 'systematic study of social numbers' began in Europe in the 1600s. Implicit in the use of numbers was a belief that a state's 'wealth and strength ... depended on the number and character of its subjects' (Porter, 1986). In England, the study was known as 'political arithmetic' when used to calculate and increase tax revenue, and as 'moral science' when employed to measure 'deviancy, of criminals, court convictions, suicides, prostitution, divorce' as empirical evidence of immorality (Hacking, 1991, p. 182). European states collected 'vast stores of information about conditions within the relevant territories' (Curtis, 2002, p. 528) during the seventeenth and eighteenth centuries. These counts required that everyone in a given territory be treated as identical so that every 'death, birth, marriage, divorce, and so on' (ibid., p. 529) could be considered equivalent. By defining the terms through which the population is known, the census manifests the political and administrative power of the state (ibid., p. 530). Some of the first counts of people were of the colonies (Hacking, cited in Rose, 1999) and census figures 'created the sense of a controllable indigenous reality' (Appadurai, 1996, p. 117). These statistics not only made governance at a distance possible for the colonial powers, they transformed the 'modes of life of non-European peoples' (Asad, 1994, cited in Kalpagam, 2000, p. 47). Statistics were also essential to legitimating colonisation since the numbers told 'stories about progress, of accumulation of wealth, control of nature, the well-being of humanity' (Kalpagam, 2000, p. 47). As such, statistics can be considered 'the most important language in the narrative legitimation of modernity' (ibid.).

During the nineteenth century, the virtual 'avalanche of numbers' (Hacking, 1991, p. 189) collected and published in Europe was part of a new way of knowing the world. As Lord Kelvin wrote in 1889, 'when you can measure what you are speaking about, you know something about it; when you cannot measure it … your knowledge is of a meager and unsatisfactory kind' (cited in ibid., p. 186). The growing reliance on numbers contributed to the establishment of bureaucracies – structures virtually synonymous with contemporary governments (Porter, 1986). Over the twentieth century, social management became more elaborate as governance relied more and more on technical calculations that help to translate 'the messy details of peoples' lives and learning … into standardised and objectified categories through which they can be counted and made administerable' (Jackson, 2005, p. 775). To standardise the messiness of reality, individuals must be comparable and this is achieved by articulating what is expected or required of individual members of a society. Once these norms are expressed in terms that are easy to calculate, such as standard costing or budgeting, the 'deviations of the person from a norm, with all their possible causes and consequences, become available for investigation and for remedial action' (Miller and O'Leary, 1987,

p. 262). Furthermore, political decisions based on this type of information insulate experts from 'external political attempts to govern them and their actions' (Miller and Rose, 2008, p. 212) because the technical nature of the data obscures the subjective judgements on which it is based.

Efforts to improve people, based on how they compare with a statistical norm, have their roots in the history of statistics. In the mid-nineteenth century, astronomers discovered that the best way to measure multiple items was to use the mean of the measurements. They found that the rate of 'error' followed a consistent pattern where half the errors were greater than the mean and half were less than the mean. This became known as the 'law of frequency of error' and is familiar to us as the bell curve. The Belgian astronomer Adolphe Quetelet applied this analysis to measurement of people's height and found that human data conformed to the pattern of the bell curve. This idea was taken up enthusiastically in Great Britain, particularly by eugenists Galton (1822 to 1911), Pearson (1857 to 1936) and Fisher (1890 to 1962). Galton was intrigued by Quetelet's use of the bell curve, but thought it should be applied to mental characteristics. He argued that 'the only secure long-term way to improve society ... was to ensure that those in the present generation with good characteristics ('the fit') had more children than those with bad characteristics ('the unfit')' (MacKenzie, 1981, p. 11). Galton's aim was to show that exceptional ability was inherited, but he soon became more interested in trying to explain variations from the norm. His contribution to statistical theory occurred when he found a way to explain how a number of variables can correlate; this marked a major shift in statistical thinking because it moved away from the determinism implied by the law of error. While eugenics as an explicit rationale for social policy fell out of favour, a range of social interventions developed over the twentieth century justified intrusion in the lives of individuals who were considered 'inefficient' (Miller and O'Leary, 1987, p. 248). Policies to address the 'problem' of adult illiteracy can be understood as examples of this type of social management.

Counting reading and writing: From census to survey

Using numerical data to define and address social problems, and to assess the effectiveness of policies, has become the primary language of political discussion in democracies (Rose, 1999), and policies can be understood as efforts to achieve the 'calculated administration of life' (*ibid.*, p. 211). In this section, I consider two different counts of adult literacy: the Canadian census and IALS. The aim of the 1994 IALS was to generate cross-national comparisons that OECD member nations could use to design 'lifelong learning, social and labour market policies' (OECD and Statistics Canada, 2000, p. xii) in order to become more competitive in the emerging 'knowledge-based society' (*ibid.*, p. 1). The OECD developed IALS to refine statistical knowledge about 'literacy' in populations of member nations where previously these countries had used census data on school enrolment or educational attainment. Both the census and IALS create 'literacy' as an object that can be measured and administered. These two numerical portraits treat individuals as equivalent units, link subjects to state revenue, and rank subjects according to articulated norms. In treating individual subjects as equivalent and interchangeable units, both studies use statistics about 'literacy' to make statements about the economic well-being of the nation as a whole. Both the census and IALS exemplify the particularly modern form of power that is indifferent to individual 'interests and aspirations' (Foucault, 1991, p. 100) while encouraging individuals to act in ways that benefit the population as a whole.

Between 1890 and 1930, the census in Canada included questions about literacy. In the census of 1890/91, individuals – excluding Indians – were asked whether they could read and whether they could write, and whether they were 'blind or otherwise defective' (Department of Agriculture and Statistics, 1893, p. vii). Among the 4.8 million adults included in that census, 84.65 per cent indicated that they could read, and 80.34 per cent stated that they could read and write (*ibid.*, p. x). The next census, ten years later, was the first to ask individuals what their mother tongue was and whether they could speak Canada's official languages, English and French. In these early counts, people were not disqualified from considering themselves 'literate' if they could read and write in a non-official language or a non-Roman script.

As the twentieth century progressed, however, what counted as literacy narrowed as questions in the census attempted to assess how well the education system was assimilating individuals to dominant practices. The 1901 census states that '[i]n a country people with so many foreign elements as Canada, it is desireable to know if they are being absorbed and unified' (Department of Agriculture, 1902, p. viii). Twenty years later, a census report discusses the fact that in communities in which a large proportion of people cannot read or write any language, fewer children attended school. The report concludes that 'illiteracy has a tendency to perpetuate itself and that the school has not only the task of educating those within its reach but also of overcoming this form of inertia' (Dominion Bureau of Statistics, 1926, p. 9). Following the 1931 census, the government published a much more detailed analysis of the correlation between literacy and schooling. This report describes illiteracy as indicative of 'the presence of a number of anti-social forces, of physical and geographical obstacles, of historical events such as dates of settlement, of the racial or nativity composition of the population, of the age distribution ... and so on' (MacLean, 1937, p. 26). This report decries the fact that several European countries 'are apparently sending to Canada the more illiterate portion of their population' (*ibid.*, p.43) and serves as a useful reminder that blaming immigrants for 'the literacy problem' is not a new phenomenon.

When the IALS was conducted in 1994, individuals were required to take the test in an official language because it is based on the assumption that nations participating in the survey are 'homogeneous countries' (OECD and Statistics Canada, 2000, p. 88). People who score below 225, out of a possible 500 points, are ranked as IALS Level 1 and described as having 'very poor skills' (*ibid.*, p. xi), regardless of whether they might be highly literate in a non-alphabetic script or a non-official language. Developers of IALS claim that it is an improvement over the earlier proxy measures because it posits literacy as a continuum rather than an attribute that people either do or do not possess. However, where nebulous 'illiteracy' allowed space for a range of literacies, the IALS definition of literacy asserts a norm that discounts other literacies.

The IALS definition builds on the distinction between literacy and functional literacy contained in the United Nations Educational, Scientific and Cultural Organization (UNESCO) 'Revised recommendation concerning the international standardization of educational statistics' (1978). While a person was literate if he (sic) 'can with understanding both read and write a short simple statement on his everyday life', people were only functionally literate if they could 'engage in all those activities in which literacy is required for effective functioning of his group and community and also for enabling him to continue to use reading, writing and calculation for his own and the community's development' (cited in Thomas, 1983, p. 26). But within IALS 'literacy' is not a set of practices that people use as needed, nor is it connected to individual or community development. Furthermore, individuals are deemed incompetent to judge their own ability to use literacy. This transformation from a range of acceptable literacies to the assertion that only one literacy counts exhibits what Fendler and Muzaffar (2008) call 'bell curve thinking': the assumption that human behaviour and attributes can and should be assessed according to the statistical distribution of a bell curve. Given that the bell curve is a representation of probability based on averages, when it is applied to education it not only creates failure but also naturalises hierarchical social organisation.

Free trade and 'literacy' as investment

A significant body of work has critiqued the assumptions and methodology of the IALS (Hamilton and Barton, 2000; Darville, 1999; Hautecoeur, 2000; Manesse, 2000; Gomez, 2000) and pointed out how OECD measures of literacy have 'push[ed] aside those other truths about literacy known through everyday lived experience of adults and the practitioners who work alongside them' (Hamilton, 2001, p. 193). IALS and subsequent OECD surveys can be seen as mechanisms whereby vernacular literacies are subordinated to dominant literacies (Barton and Hamilton, 1998) in the interests of social management. These surveys certainly are the source of the frustration many practitioners feel about the 'competing and sometimes conflicting interests [of] … funders and users of literacy services' (Jackson, 2005, p. 775). But the impacts of the OECD survey results have a particular character that is connected to the specific historical moment in which they arose.

It is worth remembering that market assessments of literacy as a form of human capital became dominant in a period of neo-liberalism. In this era, many OECD member nations drastically cut funding for public income support programmes – such as welfare, unemployment insurance and pensions – and began to enact policies that required people to adopt entrepreneurial 'values, norms, desires and dispositions' (Edwards, 2008, p. 29). The neo-liberal approach posits that people are not social beings but economic units. As such they are expected to take responsibility for their own well-being (Ilcan, 2009) and to use 'market-based values in *all* of their judgements and practices in order to amass sufficient quantities of "human capital" and thereby become "entrepreneurs of themselves"' (Hamann, 2009, p. 38). In this context, the OECD surveys can be seen as technologies of neo-liberal governance. Literacy is a 'direct measure of human capital' (Boudard and Jones, 2003, p. 198); IALS claims to assess whether subjects are 'fit' or 'unfit' to participate in society. The levels articulated in these surveys clearly state the norms against which everyone should measure themselves; they articulate exactly what kind of literate subject one is expected to be in order to 'count' as a productive member of society. People who have not attained Level 3 – defined as '[a]dequate to cope with the demands of everyday life and work in an advanced society' – are deemed to be unfit, as they are 'below the internationally-accepted standard for coping in a modern society' (Canadian Council on Learning, 2008).

But aggressively asserting something does not necessarily make it so. Adult literacy workers across OECD nations are immensely frustrated, stuck as they are in the gap (Jackson, 2005) between the idealised literacy of OECD framings and the lived realities and multiple literacies of the adults who attend the programmes where they work. Literacy workers' frustration is an embodiment of dissatisfaction with how policies based on the OECD's market-logic model focus more on the 'strong plausible link between literacy and a country's economic potential' (Statistics Canada, 2011) than on the lived experiences of people who struggle with print. Their frustration is a sign of how market-oriented policies are 'further deepening the gap between social groups whose unequal access to the knowledge economy has nothing to do with an ability to decode the alphabet' (Hernandez-Zamora, 2010, p. 185). During the era in which adult literacy policies became aligned with the IALS statistics, income disparities increased dramatically and people living in poverty were disproportionately indigenous people and racialised people, particularly women. In Canada, policies based on the OECD framing ignore the fact that close to 'half of the wage gap' between Aboriginal and non-Aboriginal workers is due to 'factors such as discrimination' (Kapsalis, 2006, p. 25) and that education alone cannot overcome this disparity. Policies also ignore studies showing that improvements in literacy skills do not translate to improved incomes for racialised subjects (Arat-Koç, 2010; Colour of Justice Network, 2007) or women (Shalla and Schellenberg, 1998).

Towards hope

Inequality and social exclusion are not new: these 'entrenched and intractable problems' (Hillier, 2009, p. 548) can be traced to the colonial era. While access to dominant literacy is not the only factor organising such injustices, it is worth remembering that education has played a significant role in establishing global inequalities (Willinsky, 1998). So what can we do now?

As this book was being written, people around the globe were gathering in cities to protest the ways in which policies that support the interests of 'the 1 per cent' are actively destroying the lives of the majority, 'the 99 per cent'. I am tempted to see similarities between those protesters and literacy workers frustrated with current policies. Both groups question the distressing inequities on which the market model thrives and both are exposing the falsehoods of neo-liberal ideologies. But while the 'Occupy' movement has used statistics to make its point, adult literacy workers and advocates have not yet found persuasive statistics that spark widespread discussion about literacy and power, or lead to meaningful change. Instead, they are stuck using the IALS statistics even as they bemoan how those numbers have influenced policy. I understand how this has happened; when the IALS results were first released, I was among those who believed that the numbers could help raise awareness and would lead to change. But now I think we need to reconsider how we use numbers. If statistics create a powerful narrative that forms categories through which we act in and upon the world, why do we continue to use framings that ignore the lives and literacies of most people? I wonder if we could work towards finding a way to count the material supports and cultural assumptions that produce a small minority as successfully literate and others as deficient? Could we facilitate change if we found ways to document what IALS overlooks, namely how those classified as incapable of coping can and do thrive and make significant contributions in their communities? Could we use statistics to describe how dominant literacy creates injustice and social exclusion? If we documented instances in which print limited people's power in their lives and communities, perhaps we could construct compelling narratives about how literacy practices are central to perpetuating inequities. Perhaps we could find ways to quantify how our communities and lives are impoverished by the neo-liberal insistence that each of us has worth only insofar as we contribute to the gross domestic product.

To imagine alternatives to market-logic literacy, we would have to move beyond deeply entrenched ideas about what counts as reading, decoding and text. We would have to examine unstated assumptions about the moral effects and economic benefits of literacy. We would have to focus on aspects of living other than consumerism and financial exchange.

We would have to acknowledge brutalities in the history of education, including literacies that serve power rather than emancipation and empowerment. We would also have to work towards mutuality, rather than domination, as the aim of communicative practices. The powerful literacy I am imagining would be one that unpacked inequalities in the 'economies of literacy' (Blommaert, 2008) and mapped inequities in access to information and resources. In contrast to the OECD's stingy market model which justifies exploitation based on deficits in narrowly conceived instrumentalist competences, this powerful literacy would set fluency in multiple languages and literacies as the norm required to support fruitful interconnection and hope for a sustainable future. Surely we can find a way to make those things count.

References

Appadurai, A. (1996) *Modernity at Large: Cultural Dimensions of Globalization*. Minneapolis: University of Minnesota Press.

Arat-Koç, S. (2010) 'New whiteness(es), beyond the colour line? Assessing the contradictions and complexities of 'whiteness' in the (geo) political economy of capitalist globalism' in *States of Race: Critical Race Feminism for the 21st Century*, (eds) Razack, S., Smith, M. and Thobani, S. Toronto: Between the Lines.

Barton, D. and Hamilton, M. (1998) *Local Literacies: Reading and Writing in One Community*. Routledge.

Bathmaker, A.-M. (2007) 'The impact of Skills for Life on adult basic skills in England: how should we interpret trends in participation and achievement?' *International Journal of Lifelong Education*, Vol. 26 No 3, pp. 295–313.

Blommaert, J. (2008) *Grassroots Literacy: Writing, Identity and Voice in Central Africa*. Routledge.

Boudard, E. and Jones, S. (2003) 'The IALS approach to defining and measuring literacy skills', *International Journal of Educational Research*, Vol. 39 No 3, pp. 191–204.

Canadian Council on Learning (2008) *Reading the Future* [Online] http://www.ccl-cca.ca/CCL/Reports/ReadingFuture/ReadingFutureReport.html#future [Accessed September 4, 2011].

Colour of Justice Network (2007) *Fact Sheets* [Online] http://colourofpoverty.ca [Accessed September 4, 2011].

Crooks, S., Davies, P., Gardner, A., Grieve, K., Mollins, T., Niks,

M., Tannenbaum, J. and Wright, B. (2008) *Connecting the Dots: Accountability in Adult Literacy — Voices from the Field*. Montreal, QC: Centre for Literacy of Quebec.

Curtis, B. (2002) 'Foucault on governmentality and population: the impossible discovery', *Canadian Journal of Sociology/Cahiers canadiens de sociologie*, Vol. 27 No 4, pp. 505–33.

Darville, R. (1999) 'Knowledges of adult literacy: surveying for competitiveness', *International Journal of Educational Development*, Vol. 19 No 4–5, pp. 273–85.

Department of Agriculture (1902) *Fourth Census of Canada 1901*. Ottawa: S. E. Dawson, Printer to the King's Most Excellent Majesty.

Department of Agriculture and Statistics (1893) *Census of Canada 1890–91 Vol. II*. Ottawa: S. E. Dawson, Printer to the Queen's Most Excellent Majesty.

Dominion Bureau of Statistics (1926) *Illiteracy and School Attendance in Canada: A Study of the Census of 1921 with Supplementary Data*. Ottawa: F. A. Acland, Printer to the King's Most Excellent Majesty.

Edwards, R. (2008) 'Actively seeking subjects?' in *Foucault and Lifelong Learning: Governing the Subject*, (eds) Fejes, A. and Nicoll, K., pp. 21–33. Routledge.

Fendler, L. and Muzaffar, I. (2008) 'The history of the bell curve: sorting and the idea of normal', *Educational Theory*, Vol. 58 No 1, pp. 63–82.

Foucault, M. (1991) 'Governmentality' in *The Foucault Effect: Studies in Governmentality with Two Lectures by and an Interview with Michel Foucault*, (eds) Burchell, G., Gordon, C. and Miller, P., pp. 87–104. Chicago: University of Chicago Press.

Gomez, S. V. (2000) 'The collective that didn't quite collect: reflections on the IALS', *International Review of Education/Internationale Zeitschrift fur Erziehungswissenschaft/Revue internationale de pedagogie*, Vol. 46 No 5, pp. 419–31.

Grek, S. (2009) 'Governing by numbers: the PISA 'effect' in Europe', *Journal of Education Policy*, Vol. 24 No 1, pp. 23–37.

Hacking, I. (1991) 'How should we do the history of statistics?' in *The Foucault Effect: Studies in Governmentality*, (eds) Burchell, G., Gordon, C. and Miller, P., pp. 181–95. Chicago: University of Chicago Press.

Hamann, T. H. (2009) 'Neoliberalism, governmentality, and ethics', *Foucault Studies*, No 6, pp. 37–59.

Hamilton, M. (2001) 'Privileged literacies: policy, institutional process and the life of the IALS', *Language and Education*, Vol. 15 No 2, pp. 178–96.

Hamilton, M. (2009) 'Putting words in their mouths: the alignment of identities with system goals through the use of individual learning plans', *British Educational Research Journal,* Vol. 35 No 2, pp. 221–42.

Hamilton, M. and Barton, D. (2000) 'The International Adult Literacy Survey: what does it really measure?' *International Review of Education,* Vol. 46 No 5, pp. 377–89.

Hautecoeur, J. P. (2000) 'Literacy in the age of information: knowledge, power or domination?' *International Review of Education,* Vol. 46 No 5, pp. 357–65.

Hernandez-Zamora, G. (2010) *Decolonizing Literacy: Mexican Lives in the Era of Global Capitalism.* Multilingual Matters.

Ilcan, S. (2009) 'Privatizing responsibility: public sector reform under neoliberal government', *Canadian Review of Sociology,* Vol. 4 No 3, pp. 207–34.

Jackson, N. S. (2005) 'Adult literacy policy: mind the gap' in *International Handbook of Educational Policy,* (eds) Bascia, N., Cumming, A., Datnow, A., Leithwood, K. and Livingstone, D., pp. 763–78. Dordrecht, the Netherlands: Springer.

Kalpagam, U. (2000) 'The colonial state and statistical knowledge', *History of the Human Sciences,* Vol. 13 No 2, pp. 37–55.

Kapsalis, C. (2006) *Occupational and Skill Parity of Aboriginal Canadians.* Ottawa: Aboriginal Affairs Directorate, Human Resources and Skills Development Canada.

Larner, W. (2000) 'Neo-liberalism: policy, ideology, governmentality', *Studies in Political Economy,* Vol. 63, pp. 5–25.

MacKenzie, D. A. (1981) *Statistics in Britain 1865–1930: The Social Construction of Scientific Knowledge.* Edinburgh University Press.

MacLean, M. C. (1937) *Illiteracy and School Attendance: A Study Based on the Census of 1931 and Supplementary Data.* Ottawa: J. O. Patenaude, Printer to the King's Most Excellent Majesty.

Manesse, D. (2000) 'Remarques critiques à propos de l'enquête internationale sur la litteratie' (Critical remarks regarding the International Adult Literacy Survey), *International Review of Education,* Vol. 46 No 5, pp. 407–17.

Miller, P. and O'Leary, T. (1987) 'Accounting and the construction of the governable person', *Accounting, Organizations and Society,* Vol. 12 No 3, pp. 235–65.

Miller, P. and Rose, N. (2008) *Governing the Present: Administering Economic, Social and Personal Life.* Malden, MA: Polity Press.

OECD and Statistics Canada (2000) *Literacy in the Information Age: Final Report of the Adult Literacy Survey*. Paris: OECD.

Porter, T. M. (1986) *The Rise of Statistical Thinking 1820–1900*. Princeton, NJ: Princeton University Press.

Rose, N. (1999) *Powers of Freedom: Reframing Political Thought*. Port Chester, NY: Cambridge University Press.

Rubenson, K. (2006) 'The Nordic model of lifelong learning', *Compare: A Journal of Comparative Education*, Vol. 36 No 3, pp. 327–41.

Rubenson, K. (2008) 'OECD education policies and world hegemony' in *The OECD and Transnational Governance*, (eds) Mahon, R. and McBrida, S., pp. 242–59. Vancouver: UBC Press.

Shalla, V. and Schellenberg, G. (1998) *The Value of Words: Literacy and Economic Security in Canada*. Ottawa: Statistics Canada.

Statistics Canada (2011) 'IALS: about the survey' [online] http://www.statcan.gc.ca/pub/89-588-x/4152886-eng.htm [Accessed September 4, 2011].

Thomas, A. M. (1983) *Adult Illiteracy in Canada: A Challenge. Occasional Paper No. 42*. Ottawa: Canadian Commission for UNESCO.

Tuijnman, A. C. (2003) 'A 'Nordic Model' of adult education: what might be its defining parameters?' *International Journal of Educational Research*, Vol. 39 No 3, pp. 283–91.

Veeman, N., Ward, A. and Walker, K. (2006) *Valuing Literacy in Canada: Rhetoric or Reality?* Edmonton, AB: Detselig.

Willinsky, J. (1998) *Learning to Divide the World: Education at Empire's End*. Minneapolis: University of Minnesota Press.

CHAPTER FIVE

Power and positioning in writing: Exploring issues of authorship and authority

AMY BURGESS

Introduction

This chapter explores issues of power and authority in relation to writing by critically examining the connection between writing development and confidence. It draws on data from an ethnographic study of the writing and identity development of students in adult literacy classes in England. Here I present an analysis of texts produced by three students in order to explore how writers are socially positioned by the discourses on which they draw in their writing and the extent to which they are able to write from a position of authority.

Drawing on the framework for investigating writer identity, proposed by Ivanič (1998) and developed by Burgess and Ivanič (2010), I focus on the writers' 'authorial selves'. I ask the questions: what discourses did the students draw on in their writing; how were they positioned by these discourses; and how did this positioning affect their development as writers? The analysis suggests that some of the most salient discourses on which the students drew positioned them as deficient and/or socially subordinate. This negative positioning undermined their confidence and impeded their development as writers. I therefore argue that difficulties with writing are not necessarily the result of students' literacy 'problems', but can be related to issues of identity. These issues may need to be addressed before real progress in writing can be made.

The class these students attended took place in a further education college in England and met for three hours once a week. It was designed for students working just below Level 1 on the national qualifications scale, and all the students were expected to sit the National Literacy Test at the end of the academic year. I visited the class weekly for four months, carried out classroom observations and semi-structured interviews and collected texts, including samples of students' writing. The data I discuss here consists of pieces of writing by three students on the topic of coming to college as an adult, which were produced during the first few weeks of the course. The tutor, Sheila, introduced the topic by engaging the students in a group discussion about their motivations for joining the course, their aspirations, and how attending the college fitted with their other commitments and interests. Sheila recorded points from the discussion on a whiteboard and the students were encouraged to make their own notes. After this the students worked individually, first producing handwritten drafts, on which Sheila provided feedback, and then using computers to word-process their final texts. The extracts from the students' writing quoted here are from the final, word-processed versions, which they produced after the tutor had corrected their handwritten drafts.

All the students were women who had left school with few formal qualifications. Two of them, Heather and Sandie, were in their thirties and had decided to join the class because they wanted to do vocational training, but felt they needed to improve their literacy in order to cope with these other courses. The other student, Marion, had recently retired from full-time employment and was considering enrolling on an Access to Higher Education course, but felt she needed to improve her writing first.

Writing and confidence

We live in a world where many aspects of our lives and activities increasingly take place through the medium of written texts (Smith, 2005). Writing plays an increasingly important role in many jobs (Karlsson, 2009) and remains the dominant medium of learning and assessment in the formal education system. Brandt argues that with the rise of the information society and the knowledge-based economy, writing is overtaking reading as the dominant aspect of literacy and that it is crucial for social justice, civic and democratic participation:

> *Writing is gaining value as a productive skill within the information economy. More critically, it is sometimes the only way to represent one's interests in a system in which so many social and political relationships*

are conducted through print ... As a productive skill, writing is also keenly linked to political voice and to the protection and exercise of free speech rights. (Brandt, 2001, pp. 196–7)

Conversely, research evidence suggests that adults who find writing difficult are considerably disadvantaged in terms of life chances, quality of life and social inclusion (Bynner and Parsons, 2006). Adult literacy educators have long sought to address these issues through pedagogy that aims to enhance students' autonomy and sense of authority (Gillespie, 2007; O'Rourke and Mace, 1992). Such aims are frequently expressed in terms of enhancing adults' confidence and this was an explicit aim of the teacher of the students I discuss in this chapter, who told me, 'my aim for them is to develop confidence in writing, that's my priority'. There is now a significant body of research claiming that literacy learning does increase adults' confidence (see St Clair, 2010). In a large-scale study of the teaching of writing to adults in England (Grief, Meyer and Burgess, 2007), learners said that they particularly valued confidence with writing and enhanced confidence and self-esteem more generally as outcomes of their courses. Because confidence is so important to learners, it is worth critically examining the link between writing and confidence. A common assumption is that difficulties with literacy reduce confidence and that improvements in literacy will therefore create greater confidence (see, for example, DfES, 2001). In this chapter I question this assumption and argue that the causality also operates in the opposite direction. Difficulties with literacy often have social causes and are bound up with issues of identity, which need to be addressed before students can make real progress.

Writing, identity and discourse

Ivanič (1998) points out that, when we write, we align ourselves with other people who write in the same way and that writing is therefore an act of identity. This aspect of writing can create difficulties for literacy students, who may be more at home with speaking and who may not see themselves as writers. Ivanič has described these difficulties in a study of mature students entering higher education, but her comments apply equally well to adult literacy students:

They will be encountering literacy practices which belong to people with social identities different from theirs. In order to take on these

91

new aspects of their identities, they need to engage in these practices; in order to engage in these practices, they need to be people of this sort. It is a vicious circle, fraught with conflicts of identity. (Ivanič, 1998, p. 68)

In order to explore the students' identities as writers, I have used a theoretical framework that connects theories of writing, identity and learning through the concept of discourse. It draws on Gee's (1996) and Ivanič's (1998) definitions of discourses as socially accepted representations of reality which entail thinking and acting in particular ways, or as 'identity kits' (Gee, 1996) that enable people to take on particular socially recognisable roles. Gee distinguishes between 'primary discourses', which people acquire without explicit teaching in their immediate family and community, and 'secondary discourses', which are consciously learnt. The greater the convergence between a person's primary discourses and those discourses that are powerful in society – such as the discourses of formal education – the easier it will be to learn the dominant discourses. This concept has been used to explain why people who belong to minority or marginalised social groups, as is the case with many literacy students, enjoy less success in education than those from dominant groups. Literacy education based on this understanding seeks to provide students with access to powerful discourses by enabling them to learn the literacy practices associated with them. However, such an approach may be limited to the extent that it requires students to align themselves closely with the discourses of formal education and in doing so to adopt identities as people who have 'problems' or who have 'failed' (Rogers, 2003). This is likely to impede their development as writers (Burgess, 2004).

I have worked with the model of writer identity proposed by Ivanič (1998) and developed by Burgess and Ivanič (2010), which distinguishes between five different aspects: autobiographical self, socially available possibilities for selfhood, discoursal self, authorial self and perceived reader. In the analysis below I focus on the authorial self. This is particularly relevant to the issue of writing and confidence because it refers to the writer's sense of authority as a writer, and the extent to which she or he conveys that sense to the reader. I explore this aspect of the students' identities as writers by looking at the discourses on which they draw in their writing, as well as particular ways of using language that are not associated with specific discourses but implicated with power relations more generally. I ask whether these discourses and ways of using language offered them the identities of people who were able to write with authority.

The first part of the analysis is concerned with the content of the students' texts and identifies some of the most salient discourses of which I found evidence. The second stage presents analysis of some of the linguistic features of the writing, using frameworks proposed by Van Leeuwen (2008) for investigating the representation in English discourse of social actors and social action. I focus on these aspects of the writing for two reasons. Firstly, writers' representations of themselves and other people are a particularly rich source of data about the kinds of identity they construct in their writing. Secondly, the subject matter of the students' texts was concerned mainly with people. Van Leeuwen's approach is particularly suitable for this analysis because his starting point and main focus is not the linguistic features of texts in and of themselves, but rather the different ways in which it is possible to represent aspects of the social world and how they may be realised linguistically. This places the emphasis on the different ways in which the social world is represented and the possible reasons for and effects of such representations. This fits with my aim, which is not to study the students' use of language for its own sake, but for what it can reveal about the kinds of identities they felt able or obliged to construct through their writing. This form of analysis has rarely been applied to texts produced by novice writers (though see Paxton, 2006), but it is useful because it can uncover the reasons why students write in certain ways, rather than focusing solely on surface features of language and judgements about 'correctness' or otherwise. In addition, I would argue that it is not possible to gain a complete picture of the students' identities without investigating the kinds of identity they constructed through their writing. Other sources of data, such as interviews and observations, provided essential knowledge about their lives and their interactions in the classroom, but these needed to be complemented by close analysis of the students' texts. I begin the next section by presenting extracts from these texts. This is followed by my analysis, starting with the content of the texts and moving on to their linguistic features.

Heather

When I was a child going to school it was something that everybody did I had an older brother and four sisters already there.

Then you move on to secondary school again you have to go and get on with it, you are all in the same boat. Then when you leave school you have choices, like going to work or college. I first went to work for many years, then I had a family which took a lot of my time up, but now my children are growing up and moving on in there lives.

So I thought what do I want to do with my life and I decided to join college, I picked the course that was right for me and enrolled. The first day was a bit scary walking in the doors of the college and everyone else seemed so young, but when I found my class and my tutor, it was more of a mixed group of people and more my age, which made you feel a bit more relaxed …

I was feeling worried that I am not progressing much but it is my self confidence that I am working on, to overcome my worries and lack of self-esteem. Last year I went in for my English level 1 exam, which I found scary, the thought of exams really frightens me. I don't really know why because nothing really bad has happened, I think it is because I don't have the confidence. I say to myself that I will fail before I have done it and then when I do fail I feel a failure and get down and depressed about it. Also I find that it is always worse when you find that other people in your group have passed and you feel, why me, it always happens to me, so I patch up my wounds and make myself carry on and try to one day get my goal and pass my exam. That would make me feel very pleased with myself and gain that confidence.

This is how I feel about my first time going to college as an adult.

Sandie

I would like to take two different courses, one on English and the other on Maths.

I first got to know about the courses, when I was visiting a local shopping centre. After I was assessed, I was contacted by telephone call, then later by letter. I did better than I thought.

After that I was asked to attend an interview, where I had two short assessment tests to see what ability I currently had. I found this very nerve racking. I was in a new place with new people, which I found very hard at first.

After the interview I went home and discussed the situation with my mum, she was very supportive and she told me 'to do whatever I needed to do!'

Several months later, I was starting to worry that I hadn't heard anything from the college. Then one day I got a letter saying, that I needed to attend the college again about enrolment, and when the courses would actually start.

The day of the enrolment came, I was very excited but also nervous about meeting lots of different people.

Marion

Today I am starting college, back to school after forty years. I'm quite excited, but perhaps there is some trepidation about what is going to happen. Will I arrive on time, will there be a parking space? Was it the Octagon, where was it? Turn right or left, am I going the right way? There seems to be an enormous amount of young people here, will I fit in? Everyone else seems to know where they are going, standing around in groups looking relaxed and chattering.

Having settled in class it's not so bad. It's friendly and relaxed, people laughing and talking, something I did not expect. My memories of school are much more formalised and serious. It's noisy, one can hear chattering from other groups in the Octagon but it's not too disruptive.

I struggle writing this essay what can I say? There are thousands of words in the dictionary, finding these words are not easy for me. It's good to start my brain working again, having to think and write things down again. Discipline was not my strongest point at school, there was always something more interesting going on out the window, someone to mess about with. This is the beginning of a new learning curve for me, it's all about learning to learn again, and something I have not had to do for a long time.

Discourses present in the students' texts

One of the main findings to emerge from analysis of the content of the texts is that the majority of the discourses position the students in subordinate roles and that this accounts for much of the difficulty they experience as writers. Furthermore, these discourses originate within the formal education system itself. The most salient discourses on which the students drew can be grouped under two headings: discourses of writing and literacy, and discourses of education. Space restrictions prevent me from presenting a comprehensive analysis of each text here, but this can be found in Burgess (2007). In what follows, I will discuss some illustrative examples from each student's writing.

Discourses of writing and literacy

One of the most prevalent discourses in the students' writing was that of literacy as nothing more than a set of skills. This discourse was instantiated, for example, in Sandie's statement, 'I had two short assessment tests to see what ability I currently had.' The notion of literacy as a set of skills which can be measured and tested is part of the dominant discourse that underpins *Skills for Life* (DfEE, 2001) and implies an identity for learners as people who are deficient or have literacy 'problems'. Tests such as the one Sandie took are diagnostic: in other words, they are designed to show what an individual *cannot* do in relation to predetermined definitions of what counts as literacy. All the students seemed to accept the negative positioning inherent in this discourse of literacy. The extent to which such positioning can undermine confidence and impede rather than foster learning is vividly illustrated by Heather's description of not passing the National Literacy Test.

Marion's comment about the process of writing her text ('I struggle writing this essay what can I say?') conveys the sense that she is concerned about being unable to produce the accepted version of literacy that would be valued in this context, and consequently of being unable to display the identity associated with it. Not knowing the appropriate thing to say in a situation is frequently a sign of a person being an outsider and not knowing the relevant social conventions (see Clark and Ivanič, 1997, p. 66 for further discussion of this point).

Discourses of education

All the women mentioned feeling uncomfortable because the majority of the students in the college were 16- to 19-year-olds. Heather summed up the feelings of all of them when she wrote that 'The first day was a bit scary walking in the doors of the college and everyone else seemed so young.' Marion explicitly likened attending college to going back to school and all these references draw on a discourse of education as something for young people. This discourse, like the discourses of writing and literacy discussed above, positioned them as outsiders or as people who did not have the same right to be present in the college as the younger students. This is significant for the students' development as writers because, as Lillis (2001) points out, who a person can be in a particular context is directly related to what they can say. An outsider does not occupy a position of authority and cannot assume the same right to have their voice heard as an insider. In the next section, close analysis of the students' texts shows how, particularly for Sandie and Heather, this subordinate positioning is reflected in the kinds of linguistic constructions they use.

How the writers represented themselves

Table 1 provides insight into the writers' authorial selves by comparing the ways they represented themselves in their texts. It reveals a contrast between Marion and the other two students. Marion makes slightly fewer references to herself as a proportion of the overall length of her writing and the most striking thing about them is that she frequently backgrounds herself. Van Leeuwen (2008) proposes the term 'backgrounded' to describe instances in texts where a social actor is not mentioned explicitly but the reader is able to infer who they are. Two examples from Marion's writing are the sentences: 'Back to school after 40 years' and 'Having settled in class it's not so bad.' In both cases we infer that she is talking about herself. Another way in which she backgrounds herself as an individual is by using the impersonal pronoun 'one' ('… one can hear chattering …'), which, as van Leeuwen notes, has the effect of generalising personal experience and is associated with relatively powerful social actors, whose higher social position enables them to have an overview of other people. Marion's general reference to herself as 'one' contrasts with Heather's references to herself as 'you'. Whereas 'you' places writer and reader on an equal footing, 'one' signals that the writer is either equal or socially superior to the reader. Marion's tendency to distance herself from her own experience through linguistic devices such as backgrounding

Table 1: Comparison of the students' representations of themselves

	Heather	Sandie	Marion
Total length of text	644 words	571 words	357 words
Total references to self, i.e. no of clauses referring to self	44	37	16
Genericised	2 (the pronoun 'you')	0	1 (the pronoun 'one')
Backgrounded	1	2	13

and generalisation enables her to reflect on and evaluate that experience. This particular way of representing social actors may be something she learnt from her reading outside the class. She talked in her interview of being an avid reader of books that might be classified as 'literary' and spoke of greatly admiring and wanting to emulate the kinds of writing she encountered in them. Whatever her personal motivation for the linguistic choices she made, it is important to note that her ability to represent herself in a relatively impersonal way, and to generalise from and distance herself from her own experience, are all abilities that are highly valued in the formal education system. They are likely to give her an advantage over other students who have not previously encountered such ways with words. Unlike them, she can present herself as an 'insider' who knows the conventions and is consequently able to write from a position of authority.

How the writers represented their own thoughts and feelings

Since all these pieces of writing give accounts of and reflections on personal experience, they all include the emotional responses and cognitive processes of the writers. The most striking feature of Sandie's and Heather's texts is the predominance of emotion relative to cognition, as Table 2 shows. Heather attributes 19 affective reactions but only eight cognitive reactions to herself, and several of the latter represent Heather herself as deficient (as in 'I think it is because I don't have the confidence'). Sandie attributes 17 affective reactions to herself and three cognitive reactions. Van Leeuwen (2008) notes that more powerful social actors tend to have cognitive responses attributed to them, whilst the less powerful tend to be portrayed primarily as feeling rather than thinking. I take this as further evidence of how Heather and Sandie are constructing themselves and being constructed as relatively powerless. Marion's writing is quite different; she makes 11 references to cognitive processes but only five to emotion, and some of the latter are objectivated (Van Leeuwen, 2008), as I discuss below. Unlike Sandie and Heather, she seems able to adopt the position of authority that is both a prerequisite for and a consequence of making cognitive rather than affective responses.

Marion represents some of her thoughts and feelings by using constructions that Van Leeuwen classifies as objectivations. This means that actions and processes that could be expressed by active verbs are instead

Table 2: Comparison of the students' representations of their own reactions

	Heather	Sandie	Marion
Total length of text	644 words	571 words	357 words
Total references to own reactions, i.e. no of clauses referring to own reactions	27	20	16
Own cognitive reactions	8	3	11
Own affective reactions	19	17	5
Own reactions objectivated	6	0	6

expressed by nouns. For example, in describing her reaction to attending the class for the first time, she writes, 'there is some trepidation'. Like her genericised and backgrounded representations of herself, these objectivations allow her to distance herself from her own experience in order to reflect on and evaluate it. She also uses the temporal structure of her text for this purpose. In her narrative she moves back and forth between the past and the present, setting up a series of comparisons between attending college and memories of her school days. This extended comparison enables her to simultaneously evaluate the present and re-evaluate the past. In contrast to Marion, Sandie uses few objectivations, presenting events and interactions in a chronologically sequenced narrative characterised by the use of human subjects and active verbs. Heather represents the events of her life in a similar way to Sandie, particularly in the first two paragraphs of her text, where the repetition of the conjunction 'then' conveys a sense of events simply happening and not having any particular causes and effects. This feature of her writing is something that could be regarded as a problem, and is in fact singled out for comment in the version of the Adult Literacy Core Curriculum in use at the time of the research, as follows:

> *Learners need to develop their knowledge of conjunctions and other connectives to avoid repetition, for example through overuse of and, then, next in chronological writing.* (DfEE, 2001, p. 109)

I would argue, however, that apparent 'overuse' of certain conjunctions is not simply a 'fault' in the writing that could be easily remedied by the kinds of practice activities recommended in the curriculum. It is actually more complex, being tied up with the writer's social position and identity as a writer. In Heather's case, the features of her writing that might be criticised as inadequate are those that both construct and reflect a social position without much authority. They suggest a writer who does not have a sense of control over the events and processes she describes and who is therefore either unaware of or not confident to comment on – to objectivate or to evaluate – causes and consequences.

Conclusion

One of the main aims of literacy education should be to enable students to expand their range of literacy practices and the range of contexts in which they participate as users of literacy. In order to maintain confidence across a widening range of practices and contexts, adults need to understand the relationship between literacy and social positioning in society in general. This entails moving beyond a view of literacy as a personal attribute, and understanding it as a set of practices that both shape and are shaped by the various contexts in which they are used. As Brandt (2001) points out, literacy education needs to include explicit attention to the power relations that structure people's access to literacy and the ways in which literacy is used as a gate-keeping device to sustain existing power relations.

This chapter offers a challenge to the view of literacy as a set of technical skills that is dominant in official policy. According to this view, adults' difficulty with writing stems from their deficiencies or 'problems' (see, for example, DfES 2001; DIUS, 2009). The investigation of these three students' writing suggests that difficulties with literacy have social causes and are bound up with issues of identity. My analysis problematises the notion that difficulties with literacy cause lack of confidence and that increased literacy will necessarily result in increased confidence. The picture is more complex than this. Literacy is closely bound up with issues of identity and people who are positioned in relatively subordinate roles are less likely to perceive themselves as having the authority necessary to participate in powerful literacies such as those associated with the formal education system.

The teacher of this class was very aware of the connection between literacy and confidence and worked hard to create a safe and supportive environment where the students could begin to develop the self-belief that would enable them to progress towards their goals. The students valued this and told me in interviews that they had developed greater confidence as a result of attending the class. They spoke, for example, of gaining the confidence to initiate conversations with other class members or to apply for jobs. These outcomes were clearly very worthwhile and important. It is appropriate to note, however, that Sheila's efforts to boost the students' confidence were being undermined by the dominant discourses circulating within the social context of the class and it would have been difficult for her to challenge these discourses. As Gee (1992) notes, discourses are resistant to internal criticism, so it is only possible to challenge one discourse from the perspective offered by an alternative. Sheila's training and professional development as a Skills for Life teacher, however, did not appear to have provided her with any alternative perspective. It was perhaps not surprising, therefore, that I did not find evidence that the notion of a one-way causal link between literacy difficulties and confidence was being questioned.

In conclusion, I argue that the teaching of writing – and the professional development of writing teachers – needs to include explicit focus on issues of identity (see Burgess, 2012, for further discussion of this point). Discourses that position learners as subordinate and/or deficient need to be recognised and actively challenged. This kind of pedagogy would enable learners to reflect on and question the discourses that may be inhibiting their autonomy. Furthermore, by developing pedagogy which pays explicit attention to the construction of the authorial self, literacy teachers could help learners gain control of the kinds of identity they portray and develop through their writing (Ivanič and Camps, 2001). Issues of identity are not an optional extra in the teaching of writing: they are central. Without an explicit focus on identity, writing pedagogy loses power and learners' potential to develop autonomy is restricted.

References

Brandt, D. (2001) *Literacy in American Lives*. Cambridge University Press.

Burgess, A. (2004) 'New discourses, new identities: a study of writing and learning in adult literacy education', *Literacy and Numeracy Studies*, Vol. 13 No 2, pp. 41–62.

Burgess, A. (2007) *Discourses and Identities in Adult Literacy Classes: Time, Networks, Texts and Other Artefacts.* Unpublished PhD thesis, Lancaster University.

Burgess, A. (2012) "I don't want to become a China Buff": Temporal dimensions of the discoursal construction of writer identity'. *Linguistics and Education.* Vol. 23(3), pp. 223–34.

Burgess, A. and Ivanič, R. (2010) 'Writing and being written: issues of identity across timescales', *Written Communication,* Vol. 27 No 2, pp. 228–55.

Bynner, J. and Parsons, S. (2006) New Light on Literacy and Numeracy: Results of the Literacy and Numeracy Assessment in the Age 34 Follow-up of the 1970 Birth Cohort Study (BCS70). NRDC.

Clark, R. and Ivanič, R. (1997) *The Politics of Writing.* Routledge.

DfEE/BSA (2001) *Adult Literacy Core Curriculum.* DfEE/BSA.

DfES (2001) *Skills for Life: The National Strategy for Improving Adult Literacy and Numeracy Skills.*

DIUS (2009) *Skills for Life: Changing Lives.* Available at www.bis.gov.uk/assets/biscore/corporate/migratedD/publications/S/SkillsforLife ChangingLives [Accessed 27 June 2012].

Gee, J. P. (1992) *The Social Mind: Language, Ideology and Social Practice.* New York: Bergin and Garvey.

Gee, J. P. (1996) *Social Linguistics and Literacies: Ideology in Discources.* Taylor and Francis.

Gillespie, M. (2007) 'The forgotten R: why adult educators should care about writing instruction' in *Toward Defining and Improving Quality in Adult Basic Education,* (ed.) Belzer, A., pp. 160–78. Mahwah, NJ: Lawrence Erlbaum.

Grief, S., Meyer, B. and Burgess, A. (2007) *Effective Teaching and Learning: Writing.* NRDC.

Ivanič, R. (1998) *Writing and Identity: the Discoursal Construction of Identity in Academic Writing.* Amsterdam: John Benjamins.

Ivanič, R. and Camps, D. (2001) 'I am how I sound: Voice as self-representation in L2 writing'. *Journal of Second Language Writing.* Vol. 10 No 1–2, pp. 3–33.

Karlsson, A.-M. (2009) 'Positioned by reading and writing: literacy practices, roles and genres in common occupations', *Written Communication,* Vol. 26 No 1, pp. 53–76.

Lillis, T. (2001) *Student Writing: Access, Regulation, Desire.* Routledge.

O'Rourke, R. and Mace, J. (1992) *Versions and Variety: A Report on*

Student Writing and Publishing in Adult Literacy Education. Avanti Books.

Paxton, M. (2006) 'Intertextual analysis: a research tool for uncovering writers' emerging meanings' in *Academic Literacy and the Languages of Change*, Thesen, L. and van Pletzen, E., pp. 84–103. Continuum.

Rogers, R. (2003) *A Critical Discourse Analysis of Family Literacy Practices: Power In and Out of Print*. Mahwah, NJ: Lawrence Erlbaum.

St Clair, R. (2010) *Why Literacy Matters: Understanding the Effects of Literacy Education for Adults*. NIACE.

Smith, D. E. (2005), *Institutional Ethnography: A Sociology for People*. Toronto/Oxford: Altamira Press.

Van Leeuwen, T. (2008) *Discourse and Practice: New Tools for Critical Discourse Analysis*. Oxford University Press.

CHAPTER SIX

Form-filling, power and the Individual Learning Plan: Tensions and tutor strategies in one adult literacy classroom

SANDRA VAREY AND KARIN TUSTING

Introduction

In recent years, many domains in which we live our lives have become increasingly textualised, including the places in which we work and learn (Iedema and Scheeres, 2003; Iedema, 2003). This is the result of an audit culture that 'is informed by practices confined to no single set of institutions and to no one part of the world' and whose concern with accountability has 'acquired a social presence of a new kind' in the past few decades (Strathern, 2000, p. 1). Indeed, in *Powerful Literacies*, Fawns and Ivanič (2001, p. 80) highlight that 'We can't even receive a parcel without having to add our signature to a specially designed form to provide official confirmation that it has been delivered', and that 'Such administrative transactions are part of an information society which increasingly controls and dominates us'.

In adult education, form-filling of various kinds now plays a very visible role, with audit culture placing increasing importance upon mandatory processes of accountability and recording (Apple, 2005). The introduction of the Skills for Life Strategy in 2001 (DfEE, 2001) signalled many changes for literacy teaching and learning in England as the policy brought with it a new curriculum framework, funding specifications, professional qualifications for tutors, and accreditation for learners. In turn, there has been an increasing emphasis on paperwork in adult literacy education in the past decade (Tusting, 2009) and individual learning plans (ILPs) have become an important 'part of a system of performance measurement based on quantifiable indicators of teaching and learning' (Hamilton, 2009, p. 221).

Why focus on the ILP?

Textualisation of the workplace has led to increasing paperwork pressures for employees across many sectors (see Troman, 2000; Jeffrey and Troman, 2004). For adult literacy tutors, paperwork such as the ILP can occupy a significant amount of time both inside and outside the classroom. When interviewing tutors in adult education in Canada, Darville (2002, p. 63) observed that 'talk often turns to "the burden of paperwork", even when no questions have directed attention to it'. Equally, for adult literacy tutors in England, ILPs are part of the 'endless change' within this sector in recent years (Edward *et al.*, 2007). Hamilton (2009, p. 221) describes ILPs as 'something they frequently talk and worry about, but were nevertheless surprised that anyone would want to research'. While paperwork may represent a time-consuming burden for many, it can prove difficult to explore the role of texts such as the ILP. The problem with researching texts in the social sciences, as Smith (2005, p. 102) puts it, is 'their ordinary "inertia" ... the local *thereness* of the text':

> *We construct them, I suppose, as a world that isn't present in our lived spaces and thus don't recognise texts as being 'active' in co-ordinating what we are doing with another or others. When we are reading, watching, or listening, somehow or another we treat texts as given; we are responding to their internal temporal organization, the shape of a song or a concerto, or the page, the chapter, what's on the monitor, but not to their* occurrence *in time and place.* (Smith, 2005, p. 102)

The first reason for focusing on the ILP in the adult literacy classroom is that, however synonymous with inertia and the mundane such texts have become, interactions with these texts in fact play an active role in coordinating the activities and learning that take place. As Hamilton (2009) suggests, ILPs also play an important role in normalising the adult literacy learner and the tutor, aligning them with particular subject positions within the Skills for Life Strategy. The ILP is situated and negotiated within the specific teaching practices and relationships that are built up in the classroom setting. Burgess (2008, p. 49) explores how, through the use of ILPs, 'teachers and students are co-opted as active agents into the processes of Skills for Life policy' and how the ILP 'mediates power and control' between the local and the global. The second reason for focusing on the ILP in the literacy classroom is therefore to explore the ways in which tutors respond to the demands imposed on them by such paperwork and the extent to which they negotiate these.

What is an ILP?

In this chapter, the use of the term 'ILP' refers to a range of paperwork and form-filling practices involving both learner and tutor in the literacy classroom. The design and content of the ILP depends on the institution, administration, provision, tutor and learners. Indeed, the visibility and use of the ILP also differs from classroom to classroom. The ILP discussed in this chapter is from one adult literacy classroom and contains a variety of forms that were completed at different stages of the course by both the tutor and her learners. Table 1 illustrates the content and use of the various forms that make up this particular ILP.

This chapter explores the role of this particular ILP in one adult literacy classroom in the north-west of England in 2010. By focusing on this one classroom, which was both a workplace and a place of learning, we contribute to research on the increasing textualisation of people's lives, and to the understanding of power and the ILP in adult literacy education. We describe processes associated with completion of the ILP in this classroom, and demonstrate that form-filling is a collaborative practice between teacher and learner. We identify the tensions and complexities that arise from these form-filling practices, focusing in particular on those aspects of the ILP for which the tutor has developed strategies to negotiate such tensions. This chapter illustrates how one literacy tutor draws on three particular strategies when responding to the demands of ILP form-filling in her classroom: mediating, sequencing and embedding. As we will illustrate, these strategies are creative approaches to fulfilling the demands placed upon the tutor and her learners.

Table 1: Overview of the ILP content and use

Form name	Description of content and use
Learner record form	Personal details, contact information, course details, disability status, ethnic origin, employer details, qualifications held
Train to gain: self-declaration of eligibility	Declaration of eligibility sections for completion by learner, employer and course provider
Summary of training needs analysis, initial assessment and learning plan	Prior learning, qualifications, work experience and other skills Group goals and personal learning objectives Initial assessment results, preferred learning style and additional support requirements
Qualification learning objectives	Individual learning objectives Key support and development needs Estimated time required for achievement of qualification
Learning styles questionnaire	Source of information for the 'Summary of training needs analysis, initial assessment and learning plan' form
Learning and review log	Record of each lesson's activities, learning and reflections, with a section to record practice test results
Mid-course review	Tutor feedback on learner progress, learner feed-back/suggestions, and revised objectives/test date
Information, advice and guidance	Completed at the end of the course to record the learner's: • future employment and learning plans, along with information required by the learner and provided by the tutor
Learner satisfaction survey	• evaluation of different aspects of the course including venue, teaching methods, content and organisation

The research, tutor and classroom

The data discussed in this chapter is from Sandra Varey's doctoral research,[1] focusing on one of the adult literacy tutors who participated in the study. Christine (the tutor's chosen pseudonym) is based in a Lifelong Learning department within a local authority in the north-west of England and the literacy course discussed in this chapter was delivered over 12 weeks for a total of 30 guided learning hours. Learners on the course were employed by the local authority. The data we draw on includes completed ILPs from three of the five learners enrolled on the course, along with tutor interview data in which the ILPs and paperwork practices were discussed.

Responding to and negotiating tensions inherent in the ILP: Lesson 1

As illustrated in Table 1, the ILP Christine uses brings together a number of policy documents and proformas. ILP paperwork is inextricably bound up with funding requirements, which creates tensions in Christine's classroom. For example, the funding implications mean that her learners must complete a number of forms in the first lesson, including the enrolment form and 'Train to gain' eligibility form. Christine described the enrolment form (designed by the Management Information Systems (MIS) team to collect the data needed to claim funding for the learner) as being 'particularly daunting'. She talked of supporting her learners to complete the form and using their responses as additional initial assessment information. However, it is clear from the way she described it that she assumes this form will be threatening for learners. She contrasts it with a new set of forms that have fewer boxes to fill in and look 'more friendly'. The enrolment form therefore creates a tension in Christine's classroom at a time when she is only beginning to establish relationships of trust with learners. As a strategy to overcome this, she therefore takes up a *mediating* role in relation to this form in lesson one.

Christine described the 'Train to gain' eligibility form, which must also be completed in lesson one, as even less user-friendly than the enrolment form. She represented it as 'a nightmare' because of its 'very legalistic' content and design. Learners must declare, for example, that they are 'lawfully resident in the UK' or that they 'fulfil the LSC's [Learning and Skills Council] residency criteria'. This could be perceived as a threat by some Skills for Life students, particularly some English for Speakers of Other Languages (ESOL) learners who might already have been engaged in protracted legal struggles to establish residency status. They must also confirm their 'employment status' and sign to acknowledge that 'if I have declared false information the provider may take action against me'. Christine represents the act of signing such a form as having potential to provoke anxiety. As with the enrolment form, the 'Train to gain' form represents a clash of understandings and priorities because, while it 'doesn't mean anything' to Christine's students, their signatures are crucial to the institution as the means by which the funding is un-locked. However, Christine is acutely aware that being asked to sign a legal document may be a threatening act for students. Again, she takes up a mediating position in this first lesson between the demands of the institution and the needs and likely responses of the students. In order to mitigate the possibility of students becoming intimidated by this 'legal-istic' form, Christine adopted the mediating strategy of 'talk[ing] around them rather than read[ing] them all out", although she also gave them the opportunity to read the form if they wished to. She also explained the purpose of the form, using mitigating language to minimise the pos-sibility of threat, and to highlight the benefits: 'I just explain that this is how we can continue to offer these courses for free'.

It is important to Christine to manage the point at which the forms are introduced in order to minimise any threat associated with complet-ing them. Although describing them as 'forms that you've got to just get through somehow', Christine explained that she would not present them at the very beginning of the first lesson. Instead, she starts with 'some kind of ice-breaker activities', carefully chosen to fit the learner group, which facilitates introductions from both the learners and Christine. The exam-ple she gave involved showing learners a tree with jelly babies sitting on different branches, in different positions and displaying different emotions – some hugging in groups, some doing adventurous activities, some fall-ing off the tree. They are asked to identify themselves with a particular jelly baby and explain why. This is a very different activity from filling in extensive statistical information and signing a legal document. Instead, this ice-breaker is multimodal, using pictures and colour, and the product is not a completed piece of paper, but a conversation. The focus is on feelings, not on facts. It is only after this conversation, which lays the basis for relation-ships within the group and knowledge of one another and one another's feelings, that Christine judges it is appropriate to introduce the potentially more threatening forms. Along with mediation, Christine therefore draws on another strategy to balance paperwork demands with the needs of her learners in the first lesson, that of *sequencing*.

Not all forms in the ILP are described as problematic or unfriendly. For example, Christine describes the 'Move on skills checklist' in a much more neutral fashion as requiring learners to indicate their achievements and generic skills, 'like decorate a room or organise a children's party'. Learners again address this form in the first lesson, but it does not re-quire a great deal of writing, demands no legal commitment, and makes sense in relation to learners' everyday activities. It highlights what they can do, rather than what they cannot. Christine does not describe it as problematic and does not deploy any particular strategies for completing it. Interestingly, this form is not actually present in the ILP record itself (see Table 1) because, as Christine explains, learners 'would keep that'. Similarly, Christine describes the 'Qualification learning objectives' form as unproblematic. It does not require any strategising, perhaps because it clearly relates to learners' aims of working towards a qualification.

By the time the 'Learning styles questionnaire' is addressed in this same lesson, however, it is not just the form itself that is important but also its relation to the earlier forms. Christine's view was that, by this point, learners started to feel that the form-filling was taking away from their learning time. They were 'waiting to do their English course ... they know why they're there, this is just another form that they have to fill in to record that intention' for external bodies. Christine therefore dislikes the way this questionnaire is presented in the learner paperwork because 'it seems like here's another form to fill in', and she 'would tend to do it as a separate activity'. By this stage, it is the volume and materiality of the forms that is problematic and Christine manages this by reframing it – presenting it not as a 'form' but as a 'separate activity' and turning it into 'a bit of a fun thing'. In addition to mediation and sequencing, we therefore see Christine drawing on another strategy to balance paperwork demands with the needs of her learners in lesson one, that of *embedding*.

Table 1 illustrates how the 'Summary of training needs analysis' form draws on a range of sources, including the Learning Styles questionnaire, to identify a learner's needs. The section on personal learning objectives is discussed during the first two weeks of the course and Christine outlined the tension that arose from it because the way in which her learners describe their own goals (for instance, 'spelling') may not satisfy the descriptions called for by the institution, namely SMART (specific, measurable, achievable, realistic and timed) targets. Christine therefore had to negotiate the tensions between terms that were meaningful to learners and terms expected by the various institutions. This required her to draw again on her mediating strategy.

Form-filling and strategies in later lessons

Many of the ILP forms discussed so far require learners and teachers to think about the future: their goals and purposes for being involved with the course. The remainder of the forms require reflection and review.

Christine described the 'Mid-course review' form, for example, as having 'worked really well'. It included a space for tutor feedback, which she filled in before the lesson, and a space for the learner's feedback. Christine felt that this openness allowed learners to express what they had achieved, whatever that was: 'you can say whatever you want and they can say whatever they want'. All of her learners had written extensively in the spaces provided in the old version of the mid-course review forms. She contrasted this with a newer version in which there was no space for tutor feedback. Instead, learners were asked questions that related much more closely to previous forms, asking, 'Have you achieved your objectives?' The notion that a course begins with setting objectives, and is judged on whether or not these are achieved, is part of the discourse of SMART targets referred to above. Christine felt this change in paperwork was a backward step and that learners found it harder to respond in this constrained way. The framing of the form is not necessarily meaningful in their terms – 'They don't actually know what objectives *are* necessarily' – and people tended to write just one or two lines, which she felt did not adequately reflect what they had actually done: 'It's not they lack literacy skills and can't fill in the form, it's just a hard thing to think about.' So although Christine had not previously needed to draw on any of the three strategies to successfully negotiate the mid-course review, this change in paperwork meant she now had to borrow from all three.

Another, more frequent, opportunity for review was provided by the 'Learning and review log' form, which was intended for completion at the end of each session. Christine found this constraining – 'sometimes it gets a bit squeezed out because of timing' – so she took a creative approach to the sequencing of this log. If there was what she calls a 'learning moment' taking place, she might pause the class and ask them to reflect on that moment in writing. There was a space for tutor feedback on the form, but she did not prioritise this, giving students maybe one or two written comments over the duration of the course. For her, immediate verbal feedback was much more important: 'Maybe that's a bit slack on my part but it's not like they don't get feedback during the course. So continually, through the course, I'll be giving them *actual* feedback, *verbal* feedback.'

Christine discussed the tension that often arises from the need to document information in the ILP. Whereas her learners may feel unsure about what to write on forms, for example, in conversation 'you get really good feedback from learners because they discuss what they've achieved and how they feel'. To respond to this tension, Christine has in the past embedded some form-filling requirements within other paper-less activities – for example, recording end-of-course verbal discussions to capture the plenitude of this feedback and extracting a few key comments to serve the auditing purposes represented by the written form. Christine felt the real pedagogical value was in the group discussion, which could not be fully captured in the ILP.

Summary of strategies

Christine's approaches and attitudes to the ILP allow us to draw out insights and understanding both about the tensions associated with the forms and the specific strategies she adopts in order to negotiate these tensions. Her goal is to enable the completion of the forms to be as productive and positive a part of the pedagogic processes as possible. The key tension identified above is between the forms that are designed for record-keeping for the MIS (particularly to unlock funding) and the structure of the pedagogic process. In interview, for instance, Christine discussed 'the dynamic and balance between what MIS and the funding require of us and what is manageable and user-friendly with the students'. Another more subtle underlying tension is between the managerial model of pedagogy implicit in the design of the form – set SMART objectives at the start of the course and regularly review progress towards achieving them – and the much more open process Christine described where she discovers her learners' feelings and hopes through dialogue.

Christine adopted a range of strategies to resolve these tensions. She placed herself in a mediating position between the forms and the learners, re-articulating parts of the forms that she felt might be threatening by 'talking around' the subject rather than reading out the forms, making the purpose of the forms explicit, explaining why they are presented in the way they are, and supporting learners in completing them. She managed the sequencing of the forms quite carefully, minimising the amount of form-filling in the first lesson by delaying what she could. She also ensured that the potentially threatening legalistic forms were addressed only after an ice-breaker activity, which was designed to elicit joint sharing of feelings and thereby develop trusting relationships in the classroom. The sequencing of paperwork appears to be a two-fold strategy: 1) the distribution of forms over the duration of the course; and 2) addressing paperwork at appropriate moments within individual lessons. Like the forms themselves, the sequence Christine employed is subject to constant change and also 'would depend on the group'.

Form-filling was also embedded within other pedagogical activities, and Christine said she was 'always trying to find innovative ways of introducing' the forms to her learners – placing them in a new context, for instance the 'fun activity' of the learning styles questionnaire, or the 'pause before coffee to reflect and record' of the learning log. This reframed the meanings of the forms, for instance by turning the learning log record into a space for verbal dialogue with students, much of which is seen as being of value in itself, without the need to be recorded in writing.

Not all ILP forms required management through the use of strategies, particularly where they related more closely to learners' own priorities, activities and meaning frameworks. However, in general the ILP paperwork is a site of 'struggle' for Christine as a tutor, something she feels 'you've got to just get through somehow'. When faced with a form that she cannot reframe and make meaningful within her pedagogical context (she gives the example of a new learner induction checklist, presented as a list of around 40 tick boxes) she feels very frustrated. The strategies of mediating, embedding and sequencing identified here are key to her finding her way through this meaning-making process.

Conclusion

We began by making the point that ILPs and other related forms can be interpreted as agents of policy, following Hamilton's (2009) analysis of the ways in which such texts align teachers and learners with particular subject positions within the Skills for Life Strategy. However, the data presented here has shown that while these forms position learners and teachers in relation to national strategy, the local meaning of the ILP is also being negotiated through the specific teaching practices, strategies and relationships that are developed in a particular setting.

Christine's strategies are mediating, sequencing and embedding. By placing herself in a mediating position between the learners and the form, Christine is also placing herself in a mediating position between the students and the various institutions within which their learning is framed. She translates the requirements of the form into a format and language that the learners can understand and engage with. Through careful management of the sequencing of the forms in the classroom, Christine is also managing their overall effects on learners' experiences, and is minimising the impact of form-filling. By embedding form-filling within other activities, she reframes its meaning and mitigates some of the potential problems brought about particularly by the volume of forms interfering with other pedagogical activities.

The context of adult literacy and numeracy education has changed dramatically in the first years of the twenty-first century, with the Skills for Life Strategy encouraging changed notions of professionalism and the sector shifting from a locally responsive approach to one where policy is more driven from the centre (Hamilton and Hillier, 2006). One of the results of this change has been to increase the number of forms that teachers and students have to complete – a very direct example of the process of increased textualisation related to an audit society with which we began this chapter. We have demonstrated here with one detailed example how such processes play out in practice, and the form-filling practices and strategies adopted by one teacher in response to them. While data from interviews with other tutors suggest they draw on a range of strategies to address these issues, in addition to those Christine adopts, the underlying tensions they describe in relation to form-filling are similar. Many of the tensions relate to the dual and potentially conflicting purposes of the forms, which have to fulfil both the administrative demands of management systems related to funding streams, and the pedagogical functions of planning and reviewing. There is also an underlying tension between the model of pedagogy assumed in the forms – setting SMART objectives and reviewing progress towards them – and the more responsive, dialogic, evolving model represented by the tutor's account. However, despite the emergence of these constraints and tensions, we have also shown that it is possible for tutors to negotiate them in creative ways that still promote the autonomy of the learner and the pedagogical practices the tutor is committed to developing.

Note

[1] Undertaken while based in the Department of Educational Research at Lancaster University and funded by the ESRC

References

Apple, M. W. (2005) 'Education, markets, and an audit culture', *Critical Quarterly*, Vol. 47 No 1–2, pp. 11–29.

Burgess, A. (2008) 'The literacy practices of recording achievement: how a text mediates between the local and the global', *Journal of Educational Policy*, Vol. 23 No 1, pp. 49–62.

Darville, R. (2002) 'Policy, accountability and practice in adult literacy: sketching an institutional ethnography' in *Adult Education and the Contested Terrain of Public Policy: Proceedings, Canadian Association for the Study of Adult Education*, (eds) Mojab, S. and McQueen, W. University of Toronto.[Online] www.casae-aceea.ca/sites/casae/archives/cnf2002/2002_Papers/darville2002w.pdf [Accessed on 29th June 2012]

DfEE (2001) *Skills for Life: The National Strategy for Improving Adult Literacy and Numeracy Skills*. Department for Education and Employment.

Edward, S., Coffield, F., Steer, R. and Gregson, M. (2007) 'Endless change in the learning and skills sector: the impact on teaching staff', *Journal of Vocational Education and Training*, Vol. 59 No 2, pp. 155–73.

Fawns, M., and Ivanič, R. (2001) 'Form–filling as a social practice: taking power into our own hands' in *Powerful Literacies*, (eds) Tett, L., Hamilton, M. and Crowther, J. NIACE.

Hamilton, M. (2009) 'Putting words in their mouths: the alignment of identities with system goals through the use of individual learning plans', *British Educational Research Journal*, Vol. 35 No 2, pp. 221–42.

Hamilton, M. and Hillier, Y. (2006) *Changing Faces of Adult Literacy, Language and Numeracy: A Critical History*. Trentham Books.

Iedema, R. (2003) *Discourses of Post-Bureaucratic Organization*. Philadelphia: John Benjamins Publishing Co.

Iedema, R. and Scheeres, H. (2003) 'From doing work to talking work: renegotiating knowing, doing and identity', *Applied Linguistics*, Vol. 24 No 3, pp. 316–37.

Jeffrey, B. and Troman, G. (2004) 'Time for ethnography', *British Educational Research Journal*, Vol. 30 No 4, pp. 535–48.

Smith, D. (2005) 'Texts, text-reader conversations, and institutional discourse' in *Institutional Ethnography: A Sociology for People*, pp. 101–22. Altamira Press.

Strathern, M. (2000) 'Introduction: new accountabilities' in *Audit Cultures: Anthropological Studies in Accountability, Ethics and the Academy*, (ed.) Strathern, M., pp. 1–18. Routledge.

Troman, G. (2000) 'Teacher stress in the low-trust society', *British Journal of Sociology of Education*, Vol. 21 No 3, pp. 331–53.

Tusting, K. (2009) 'I am not a "good" teacher; I don't do all their paperwork': teacher resistance to accountability demands in the English Skills for Life Strategy', *Literacy and Numeracy Studies*, Vol. 17 No 3, pp. 6–26.

CHAPTER SEVEN

Learning literacy for citizenship and democracy

JIM CROWTHER AND LYN TETT

Since 2001, there has been a growth of contradictory pressures for innovative and plural literacy practices alongside a narrowing of literacy to functional skills for work and employability (see the chapters in this book by Street, and Hamilton and Tett). These trends have made the task of addressing how literacy contributes to citizenship and democracy more necessary and more difficult, particularly in the context of economic crises, austerity programmes and the impact of globalisation that has increased the numbers of migrant workers, refugees and asylum seekers. The task is more *necessary* in the sense that the democratic impulse that has informed the rise of community education in Scotland has been diminished (see Tett, 2010). It is more *difficult* in terms of finding the spaces for literacies work that is not directly linked to a narrow policy agenda framed by concerns for social cohesion or employability.

It should be clear that there is no necessary link between learning for citizenship and democracy as an outcome: the former may result in conformity and uniformity rather than the dissent and difference that characterise genuinely democratic societies (Biesta, 2011). In this chapter, we draw on material from a Scottish context in order to ask what kinds of literacy contribute to extending the ability of people to shape the forces and decisions that impact on their lives as well as deepen the experience of democracy as a way of life.

The skills of reading and writing are important for an active and informed citizenry. However, the practice of democracy involves much more than reading the names on a form and marking a ballot paper with a cross in order to vote. Whilst not demeaning the important choice this literacy skill involves, one of the central themes of democratic life is the extent to which people can participate in the processes of decision-making in all aspects of communal and public life. It is quite obvious that formal equality of voting rights does not translate into equal levels of influence. Inequalities of wealth and power generate inequalities of political influence in all spheres of life (Brookfield and Holst, 2011). To work towards extending and deepening democracy, we argue that literacy practice makes an important contribution as part of a broad political literacy that provides opportunities for adults to make power more visible as well as to make it more accountable.

Inequalities in powerful forms of literacy, differential access to information and the application of persuasive communication skills must be considered as part of the way that wider inequalities of power are systematically reproduced. If democracy is to become instantiated in everyday life, political representatives, public institutions and services, the activities of those who work for them (e.g. doctors, teachers, welfare workers), community organisations and groups have to be accountable to the people they represent or work for. Literacies education should therefore contribute to enabling people to interrogate the claims and activities offered on their behalf and, in turn, encourage them to develop the skill, analysis and confidence to make their own voice heard and, where necessary, take action to assert it.

We live in times where there is a widening gap between the information 'rich' and the information 'poor': a phenomenon affecting relations between different countries as well as relations within society (Castells, 2003). The volume of textual and non-textual information is increasing whilst our ability and time to make sense of it decreases. How can people effectively participate and claim back some control over their lives? We should not, of course, assume that because some adult students lack techniques of reading and writing they are incapable of critical inquiry. The assumption that 'illiteracy' implies a deficit person has to be strongly resisted. In the context of engaging with adults educationally, we subscribe to Jackson's (1995, p. 185) view that 'adults bring something which derives both from their experience of adult life and from their status as citizens to the educational process'. This in turn has implications for the literacy curriculum and what it seeks to achieve. Moreover, policy interest in citizenship and social inclusion, we argue, presents an opportunity to go beyond the limited – and limiting – functional way of thinking about literacy and a deficit model of literacy students. We therefore need to subscribe to an understanding of citizenship that engages with the issues and concerns that adults face and adds to their capacity to develop individual and collective control of their lives.

Discourses of citizenship

Educational practice is an intellectual task prior to becoming a practical accomplishment. In the context of literacy for citizenship and democracy, it is necessary to explore some of the terrain of thinking that can be a resource for educational engagement. As Carr and Hartnett (1996) pointed out:

> *The only kind of civic education which can prepare people as citizens for life in a fully democratic society is one which acknowledges both that the meaning of citizenship is perennially the subject of contestation, and that it is through this process of contestation that the relationship between the citizen and the state is being continuously redefined.* (1996, p. 82)

How we think about citizenship and the relationship between the state and its citizens therefore shapes how we construct it as a problem to address educationally. A current policy debate is about the appropriate balance between the rights and duties of individuals and the state (see Hamilton and Pitt, 2011). The UK's Coalition Government has embarked on a series of austerity measures aimed at cutting welfare benefits and reducing the public sector, in the belief that people have become too dependent on the state and that the solution is to make individuals and communities more resilient and capable of taking care of themselves (Crowther and Shaw, 2011). In this context, rights become increasingly contingent on fulfilling duties.

Marshall (1950), in his seminal analysis, makes the distinction between three types of rights essential for understanding citizenship. The first, civil rights, involve individual freedom of the person, of speech and so on. The second, political rights, concern the extension of the franchise to enable people to share political power. Finally, social rights indicate the right to economic welfare, social security, health and education as a context in which other rights are exercised. The undermining of social rights is therefore counterproductive to developing active citizenship, and yet the 'big society' – which depends on people having the time, resources and commitment to volunteer – is another policy goal for the UK government. However, it is sometimes within such contradictions that the possibility for critical and creative educational work can occur.

Another educationally important way of thinking about citizenship is that which distinguishes between its social and political nature. Citizenship as a political identity relates to the kind of rights and responsibilities explained in the paragraph above. Important as these issues are, they do not capture all of what it means to be a citizen. Citizenship as a social identity refers to the roles and sense of belonging that one has in society. Whilst policy is usually interested in both, the emphasis on citizenship as a social identity foregrounds issues of social integration, difference and diversity, and the common bonds people subscribe to – or, more pointedly, the absence of these bonds. The issue of social identity as an aspect of citizenship is an important issue in a number of Western societies today, particularly in the context of social, cultural and political processes of discrimination (which create an 'other' category for particular groups such as disabled people). The context also includes globalisation, the migration of people and the growth of refugees and asylum seekers. The debate on citizenship has inevitably focused on the acquisition of the national language, on clothing and on wearing religious icons that appear to separate people from the wider culture. However, this can lead to a contradiction between the discourse of citizenship that focuses, on the one hand, on social identity and leads to framing difference and diversity as a problem for social integration, and, on the other, on a political identity that involves plurality as a hallmark of an open, free and democratic social order (Biesta, 2011).

There is also an important difference between citizenship as an ascribed status and citizenship as an asserted practice (Lister, 1998). The former refers to the legal rights people possess as members of a society and may lead us to think about education for citizenship in terms of understanding our formal rights. This might involve education for understanding the role of elected representatives, how to vote, the nature of political parties, the responsibility of democratic institutions and so on. The emphasis on citizenship as an asserted practice, however, recognises that formal rights have often to be realised by actively claiming them through a political process that involves organisation, making claims, mobilising support, taking action and campaigning – amongst other things – to ensure that formal rights are enacted. Challenges to existing representative institutions and procedures by social movements could constitute an infringement of democracy – from the perspective of it as a formal and legal status, rather than an arena in which legitimate politics are carried out. However, it is politically naïve in the extreme to assume governments merely look after our rights. It seems wiser to expect that rights have to be continually argued and struggled for. After all, where did our existing rights come from? If we have not reached the end of history, where will the forces for new rights come from? The question, then, is about how people learn to claim their rights of citizenship as distinct from being taught how to be citizens.

Finally, we concur with Martin (1999) who draws attention to the distinction between the rhetoric of policy and the discourses that inform them. The rhetoric can be seductive (e.g. promoting active citizenship) and may be appealing, whereas the discourses that give policy meaning are often more limiting than the rhetoric suggests. In the context of educational work with adults, he identifies two dominant economistic discourses of citizenship that position the adult learner as either a worker/ producer or as a customer/consumer. In the first, education is equated with training for work. In the second, education is understood as a commodity to be bought and sold. Both are reductionist in that adult learning is seen only in economic terms. As Martin goes on to say:

> *It is not, of course, that these economistic discourses do not matter – self-evidently, they do. Rather, it is that they simply do not account for enough of what adult education, let alone lifelong learning, should be about. We are not just servicers of the economy or traders in the educational marketplace. On the contrary, our interest lies in enabling people to develop to their full potential as 'whole persons' or rounded human beings. This suggests that adult education should help people to engage in a wide range of political roles and social relationships that occur outside both the workplace and the marketplace. We are more than simply creatures of the cash nexus.* (1999, p. 17)

There are various examples of both types of the above in adult litera-cies. In relation to the adult learner as a producer/worker, the basis of much current policy is aimed at providing young adults with basic skills in reading, writing and numeracy, amongst other things, as prerequisites for entering the job market. In Scotland today, recent policy proposals for post–16 educational reform focus entirely on education for work to the exclusion of everything else (Crowther, 2011). Unemployment, particularly for young people in the 16- to 19-year-old bracket, takes precedence in a misleadingly titled proposal, *Putting Learners at the Centre* (Scottish Government, 2011). Public funding to support literacies provision is fixated on skilling (young) people for work which, it is claimed, is good for the economy in terms of relieving skill shortages and good for the individual who is more likely to find work and improve the level of their income. The assumption made from this economistic perspective is that literacy is the same thing for everyone since it is only necessary as a functional skill for work. However, what is regarded as 'functional' cannot be understood outside the processes that define it, and differentially distribute it, to different groups. Decoding words and texts cannot simply be understood as a neutral skill. For example, what is functional rarely includes the ability to control or influence the decisions that affect people's lives – but surely these are essential too for everyday life at home, in the community, at work and in society? (Crowther, *et al.*, 2003; Brookfield and Holst, 2011.)

The other discourse of the adult learner as a consumer has been present in adult literacy work where the learner is depicted as a reluctant participant who is failing to fulfil their duty to obtain work. The literacy student as reluctant consumer is to be encouraged to shake off the stigma of illiteracy and participate in a learning programme so that they take responsibility for their own welfare. One of the consequences of realigning rights as being dependent on duties is that the voluntary status of adult education provision is increasingly being undermined by coercive penalties for failure to engage in improving literacy skills. 'Welfare to workfare' measures, which involve cuts in benefits for failure to comply with training programmes, are a case in point (DWP, 2011). Moreover, as rights become contingent on duties, they no longer have the status of rights because they cannot be claimed unconditionally.

In summary, we agree with the disabled scholar and activist Michael Oliver (1996) who remarks that 'when the relationship between the state and its population is in crisis, citizenship becomes the device whereby such a crisis is talked about and mediated'. This discourse is primarily one that occurs at a policy and political level rather than at a practitioner level, but, as Freire (1973) reminds us, education is politics and to wash our hands of the situation is to side with the powerful. To refuse the choice is to make one. The competing discourses of citizenship, and the diverse problems they seek to address, raise dilemmas for practitioners but also offer exciting options to open up educational possibilities for engagement and negotiation with students – and this is an important task for the educator interested in both citizenship and democracy.

Starting points for a political literacy education

Whilst literacy for citizenship and democracy has to address making power visible and accountable, this is not always the starting point for engagement with adults. Building a curriculum has to recognise that many people want to acquire literacies for a variety of purposes – initially, the dominant motive is most likely to be an instrumental purpose related to an everyday life problem. In the context of the life of migrants, the motive for participating in English language provision may be to achieve literacy competence to pass the citizenship test set by the government so that they can acquire the formal rights they are denied without this status. Important as it is to meet such needs, literacy practitioners have to keep in mind that initial motivations for learning are not necessarily fixed. They can change as individuals acquire fresh views about the value of education for their lives and begin to become aware of a wider range of purposes it can serve. On the other hand, people often desire to get involved in community life but are hampered by low self-confidence and low self-esteem, which the acquisition of literacies can transform (Tett and Maclachlan, 2007).

One of the strengths of the social practice perspective of literacy is that it grounds these activities in the ecology of everyday life (Barton, 1994), which enables the literacies practitioners to develop a broad curriculum through which the acquisition of skills can be addressed. At the same time, adults' expectations of literacy have been shaped by previous experience, particularly in schooling that treats literacy broadly as a neutral, cognitive, skill. Developing literacy learning for citizenship and democracy involves working with, as well as against, the grain of cultural and educational expectations that students bring to provision.

The approach we are advocating for political literacy connects with a rich and long tradition of educational philosophy in Scotland that juxtaposes education with wider issues of a democratic way of life. The tradition of 'democratic intellectualism' was part of a debate related to a claimed meritocratic form of university education that was specific to the curriculum of these institutions. It was not seen as a project *outside* these institutions nor was it, in all likelihood, seen as a feasible project for the mass of people. Nonetheless, we would argue that the principles that inform it do connect with the aspiration for a critical and questioning citizenry and can be adapted for political literacy work in communities amongst a broader range of people.

Alexander and Martin (1995) argue that this educational tradition '… provides the basis for a distinctive vision of a rich and humane civic culture that is worth working for and requires the commitment of all democratic adult educators'. Briefly, democratic intellectualism dates back to the Scottish Enlightenment and refers to the role of higher education to engage all students in the study of first principles in a commonly understood way through the study of subjects such as philosophy. The problem this sought to address was that of over-specialism and a narrow technical rationality of how to get things done rather than why they should be done in the first place. The case for a 'common sense' approach pointed to the need to get to the root issues, in a democratically informed way, before questions of detail were addressed.

Writing about the influence of George Davie as an exponent of this tradition, Murdoch (1999) points out that:

> *The key notion to take from Davie's ideas is that the expert's knowledge is inherently incomplete. In short, the narrow focus of the specialised expert creates blind spots. The point about a generalist approach such as democratic intellectualism is not that non-experts have a right to scrutinise the work of the expert, but that the work of the expert is only complete in the light of such scrutiny … Thus, others in the community, by virtue of their lack of expertise (which gives them a different perspective from that of the expert), have a responsibility to comment on these blind spots.* (1999, p. 85)

In such a perspective, a politically literate community is the foundation of democratic life. Davie's argument for a democratic intellect where non-specialists are encouraged to interrogate specialists is seen as a vital part of a healthy society. An educated community of specialists is unfit to govern without the process of scrutiny argued for. They become, in effect, intellects without democracy. Whilst this argument was used within universities, there is no reason why it cannot be applied and adapted to other areas of adult education and adult literacy.

The issue for the adult literacies worker is how to develop a curriculum that can facilitate the mutual illumination of blind spots in the sense referred to above. This would necessitate a dialogue between tutor and student to scrutinise the claims of specialists based on the premise that all have a valid contribution to make. An essential component is to engage the critical intellect of people in a way that motivates and stretches them, and enables them to engage with public issues. Developing political literacy is therefore integral to being an adult citizen in a democratic society. If people are to gain a voice – to question and speak back to power – they will need the confidence and authority that comes out of experience, reinforced and tempered by study. In the context of citizenship, notions of literacy that focus purely on functional skills – which ignore the struggles over rights and responsibilities, the social and political nature of citizenship, and its formal status, which may not be realised in practice – might easily end up diminishing citizenship to economistic prerequisites. These are unlikely to provide opportunities for people to read the meaning beyond, or between, the lines and the interests behind the meaning.

We would agree with Green's claim (cited by Lankshear, 1998) that literacy involves three levels. The first, an operational level, involves competence in reading and writing; the second, cultural literacy, involves understanding the meaning embodied in communications and texts; the third, critical literacy, involves understanding how some meanings are selected and legitimated whilst others are not. The difficulty, of course, is working these levels together in practice. The example of the Glory and Dismay Football Literacy Programme is a case in point (see the chapter in this book by Player).

An example of literacy contributing to citizenship as an asserted practice is described by Gillian Lawrence's (2003) work with the Democracy, Disability and Society group, which was based in an outer city estate in Edinburgh. She describes the growth and emerging identity of the group as a campaigning organisation to assert the rights of disabled people living in the area who were also interested in pressing for policy changes to benefit disabled people across the city. One example was a campaign to influence transport facilities by identifying and describing the barriers disabled people face, particularly in relation to buses and taxis. This was followed up with a campaign of awareness-raising material and a training pack for taxi drivers, distributed by taxi licensing authorities. A touring exhibition and a transport event attended by policy decision-makers and bus and taxi companies was also part of the project's literacies activities.

The demand for more accountable democratic institutions in Scotland also created the impetus for literacy and citizenship activity, which reflects a number of the issues referred to in this chapter. One of the arguments for the Scottish Parliament was the need for a closer relationship between the people and its politicians. This led to a number of voluntary organisations working together to produce critical and creative literacy resources to explain the Parliament and the role of its members and show how people could engage with formal political processes and procedures and, if necessary, participate in campaigning activities outside the Parliament (WEA, 2009). Students are able to engage with the subject through a range of materials that use a variety of different communications media – including political poems, political songs, banner making, video clips, tables of information, word matches, websites and so on. A rich resource is provided for a broad literacy programme that raises awareness and develops skills. The curriculum covers the vocabulary of politics, the conventions of writing and speaking in the Parliament, the protocols for engagement with politicians and political parties, and a comparison of these practices and the practices of campaign groups that mobilise people by operating outside of formal political institutions. The way in which politics as a discourse shapes thinking about policy problems and solutions adds to the curriculum for literacy activity, which extends citizenship and deepens democratic life.

Conclusion

It is by no means easy to build a literacy curriculum that enables people to make real choices about what being a citizen means and how they can contribute to democratic processes. To do so will require enthusiasm, determination and imagination on the part of the practitioner as well as an awareness of the range of issues posed by literacies for citizenship (as explored in this chapter). In the context of understandable concerns for people's capacity to have a productive economic life, we must avoid simultaneously reducing the possibilities for a democratic one. If policy-makers cannot see this, then it is up to practitioners to create the spaces for this work.

What should be avoided is both cynicism and apathy about the contribution that literacy can make to the issue of citizenship in people's lives. Adult literacy practitioners need to be reflexive about the assumptions they make about the 'limit situations' of the people they work with. Moreover, the limitations of the dominant policy discourses on the meaning of citizenship have to be contested. Democracy and citizenship are too important to be left to the policy-makers and politicians. If we do so, what kind of democracy are we living in? Educators must develop a space for critical and creative work that imparts genuine skills and understanding whilst developing the confidence of people to play an active and informed role in the issues that are important to them. Education needs to be a resource for individuals and collectivities to take some control over their lives by providing opportunities for a broad and stimulating curriculum that firmly embraces learning for democracy. Hirshman (1970) argued that people respond to changes either by expressing their loyalty, exiting and opting out, or using their voice to speak up for their rights. The suggestions we have made aim to maximise the 'voice' option because to 'exit' or merely to express loyalty involves conforming to the dominant order which, in turn, diminishes democratic life.

References

Alexander, D. and Martin, I. (1995) 'Competence, curriculum and democracy' in *Adults Learning, Critical Intelligence and Social Change,* (eds) Mayo, M. and Thompson, J., pp. 82–96. NIACE.

Barton, D. (1994) *Literacy: An Introduction to the Ecology of Written Language.* Blackwell.

Biesta, G. (2011) 'We need better democracy, not better citizens', *Adults Learning,* Vol. 23 No 2, pp. 226–33.

Brookfield, S. D. and Holst, J. D. (2011) *Radicalizing Learning: Adult Education for a Just World.* San Francisco: Jossey-Bass.

Carr, W. and Hartnett, A. (1996) 'Civic education, democracy and the English political tradition' in *Beyond Communitarianism,* (eds) Demaine, J. and Entwhistle, H., pp. 64–82. Macmillan Press.

Castells, M. (2003) *The Internet Galaxy.* Oxford University Press.

Crowther, J. (2011) 'Too narrow a vision', *Adults Learning,* Vol. 23 No 2, pp. 14–15.

Crowther, J., Martin, I. and Shaw, M. (2003) *Renewing Democracy in Scotland: An Educational Resource Pack.* NIACE.

Crowther, J. and Shaw, M. (2011) 'Education for resilience and resistance in the "big society"' in *Surviving Economic Crises through Education,* (ed.) Cole, D. Frankfurt Am Main: Peter Lang.

DWP (2011) *The Work Programme* [Online] http://www.dwp.gov.uk/policy/welfare-reform/get-britain-working/#britain [Accessed 17 December 2011] Department for Work and Pensions.

Freire, P. (1973) *Pedagogy of the Oppressed.* Penguin.

Hamilton, M. and Pitt, K. (2011) 'Challenging representations: constructing the adult literacy learner over 30 years of policy and practice in the United Kingdom', *Reading Research Quarterly*, Vol. 46 No 4, pp. 350–73.

Hirshman, A. (1970) *Exit, Voice and Loyalty*. Cambridge, MA: Harvard University Press.

Jackson, K. (1995) 'Popular education and the state: a new look at the community debate' in *Adult Learning, Critical Intelligence and Social Change*, (eds) Mayo, M. and Thompson, J., pp. 82–96. NIACE.

Lankshear, C. (1998) 'The educational challenge of the new work order: globalisation and the meanings of literacy', *Concept*, Vol. 8 No 2, pp. 12–15.

Lawrence, G. (2003) 'Learners as teachers: democracy and social action in community-based adult literacies practice', *Concept*, Vol. 13 No 1–2, pp. 6–10.

Lister, R. (1998) 'In from the margins: citizenship, inclusion and exclusion' in *Social Exclusion and Social Work: Issues of Theory, Policy and Practice*, (eds) Barry, M. and Hallet, C., pp. 26–38. Russell House Publishing.

Marshall, T. (1950) *Citizenship and Social Class*. Chicago: Chicago University Press.

Martin, I. (1999) 'Adult education, lifelong learning and active citizenship', *Adults Learning*, Vol. 11 No 2, pp. 16–18.

Murdoch, M. (1999) 'The significance of the Scottish generalist tradition' in *Popular Education and Social Movements in Scotland Today*, (eds) Crowther, J., Martin, I. and Shaw, M., pp. 83–94. NIACE.

Oliver, M. (1996) *Disability: From Theory to Practice*. Macmillan.

Scottish Government (2011) *Putting Learners at the Centre: Delivering our Ambitions*, [Online] http://www.scotland.gov.uk/Publications/2011/09/15103949/0 [Accessed 17 December 2011].

Tett, L. (2010) *Community Education, Learning and Development*. Dunedin Press.

Tett, L. and Maclachlan, K. (2007) 'Adult literacy and numeracy, social capital, learner identities and self-confidence, *Studies in the Education of Adults*, Vol. 39 No 2, pp. 150–67.

WEA (2009) *Political Literacy Resource Pack*. Workers' Educational Association. [Online] www.aloscotland.com/alo/viewresource.htm?id=519 [Accessed 16 June 2012].

SECTION THREE

RESISTANCE AND CHALLENGES

CHAPTER EIGHT

Affective power: Exploring the concept of learning care in the context of adult literacy

MAGGIE FEELEY

The whole thing about our childhood was to keep us down. Edu-cation was too good, too powerful for us. If we had been able to read and write we would have become stronger; but by keeping us down we were vulnerable and they could abuse us. (Tania, woman aged 52 who left industrial school with unmet literacy needs)

Introduction

Tania's words illustrate the emancipatory potential of learning and the vulnerability felt by many excluded from literacy use. Access to powerful literacies emerged from the study discussed below as inextricably linked to matters in the affective domain – to love, care and solidarity. This is not news. Adult literacy learners are constantly reminding us about the im-portance of relational aspects of the learning process, yet these affective issues have received relatively little academic or pedagogical attention. We know that in other social contexts the complex role of care is often unrecognised, undervalued and overshadowed by economic concerns (Lynch *et al.*, 2009). Affective aspects of teaching and learning have also been perceived as a natural, often gendered phenomenon, for which no additional training or resources are necessary (Gannerud, 2001).

Despite general neglect, recognition is growing across the educational spectrum that affective matters are an important part of how and what we learn. Studies have begun to focus on a range of issues such as: care and the school curriculum (Cohen, 2006; McClave, 2005); teachers' emotional labour (Hargreaves, 2000, 2001); the role of the affective domain in educational ideology (Lynch *et al.*, 2007; Lynch *et al.*, 2009); a school ethic of care (Noddings, 1992; 2006; 2007) and mothers' care labour in children's education (O'Brien, 2005; 2007; Reay, 2000). This chapter now takes a literacy turn to explore and record the relationship between literacy and care equalities and inequalities. Coining the concept of 'learning care', I argue that affective dimensions of equality are pivotal and powerful in establishing more just literacy outcomes (Feeley, 2009; 2010). My hope is that a focus on equalities and inequalities of care will bring a fresh perspective for all of us concerned with literacy matters and working for greater social justice.

Literacy, care and equality

The chapter is written from an equality studies and new literacy studies perspective that defines literacy as a form of social practice with powerful potential for individual and collective change.[1] If we accept that literacy is socially situated and a tool in the struggle for social justice, then understanding the unequal nature of that social backdrop is important. An equality perspective (Baker *et al.*, 2004; 2009) provides a base from which to examine aspects of the wider, hegemonic social context in which literacy and care are located.

The equality framework developed in the Equality Studies Centre, University College Dublin (Baker *et al.*, 2004; 2009) provides the conceptual basis for this study of affective aspects of literacy and the development of the notion of learning care. Those who developed the framework describe their ultimate vision of equality of condition where 'people should be as equal as possible in relation to the central condition of their lives' (Lynch and Baker, 2005, p. 132). The potential for such equality of condition is located in four overarching and interconnected social systems: economic, cultural, political and affective. These are the arbiters of interrelated socially situated disparities, including those that are literacy related (Baker *et al.*, 2004; 2009, Chapters 1, 2 and 4).[2]

In relation to literacy, the equality framework generally provides a language and structure for a holistic, multidimensional conceptualisation of literacy. It allows us to identify a range of literacy events and practices – for economic, cultural, political and relational purposes. It provides a systematic method for identifying causes and outcomes of unmet literacy needs – poverty, powerlessness, marginalisation, exclusion and degrees of isolation. Those with fewer resources, less voice in decision-making, lower status and poorer care are more likely to be denied access to powerful literacies than those who are socially privileged. More positively, the different equality contexts suggest actions that might be transformative in reducing literacy inequalities. For example: increasing the resources of individuals and groups that experience educational disadvantage; valuing diverse vernacular language and literacy uses in different contexts and in the lives of those outside the mainstream; using literacy as a Freirean praxis tool for empowerment and change; moving away from atrophying, functional learning for productivity towards learning that is rooted in care and respect for people's dreams and aspirations. The ideal of 'equality of condition' described by Lynch and Baker (2005) holds rich possibilities for new perspectives on adult literacy.

A focus on the structural roots of social inequality exposes the deception in the deficit literacy discourses that fixate on dysfunctional individuals, families, schools, social groups and communities, and suggests that these are just (and unjust) distractions from the real issues and the powerful vested interests that actively conceal them (Lynch, 1999). The inclusion of the affective system in a framework for thinking about inequality is novel and although in reality they are all inextricably entangled, here the care strand is singled out for specific attention.

A relational method of enquiry

The voices and ideas that are the backbone of this chapter were gathered as part of a four-year ethnographic study (2004 to 2007) and continue to be informed by ongoing work within the same community. A critical case study carried out in the Lighthouse Centre,[3] with survivors of institutional abuse in Irish industrial schools, illustrates how inequalities of care pivotally interact with more recognised disparities in the economic, cultural and political context.

Industrial schools were first established in Scotland, operated throughout Britain under the 1857 Industrial Schools Act and were extended to Ireland in 1868. They were intended as a complement to the Reformatory School system with the remit of providing state care and education for children whose family life was deemed no longer viable. Although known to be exceptionally punitive, the schools were allowed to operate virtually without either challenge or sanction for over one hundred years. In 1970, the Kennedy Report (Government of Ireland, 1970) was highly critical of the system and the decades that followed saw survivors speaking out about their experiences so that the extent of their multiple abuses became public. In 1999, the State apologised to survivors, instigated a redress system and established an education fund for survivors and their families. The Lighthouse Centre was established in 1999 by a group of survivors to provide healing through adult learning opportunities; adult literacy is a core part of the work of the Centre.

This is not just a historical or local matter. The Irish experience of education that is used to further disempower oppressed groups has produced echoes in other contexts,[4] all of which offer insights into persistent contemporary basic educational inequalities. These educational injustices are arguably still the lot of individuals and groups that are less cared for or cared about within contemporary social structures (Noddings 2006; Engster, 2007).

In the empirical study, learning care is explored through its absence from the lives of those for whom life and learning were the antithesis of affection. For these research participants, literacy outcomes mirrored the (often negative) levels of care in their lives. Although with a less physically violent expression, such disregard and harm continue in the care-less educational experiences that continue to occur today and result in persistent unmet literacy needs in both developed and developing countries (UNESCO, 2006; CEC, 2008; OECD, 2009).

Alongside the extensive ethnography, the study sample of 28 adults, aged between 40 and 65, took part in semi-structured interviews and a series of follow-up, feedback focus groups. This age cohort reflected the majority mainstream grouping involved in adult literacy and there is considerable overlap between the experiences of survivors and other learners in the contemporary literacy field (Bailey and Coleman, 1998; DES, 2006). It was decided to sample in terms of (self-defined) literacy status on leaving school so that comparison could be made between those who had learned literacy while in the care of industrial schools and those who had not. In this way, the significance of care within the learning process became more clearly discernible.

The centrality of care

The findings of this empirical study have indicated a model of literacy learning care that builds on the work of Kathleen Lynch (2007). She proposed a model of three concentric circles of care relations – primary, secondary and tertiary contexts where care is given and received. Each level of care is associated with a form of work: love labour in primary care relations, care work in secondary care relations and the collaborative agency involved in solidary activity. Activity in the affective domain is key to well-being in every aspect of our interdependent lives (Engster, 2005; Lynch *et al.*, 2009). To be meaningful, care moves beyond sentiment and intent to become realised in effort and actions that aim to benefit care recipients and this equally holds true for learning care. Within these wider circles of care, learning care refers to the impact of care on our capacity to absorb and retain new knowledge and skills.

The process and outcome of literacy acts and events, and learning how to perform them, is almost always social and relational. Nevertheless, until recently, learning to read and write has been viewed as a purely cognitive matter (Lankshear and Knobel, 2003). As construed here, learning care describes the affective attitudes, emotions and actions, both paid and unpaid, that dynamically influence individuals and groups in learning literacy. Learning care is both given and received. It involves caregivers and recipients and these relationships are reciprocal (Feeley, 2009; 2010). The affective aspects of supporting and facilitating language and literacy development involve skill, effort and insight and as such need to be learned and resourced.

The history of survivors of institutional abuse is a stark reminder that not everyone in society profits equally from care-giving. This in turn has a knock-on effect on all aspects of human development that care promotes and sustains, including literacy. Ethnographic research with survivors suggests four discreet but interconnected sources of learning care with a distinct and combined relevance to the field of literacy.

Four types of learning care relationships

1. **Primary learning care** in loving relationships is experienced within the family or alternative primary care centre. In adult literacy, inequalities in this area are recognised in the attention now given to family literacy and the need to enable and resource parents to support children's language and literacy development and interrupt cycles of educational disadvantage.
2. **Secondary learning care** occurs in caring relationships in schools, colleges and other places of adult learning. The need for ongoing support with traditional and new literacies is becoming widely recognised and the case for a relational emphasis in embedded or

integrated approaches to literacy in all sectors has been well made (NRDC, 2005; Hegarty and Feeley, 2009).

3. **Solidary learning care** is often experienced informally, in solidarity with peer learners and communities of interest. Much adult literacy work includes and exemplifies a collaborative approach to learning where groups encourage and support each other in language and literacy development and practice. The National Adult Literacy Agency (NALA) Learners' Forum is an example of how solidary learning care can be resourced and facilitated and learners empowered to become literacy activists (Cox, 2010).

4. **State learning care** is defined here as the degree of attentiveness given by the state to ensuring structural equality (equality of condition) across all the contexts that influence family, school and community capacity to support literacy learning. This is a weak link in the care chain and evidence of an absence of state learning care is apparent in persistent social and educational inequalities and the reluctance of states to provide real resolutions to this inequity.

How the data helped clarify these different types of learning care is outlined below.

Primary learning care

Irrespective of age, for most people, the 'natural' locus of learning care is undoubtedly the family or primary care centre, where nurturing relationships promote and model all aspects of human development, including literacy. For the 28 participants in this research, the main source of primary care was the industrial school although some also had early or intermittent opportunities for care with their family of origin or in foster care. Fifteen respondents left school with their literacy needs met or partially met. The remaining 13 could use little or no literacy. In the majority (87 per cent) of cases of those who had either met or partially met literacy needs when leaving school, there was a discernible link with levels of consistency in positive primary care relationships. Similarly, of the 13 who finished school with unmet literacy needs, 11 (85 per cent) had no family life or consistent family relationship while in care. The conclusive trend in the data therefore established a strong link between continuity of primary care and positive literacy outcomes.

The capacity of the respondents' families to offer care in the home was negatively influenced by extremes of poverty, the disrespect that comes from perceived moral inferiority and the powerlessness of those without privilege to challenge a rigidly authoritarian system. Where some degree of stability was possible in the home, and education valued and promoted, a positive experience of literacy could be traced back to an early age:

> My life has been a pattern of in and out of care but I have very vivid memories of my life before I went, say when I was three or four ... learning words at home with my mother ... storytelling. And then when I did go to school we weren't allowed to eat until our homework was done. There is a bit of a perfectionist in me as well and maybe it's because I remember my mother always checking over our homework. You need that kind of approval. It is a kind of a nurturing thing you know. (Carol, woman aged 50 who left school with met literacy needs)

Authoritarianism and regimentation were the pervasive order of the day in a culture where children were identified with the perceived failings of their family. The goal of industrial schools was control and the production of docile, obedient, manual and domestic labourers for deployment in religious enterprises or in wealthy families. Nevertheless, those who were sustained in any affective family framework could be encouraged and motivated by that relationship or even the memory of it. Kevin had been at home until he was seven and could clearly name the role of primary care relationships in learning:

> The way I look at it is that some people did well because they were connected with their families outside. They had their families to support them. They were able to concentrate better. Their thinking was different. People that did well at the school had their families looking after them. (Kevin, man aged 56 who left school with partially met literacy needs)

More recent research with disadvantaged parents about their understandings of family literacy also shows an awareness of the synonymous nature of early literacy and primary care (Hegarty and Feeley, 2010, p. 51):

> Actually when I am doing homework with the young fellow he is kind of sitting up and kind of leaning against me as if to say I am

well supported here. He feels safe. So I think love should go in there. When they come in from school they come to me for a hug and the same before they leave in the morning. That is their support. (Parent aged 42 with four children)

Secondary learning care

Accounts of secondary learning care in the industrial school were re-plete with details of time spent in the tension and fear that accompanies the threat of aggression and harm. Within that learning environment, corporal punishment and public humiliation were commonplace. In the immediate context, learning was blocked by terror and concerns with self-protection and survival. In the longer term, the abuses that were experienced resulted in damaged self-esteem, negative associations with the learning process and an inevitable mistrust of teachers and author-ity figures. Kevin was seven when he went into care and became fearful of learning:

> *I didn't like the school there. I hated it. There was a terrible tense atmosphere. And like you would be looking at them to see if they were in a bad mood. There was always somebody getting a right beating. And you were tense all through the class and afraid. If you got something to do you would be scared. I didn't like it – it was too tense.* (Kevin, man aged 56 who left school with partially met literacy needs)

In addition to the pervasive sense of angst, large classes were managed as batches with no allowance for different learning styles. Those who were left-handed were demonised and brutalised:

> *I was a twin and we were both left-handed. We were beaten into writing with our right hands and I think it really upset our brains. I picked it up quickly but my brother didn't and he went through hell for it. They used to say it was evil – a sign of the devil and all that. 'I will beat the devil out of you.' I used to be frustrated that my brother didn't grasp it quickly enough to save himself from beatings.* (Bridget, woman aged 51 who left school with met literacy needs)

Literacy learning was robotic and anyone unable to grasp reading and spelling through primarily auditory methods was additionally disadvantaged. In some cases children attended 'outside' school where they reported that they were constantly reminded of their inferiority. Within both 'inside' and 'outside' school, Irish Travellers, orphans, those of mixed race, those perceived as morally defective because their parents were unmarried and those with learning difficulties all attracted additional abuse and disparagement. An absence of primary care was used systematically and maliciously to explain and legitimate the withholding of secondary learning care. The lack of a positive school learning experience in turn made learning in adulthood more daunting, suggesting that the four types of learning care outlined here have a dynamic and interconnected relationship.

Secondary learning care in adult literacy

The findings of the study in the Lighthouse Centre provided much evidence about the need for care-full approaches to all aspects of the adult literacy learning process. One man remarked that 'sometimes as an adult you can feel that you are being left at the back of the class too'. It is hard for adults to unlearn their fearful learning patterns. People display their long, often visceral, memories in almost imperceptible but ever-present responses. They wince at sudden movements, closed doors, loud noises or someone approaching from behind. One woman persistently hits herself for making small errors in reading and spelling. As well as learning literacy, people are also learning about making new relationships with themselves, with others and with their past; tutors have discovered the need to make room for this. Literacy tutors are constantly patrolling the borders between past and present, deflecting and disarming negative echoes and substituting positive learning experiences. In this, they are attentive to learners' real condition, holding in mind their sensitivities and mapping different and effective routes to good literacy outcomes. This is all about care. It is not just about attitude and intent but also about strategic action. Secondary learning care is less about sentiment and more about skilful, respectful learning facilitation. It accurately and insightfully recognises individual and group needs, provides appropriate resources and pursues empowering methodologies that allow people to flourish.

Solidary learning care

More than half of the participants in the research had begun to learn literacy in adulthood. Primary and secondary learning care relationships provided a bridge back into learning. This was through successful adult relationships, the desire to make a positive contribution to children's lives, and the liberating personal counselling process established in the aftermath of the State apology to those abused while in its care. Positive experience of care in adulthood enabled survivors to develop greater self-esteem, a more solid sense of identity and consequently renewed hope that learning literacy was possible.

In the Lighthouse Centre, the sense of shared history and collective struggle for justice formed a bond for survivors of abuse in industrial schools. Institutional life left little time or space for friendship or solidarity and group learning was not on the pedagogical menu. It was only in later life that survivors began to savour the benefits of community solidarity and the second chance it provided for learning literacy. As well as those whose return to learning was enabled by new relationships of primary care in adulthood, the bond that formed around a common experience of abuse and neglect has also been transformational in attracting people back to literacy:

> *I think that there is actually a lot of solace for people who maybe have felt quite alone that they come into a place and realise that people do have some form of shared history, some sort of shared continuing difficulties and that actually binds them together as a group. One of the features of the groups is that they do very much look out for each other, especially new members of the group. They try to welcome them in and a lot of support is actually peer-to-peer support.* (Lighthouse Centre worker)

Collaborative approaches to learning took on added significance in the context of shared struggle and explaining the difficulty of learning in authoritarian, repressive environments became part of processing the past and taking power and control over the present. The need for tutors to adopt a facilitative and sensitive approach to group work gains added weight when learners are particularly attuned to the subtle expressions of negative aspects of power.

State learning care
The majority of the research participants (68 per cent) asserted that the State neglected its direct responsibility to monitor the quality of care and education offered to them as children. Respondents described feelings of abandonment that transcended their immediate family and extended

to the wider population. They saw an irony in the fact that they were taken away from families who were perceived to be unfit to offer care and supervision, only to be neglected in the alternative state provision.

Despite the fact that orphanages were designed to educate us and protect us from the ills of society, we received only minimal education and most of us were illiterate. Lack of education deeply affected every aspect of our lives, leaving us unprepared for and fearful of the world outside the institution. (Fahy, 1999, p. 54)

Many attributed the loss of their primary care centre to wider structural inequalities. Unemployment, poverty, ill health, emigration, family breakdown, moral opprobrium and cultural powerlessness resulted in children being taken into state care and subsequently experiencing abuses that impacted negatively on their ability to learn literacy. State care-lessness was therefore causal both in their original disadvantage and their subsequent neglect in the industrial school. In later years, the State's acknowledgement of its neglect of survivors did much to relieve the stigma that is still widely attached to unmet literacy needs. In this case, educational disadvantage was clearly identified as an integral part of the wider package of social harm and inequality that was beyond individual control.

A chain of care

Like Freire (1997) in his later text, *Pedagogy of the Heart*, one of the research participants, Bridget, argued for an ideal, inclusive, participative view of the state where interdependency is recognised and acted upon by all. Placing limits on those for whom we should have concern meant she and others were pushed to the margins of care. She proposed that our interrelatedness brings with it responsibilities that make us inalienably part of one another and accountable for what happens to our fellow beings.

Do you know it might sound simplistic but it is every adult's responsibility to ensure that every child is educated. If we all just look after our own — that is why we were the way we were. Those adults who couldn't look after us were equally abandoned by all the adults who could have helped out but instead abused them every way they could. (Bridget, woman aged 51 who left school with met literacy needs)

141

In her analysis, Bridget identifies the links in the chain of care at primary, secondary and tertiary level that are underwritten by the intent and actions of the state and civic society.

Lifelong learning care

The case for lifelong learning care outlined here matters because literacy inequalities persist and are clearly located in individuals and groups that are treated with less value and importance than others. For literacy practitioners this is significant, not just in providing a new perspective on the social practice context, but also in beginning to identify what learning care means in terms of literacy work.

Those who learned literacy in industrial schools identified continuity of primary care as a decisive factor and family literacy is an immediate way of supporting disadvantaged families in this literacy support role. Primary learning care was a source of self-esteem, gave some security of identity and afforded the protection of a caring family presence. School was tense and unforgiving, and repressive. Low expectations of learners became self-fulfilling as trust was repeatedly betrayed and hopes of learning were paralysed by care-less relationships and impoverished pedagogy.

Secondary learning care in the context of adult literacy suggests a process that delivers on high expectations for all learners through insightful, creative learning relationships grounded in skill and expertise adapted to meet diverse needs. An important aspect of adult literacy learning is the respectful sharing of power between learners and tutors and the enabling of new patterns of power through solidary learning care between peers.

The unequal social context is pitted with assumptions about who can and who will learn literacy, whose language merits recognition and reproduction, and what styles of learning are privileged in school and adult learning environments. These issues have affective dimensions that are easily overshadowed by the pervasive imperatives of accreditation, performativity and profit.

Research carried out with survivors of institutional abuse in Irish industrial schools suggests that understanding inequalities in the affective domain is pivotal to literacy work. While home is undoubtedly the primary place of care, and secondary care in school and adult learning can be transformational, the capacity of the family (and the school) is determined, to a great extent, by the state's achievements with regard to creating a more equal society. The state enables or restricts the policies and systems that shape how egalitarian a society is and whether its goods are shared in a fair and just manner (Baker, 1987; Baker et al., 2004). The legislative and policy decisions made by the state, in practice, constitute choices about learning care equality and this is evidently as true today as in the excesses of care-lessness that were experienced in the industrial schools of the past.

Notes

[1] NALA defines literacy thus: 'Literacy involves listening and speaking, reading, writing, numeracy and using everyday technology to communicate and handle information. But it includes more than the technical skills of communication: it also has personal, social and economic dimensions. Literacy increases the opportunity for individuals and communities to reflect on their situations, explore new possibilities and initiate change.' (NALA, 2011, p. 8)

[2] *Equality: From Theory to Action* (Baker et al., 2004; 2009) elaborates the equality framework in fine detail and illustrates the interaction of the four equality/inequality contexts in a number of practical examples. These include an egalitarian perspective on education in Chapter 8 that has much relevance to the specific context of literacy.

[3] Pseudonym

[4] In Canada, New Zealand and Australia, there are similar accounts of aboriginal and marginalised people being taken into institutions where they were subjected to authoritarian regimes and extreme attempts to erase their cultural identity. A repressive regime of discipline and punishment like that described by Foucault (1975) was commonplace in many educational establishments in the first half of the twentieth century and was further intensified in institutions that were ironically part of the 'care' apparatus of the state.

References

Bailey, I. and Coleman, U. (1998) *Access and Participation in Adult Literacy Schemes*. Dublin: NALA.

Baker, J. (1987) *Arguing for Equality*. New York: Verso.

Baker, J., Lynch, K., Cantillon, S. and Walsh, J. (2004) *Equality: From Theory to Action*. Palgrave Macmillan.

Baker, J., Lynch, K., Cantillon, S. and Walsh, J. (2009) *Equality: From Theory to Action*. Palgrave Macmillan.

Cohen, J. (2006) 'Social, emotional, ethical and academic education: creating a climate for learning, participation in democracy and wellbeing', *Harvard Educational Review*, Vol. 76 No 2, pp. 201–37.

CEC (2008) *Progress Towards the Lisbon Objectives in Education and Training: Indicators and Benchmarks*. Commission of the European Communities.

Cox, W. (2010) *The Impact of NALA's Student Development Work 2007–2010*. Dublin: NALA.

DES (2006) *Joint Committee on Education and Science: Adult Literacy in Ireland*. Department of Education and Science. Dublin: Government Publications.

Engster, D. (2005) 'Rethinking care theory: the practice of caring and the obligation to care', *Hypatia*, Vol. 20 No 3, pp. 50–74.

Engster, D. (2007) *The Heart of Justice: Care Ethics and Political Theory*. Oxford University Press.

Fahy, B. (1999) *Freedom of Angels: Surviving Goldenbridge Orphanage*. Dublin: O'Brien Press.

Feeley, M. (2009) 'Living in care and without love: the impact of affective inequalities on learning literacy' in *Affective Equality: Who Cares?* (eds) Lynch, K., Baker, J. and Lyons, M. Palgrave.

Feeley, M. (2010) 'Literacy learning care: exploring the role of care in literacy learning with survivors of abuse in Irish industrial schools', *The Adult Learner: The Irish Journal of Adult and Community Education*, pp. 72–90.

Foucault, Michel (1995) *Discipline and Punish: The Birth of the Prison*. New York: Vintage Books.

Freire, P. (1997) *Pedagogy of the Heart*. New York: Continuum.

Gannerud, E. (2001) 'A gender perspective on the work and lives of women primary school teachers', *Scandinavian Journal of Educational Research*, Vol. 45 No 1, pp. 55–70.

Government of Ireland (1970) *Reformatory and Industrial Schools in Ireland* (Prl. 1342, Kennedy Report). Dublin: Government Publication.

Hargreaves, A. (2000) 'Mixed emotions: teachers' perceptions of their interactions with students', in *Teaching and Teacher Education*, Vol. 16 No 8, pp. 811–26.

Hargreaves, A. (2001) 'Emotional geographies of teaching', *Teachers College Record*, Vol. 103 No 6, pp. 1056–80.

Hegarty, A. and Feeley, M. (2009) *Literacy-friendly Further Education and Training*. Dublin: NALA.

Hegarty, A. and Feeley, M. (2010) *Taking Care of Family Literacy Work: An Enquiry with Parents About their Experience of Nurturing Language and Literacy in the Home*. Dublin: NALA.

Lankshear, C. and Knobel, M. (2003) *New Literacies: Changing Knowledge and Classroom Learning*. OU.

Lynch, K. (1999) *Equality in Education*. Dublin: Gill and Macmillan.

Lynch, K. (2007) 'Love labour as a distinct and non-commodifiable form of care labour', *The Sociological Review*, Vol. 55 No 3, pp. 550–70.

Lynch, K. and Baker, J. (2005) 'Equality in education: an equality of condition perspective', *Theory and Research in Education*, Vol. 3 No 2, pp. 131–64.

Lynch, K., Baker, J. and Lyons, M. (eds) (2009) *Affective Equality: Love Care and Injustice*. Palgrave.

Lynch, K., Lyons, M. and Cantillon, S. (2007) 'Breaking silence: educating citizens for love, care and solidarity', *International Studies in Sociology of Education*, Vol. 7 No 1–2, pp. 1–19.

McClave, H. (2005) *Education for Citizenship: A Capabilities Approach.* Unpublished PhD thesis. UCD Equality Studies Centre, University College Dublin.

NALA (2011) *Providing Leadership in Adult Literacy: Strategic Plan 2011–2013*. Dublin.

NRDC (2005) *Embedded Teaching and Learning of Adult Literacy, Numeracy and ESOL: Seven Case Studies of Embedded Provision*. National Research and Development Centre.

Noddings, N. (1992) *The Challenge to Care in Schools: An Alternative Approach to Education*. New York: Teachers College Press.

Noddings, N. (2006) 'Educating whole people: a response to Jonathan Cohen', *Harvard Educational Review*, Vol. 76 No 2, pp. 238–42.

Noddings, N. (2007) *Philosophy of Education,* 2nd edition. Boulder, Colorado: Westview Press.

O'Brien, M. (2005) 'Mothers as educational workers: mothers' emotional work at their children's transfer to second-level education', *Irish Educational Studies*, Vol. 24 No 2–3, pp. 223–42.

O'Brien, M. (2007) 'Mothers' emotional care work in education and its moral imperative', *Gender and Education*, Vol. 19 No 2, pp. 159–57.

OECD (2009) OECD *Programme for International Student Assessment (PISA)*, Paris: OECD.

Reay, D. (2000) 'A useful extension of Bourdieu's conceptual framework?: emotional capital as a way of understanding mothers' involvement in their children's education?', *The Sociological Review*, Vol. 48 No 4, pp. 568–85.

UNESCO (2006) *Education for All: Literacy for Life*. Paris: UNESCO.

Wilkinson and Pickett (2009) *The Spirit Level: Why More Equal Societies Almost Always Do Better*. Allen Lane.

CHAPTER NINE

Empowerment in educational processes: Feminist reappropriations

MALINI GHOSE AND DISHA MULLICK

Introduction

The term 'empowerment' has been rigorously discussed and analysed in literature on development and policy in the last 20 years. In this paper, drawing on the work we have been involved in at Nirantar, an organi-sation based in India,[1] we try to probe reflexively the continuing sig-nificance of the idea. Empowerment has been a central theme in our feminist praxis, and here we relook at the meaning of education in the lives of women who have been through interventions that have claimed to be empowering.

The paper follows two parallel trajectories. It briefly describes two interventions that Nirantar was involved in designing and working on, and shows how they were embedded in the lives and contexts of women participants. In doing this, it traces the changes and continuity in Niran-tar's educational programmes in terms of context, content and pedagogic principles. Further, mapping the lives of a set of women who had been through these empowering interventions, we interrogate the value of the concept of empowerment in the context of educational processes. How has their experience of education moulded their lives? To what extent does a content and pedagogy (that may have been empowering within a certain space and time in participants' lives) have continued impact in a different context? Our analysis reiterates the importance of process tied in with outcome, in the transaction of educational work, and in the way education permeates the lives of women.

147

The paper is structured as follows. Firstly, there is a brief section that maps the conceptualisation of empowerment through some of the literature that has influenced our understanding of the term in our work. The second section introduces the two educational interventions that we analyse in this paper – the Mahila Shikshan Kendra (MSK), an eight-month residential learning programme run by Mahila Samakhya in collaboration with Nirantar from 1994 to 1997, and *Khabar Lahariya*, a rural newspaper and continuing education programme that brought women into the arena of media production. We reflect on the pedagogy in both these interventions in terms of the spaces and processes for empowerment that they enabled. The final section, drawing on a tracer study conducted with some of the women involved in the MSK, makes some concluding observations about the relevance of empowerment in the context of specific educational programmes.

Building a conceptual understanding of empowerment

Over the past few decades, activists and scholars, as well as national and international players, have seen the potential in the concept of empowerment. It has been employed to varied ends across disciplines such as development, education, economics, psychology and the study of social movements and organisations (Page and Czuba, 1999). Perhaps the most useful understanding of empowerment is that it is concerned with power and power relations, and the change or distribution of power between groups and individuals (Sen and Grown, 1987; Batliwala, 1994; Stromquist, 2009). The conceptualisation of empowerment that feminists have used, and which is closest to our own as feminist educators, sees it as a process that 'enhances disadvantaged ... individuals or groups to challenge and change ... existing power relationships that place them in subordinate economic, social and political positions' (Agarwal in Nagar *et al.*, 2006, p. 30). This moves away from the outcome-focused use of the term in the national and international development discourse, and also locates it in the realm of political awareness and transformation. Feminists in the Indian context have engaged with the Freirian concept of conscientisation in their work on women's empowerment, seeing it as a process that involves the pedagogic creation of a collective time and space where women 'analyse their environment and situation, recognize their strengths, alter their self image, access information and knowledge ... aimed at gaining greater control over resources of various kinds' (Batliwala, 1994, p. 26). More recent work on empowerment in the Indian context has seen it as a 'translocal assemblage', 'a shifting formation and flexible technology of government' (Sharma, 2008, p. 2), taking on specific meaning from the contexts in which it is used – in the field of political transformation, as well as in the neo-liberal lexicon of international development agencies – and yet constantly evolving, dynamic and unpredictable.

Political rhetoric as well as government policies have capitalised on the term empowerment, dividing it into result-oriented parts such as 'social empowerment' and 'economic empowerment', or using it as a term to describe the positive change that is a desirable outcome of policy interventions framed in a developing, market-oriented, skill-driven economy. The increasing focus on the need to measure results and the complexities of 'measuring' intangible processes and outcomes continues to be a knotty area and often takes away from engaging with deeper structures and constructs that are embedded in the concept of empowerment.

More recently, the proliferation of media and communications technologies has brought into the development discourse issues of access to and production of information, and who and what contributes to the creation of knowledge in society. The United Nations Educational, Scientific and Cultural Organization (UNESCO), in its Media and Information Literacy theme, brings these issues into the realm of education and learning processes. Media becomes an important pedagogical tool for empowerment in democratic societies, involving access to information and the development of skills such as critical understanding of content and the ability to participate in this arena of information. In the last decade, research studies have been designed to assess the potential of 'new media literacies' – the use of interactive, collaborative digital media, especially facilitated by the Internet – in creating 'participatory cultures' (Jenkins *et al.*, 2009). These signal the positive effects of increased democratisation of media and information in a context where media production is less centralised and can be shared, discussed and modified from various locations.

In India, information and communication technologies (ICTs) have, over the past decade, found their way into education policies at the primary, secondary and adult level. The most recent national adult education scheme, Saakshar Bharat (2010), mentions that 'ICTs can be creatively used to close the digital divide – where computer proficiency is not just seen as a marketable skill but one that enables access to information and helps sustain literacy skills. ICT and other technologies, therefore, will have to be extensively used to achieve the National Literacy Goals.' Our concern has been the access and engagement of women, especially those from marginalised and poor communities, in the sphere of communication technologies and information production. What are the possibilities of empowerment for women in this highly contested arena? A feminist and empowering engagement with information and media necessitates an ability to proactively engage in the information landscape, to interrogate and contribute to it.

Considering feminist education at work

In this section, we briefly describe two different feminist educational interventions designed by Nirantar over the past two decades, and reflect on the ways in which empowerment figured as a pedagogical element, as well as in the outcomes of these processes.

The Mahila Shikshan Kendra: a feminist learning space

The MSK women's education centre, set up in Chitrakoot district of Uttar Pradesh, north India, in 1995, was an eight-month residential educational intervention for women and girls from marginalised communities. It was part of a larger government programme called Mahila Samakhya (MS), which roughly translates as Education for Women's Equality.[2] Between 1994 and 1997, Nirantar worked closely with the MS Programme in Banda and Chitrakoot districts to develop curriculum, training and implementation strategy for the MSK. The rural women and girls who attended had participated in basic literacy programmes but wanted to make longer-term investments in their education.[3] In the MSK, we worked on creating a curriculum based on pedagogical principles that informed popular education programmes elsewhere in the world, that drew on participants' lives and experiences, interrogated the relationships between the teacher and participant, and used these as the basis for empowering education strategies. Traditional hierarchies of knowledge and disciplinary boundaries were pushed out, and the curriculum instead centred on the lifeworld and experiences of the women participants. It also attempted to integrate an understanding of the interplay of structures of power such as gender, caste and class into the content and pedagogy of all curriculum content.

The MSK programme had clear learning goals in terms of reading, writing and numeracy, but we also spelt out a framework to unpack 'empowerment'. We expected that the curriculum and pedagogy at the MSK should first enable women to analyse structures of power, including gender, and then use this understanding to interrogate, negotiate and change such relationships, both in the private and public sphere. To be able to do this, women should be confident and develop a positive sense of self. We also expected that undergoing the MSK course would enable women to enter, engage with and alter the public domain, continuing their education and learning process further.

Knowledge, power and information in feminist educational processes

In determining the course content, we broke down traditional 'subject' boundaries used in curricular design. Instead, along with the participants and teachers, we developed a curriculum framework that began from their lives and contexts and focused on the themes of land, water, forest, health and society. So, for instance, the curriculum content on water involved a discussion of the relationship of women and women's work to sources of and access to water. We also discussed the structure of caste, and how and why this affected the access to water. Women provide water for the household by fetching it from public sources like wells and ponds. Reflecting on this daily lived experience the participants were able to understand the intersection of structures of gender, caste, class and ethnicity: when, from where and how much water women could access greatly depended on their class and caste. We traversed the history and location of different social movements relating to water – for instance, the Narmada Bachao Andolan movement against the building of a large dam on the river Narmada – and also spoke about the importance of the river on the lives and livelihoods of men and women who lived along its banks. Of course, the curriculum also included 'scientific' content, like understanding of the processes of evaporation and condensation, the properties of water and so on. A holistic perspective, and one that enabled participants to view the world around them more critically, was thus developed through the MSK curriculum.

However, the notion of an 'alternative' curriculum in which the source of knowledge is not only scientific, or formal disciplines, but uses women's understanding and knowledge of their worlds as a starting point and establishes that, too, as valid as textbook knowledge, is not as simple as it may at first seem. If feminist pedagogy is a 'notion of learning as constructed not just in individual minds but also through the interaction of a community of knowers' (Maher and Tetreault, 2001, p. 22), then what happens when 'authority' of knowledge becomes a questionable thing and when 'positionality' becomes key in the creation and transaction of knowledge? Our objective may have been to make the positions and world views of the rural women participants visible in the educational process, and shift the balance of power between disciplinary or 'scientific' knowledge and non-disciplinary or indigenous knowledge, but the participants themselves were not passive in this process and in fact played an active role in determining what knowledge they wanted to have access to.

Consider, for instance, the response of a participant soon after she came to the MSK:'We know about our forests and trees ... We know what sources of water we have in our village and the problems around it. All you do is listen to us and give back what we have told you. What do you have to give us? Tell us what we do not know' (field notes in Ghose, 2001, p. 306). Our pedagogy, we soon realised, could not be limited to mainst ream knowledge versus the participant's systems of knowing. It had to enable the participant to know both these systems, and the location of power within them, and negotiate both these worlds with some degree of autonomy. An analysis and methodology had to be designed towards this end. So, for instance, sessions on volcanoes and earthquakes used participants' stories of how earthquakes occurred with the shifting of position of the snake god alongside exercises in which they made models of the earth with their hands and understood its geomorphology.[4] These sessions were amongst the most vividly recalled by participants. When asked why they remembered these topics, they said, 'It was so interesting, it was a new way of looking at the earth and understanding phenomena like the earthquake which we were familiar with. We had so much fun making models of volcanoes – doing these "practical" exercises have embedded these concepts in our mind' (Joshi and Ghose, forthcoming).

Feminist pedagogies in the landscape of media literacy

The second educational intervention we would like to discuss is *Khabar Lahariya*, a newspaper that Nirantar initiated in 2002 after the MS programme withdrew in Chitrakoot. The idea came from the success of a broadsheet, *Mahila Dakiya*, which involved MSK participants in its writing and production as a way for them to use their nascent literacy and information skills. This broadsheet, in Hindi and the local language, Bundeli, was intended for a predominantly local, female, neo-literate audience (although its readership soon swelled beyond this). It became so popular in the area that, after MS withdrew, the women contributors and readers demanded it be reinstated. *Khabar Lahariya* was conceptualised as a local language newspaper that would be run by a team of women journalists from marginalised communities and who had varying levels of literacy. It was a way in which women could be part of producing reading material that would sustain their fragile literacy, but it was also an attempt at subverting conventional gender roles and bringing women out into the public sphere of information, news, governance, politics and more.

A few of the women who had been at the MSK (some of whom had worked passionately on *Mahila Dakiya*) and showed interest both in continuing their education and in working, became the first of *Khabar Lahariya's* reporters. The process of strengthening their reading and writing was accompanied by a rigorous training in reporting, interviewing, marketing, politics and, eventually, the technical skills of desktop publishing (DTP) and Internet use. In this section, we use *Khabar Lahariya* as a take-off point to show the potential of media and new media as (feminist) pedagogical tools in educational interventions with women.

> *With KL, there were different kinds of information. Never, till KL, did I know what a newspaper was, who produces it, and how ... In our trainings, we used to talk about many things ... journalism, our rights, photography, computers ... I've travelled outside for trainings, gone for big sammelans. Heard people talk about their experiences, read about people's lives. When I saw the world outside, I understood myself.* (Kavita, ex–MSK participant and editor, Khabar Lahariya)

> *When I first used to hear website addresses on the radio, I used to wonder what these are and how you see them! Now there are so many ways that the computer has made life easier. We can type our own stories, email them for instant feedback. We can get stories – especially national and international – off the Internet. We never had these sources of information before. We're not dependent on mainstream papers. We did a story on malnutrition and we used BBC Hindi as a source, we could get statistics on the number of Dalit children dying of malnutrition. You don't get those statistics in other papers.* (Meera, editor, Khabar Lahariya)

While it began as a continuing education programme, *Khabar Lahariya* soon grew beyond this objective and brought women into the public domain, participating in the production of media. If stepping across the

line between private and public spheres was an empowering and transformative experience in the lives of the women at *Khabar Lahariya*, one
might argue that this transformation was catalysed through access to
new domains of information. As women with varied education levels
and from marginalised communities – Dalit, Muslim or tribal – the
Khabar Lahariya journalists are constantly open to ridicule and contestation. Their training to be journalists has involved not just building skills
in rural reporting and newswriting, but also developing an understanding
of the structures that constantly challenge their presence and mobility
in public – gender, caste and religion. Lastly, their levels of information
about local, regional and national politics were continuously built up, a
domain from which they had been historically marginalised.

The analysis and writing on politics was one crucial area where gender, caste and education intertwined to obstruct the journalists, despite
workshops, readings and in-depth discussions over the years. Here, for us as
trainers and educators, a dilemma emerged. We still believed in our feminist educational principles that focused on the learning, perspectives and
experiences of women, and that hierarchies of dominant and mainstream
knowledge should be interrogated by these. However, these women journalists required access to and understanding of mainstream politics to negotiate it on their own terms. Access to new communications technologies,
while it has not taken away from the deep rootedness of this dilemma, has
levelled the playing field in some way. Access is still limited, and requires a
level of literacy that not all in the group possess. However, even in a limited sense, accessing and being familiar with technology is significant for a
group conventionally kept at a distance from education and information
of any kind. It is empowering in that it marks a shift in the centre of power
that controlled information and knowledge. The technology democratises
access to a wider pool of information in which the women journalists
participate to strengthen a political and critical understanding of the world.

The possibilities of new media

> *The Internet, I think, is a way to send news, information (*khabar*)
> … Isn't it? Like, if you send an email, you create a blog and send it
> to someone. You can type things, use photos … So whatever photo
> I saw and I thought was beautiful, I clicked on it and made it big.
> I thought, let me send this to someone.* (Rukhsana, participant,
> new media training)

If I had the camera in my hand, or the microphone, then I felt a strength inside. I felt that I could ask questions, take photos. When we were taking photos in the market, I didn't feel like we were ordinary people. I felt like I was a reporter, and if I had to take a photo, no one could stop me. (Sahar, participant, new media training)

In a recent training process with young Muslim and Dalit women in Banda, including members of the *Khabar Lahariya* team, we used the teaching of new media skills – digital photography, videography, Internet/blogging – as the central pedagogical tool. While a large part of the discourse on ICTs in India is limited to 'bridging the digital divide', this educational intervention sought to move further, to facilitate women's engagement in changing the landscape of new media production. Access to new media and ICTs is an important concern, but whether and how women, and especially neo-literate women from marginalised communities, can confront multiple structures of power to impact the content of new media – yet another mainstream system of knowledge – was the basis of this intervention. Much exists in the slowly proliferating literature on new media (Jenkins, *et al.*, 2009) on the 'participatory cultures' it makes possible, and the opportunities for an empowering and democratised engagement in civic life. Where do neo-literate women figure in this domain?

The new media training was conceptually framed within a feminist understanding of how communication and media skills can be empowering. An analysis of the content of mainstream traditional and new media content raised the issue of the marginalisation of women's voices; access to stories, films and YouTube videos about women close to the contexts of the participants showed the importance of documenting and archiving personal stories. Further, the experience of moving around in public spaces to create print or visual media content during the workshop (and ultimately, the withdrawal of participants who had been spotted in the street by male family members) forced a critical discussion about control over the mobility of women.

Gender and empowerment were not discussed during the workshop, but the pedagogy of the workshop was conceptually based on these. Participants learnt to type, to send emails and search the Internet; they shot portraits, photo features and short films in the town. At the end of the training, a blog was created, on which the participants uploaded the content they had created over seven days. In the viewing and discussion of participant emails, typed life stories, photographs and films, and around the process of creating these, however, it was clear that when women from the margins have the skill and the opportunity to be at the centre of knowledge production, the outcome is deeply empowering. In using the new media technologies and creating their media content, the women turned their gaze on the society that saw them as 'foreign' to the public spaces they were shooting in; they questioned the control over their bodies and their lack of mobility. Discussions and use of the Internet raised issues of their lack of access to information about people, places, issues, rights and entitlements – from places of historical significance, to government schemes for education, to news. Shooting a film, sending an email, uploading a blog post – even in the transient moment of a training session, these were moments of rupture in the conventional paradigm of knowledge production.

> *If I had a chance to ask a lawyer and a judge some questions, I would ask them this: If you can get a judgement on a case in two years, why do you drag it for five or ten years? If you can't understand the problems of people who come to you with their cases, then I think we could do more speedy and better justice to them. Maybe it's to avoid problems like this in the court that people would rather suffer injustice.*
> (Sahar, first blog post)

Empowerment in the unfolding of women's lives

In this final section, we look at the lives of three women who have been part of the educational interventions described above, and attempt to un-pack the idea of empowerment in the trajectories their lives have taken.

Kavita (32) came to the MSK at the age of 12, and through her own longing for education, and continued contact with women's organisa-tions and individuals from her MSK days, managed to study further in spite of her early marriage, resistance from her family, poverty and other factors. She was one of the earliest members of the *Khabar Lahariya* team, and her own journey of struggling with social structures to establish herself has paralleled the newspaper's over the last ten years. Shivdevi (around 40) and Shivmani (around 35) are much newer entrants to the team, and had little or no contact with formal education, or any indi-viduals or organisations over the last 15 years.

The journey from home into the world

> [after MSK], I got stuck in domesticity, and was not able to study.
> I didn't have a husband either who would support my education. I
> did all the work in the house, supported my children, their education,
> their medical expenses ... I was a saheli[5] for 2–3 years. It paid 500
> rupees, I couldn't manage my expenses with that much ... I went
> to Maharastra to work .... I came back and built my own house.
> I had three children, and I wanted them all to study further. I met
> Aarti Didi. She said, your writing is good, why don't you work with
> Khabar Lahariya? (Shivmani)

All three women we interviewed showed similar trajectories after they
left MSK. Only Kavita managed to study further, but they were all
trapped by the demands of domesticity and poverty, at least for a while.
Finding ways out of these traps were contingent on various factors –
most often a chance meeting (and in Kavita's case, continued contact)
with someone from their MSK days, field workers from local organisations, teachers, members of Nirantar or MS. What is striking, however, is
the mobility they all displayed and the tenacity with which they made
certain decisions, even before they came to *Khabar Lahariya* – in terms of
where they stayed, and how they supported themselves and their families. Leaving home to access education, and that education itself, did not
reduce the power of the structures they lived within, but it opened up
the world as a place they too could explore, that offered them ways and
means to confront the circumstances of their lives.

As others see us

> Upper caste men think that we are of 'that' caste ... that we keep
> roaming around. They say, why do you do this kind of work, being
> women? I said – his wife is a teacher, she keeps coming to Banda – if
> your wife goes to teach, doesn't she pass through villages and roads?
> Do you go with her, keep your hand on her arm always? [laughs] So
> then he didn't answer, he was quiet. (Shivdevi)

In the eyes of the patriarchal, class- and caste-ridden society in which
the women were located, moving outside the sphere of the private
to earn money for the family, and moving around as journalists, were

significantly different. Education provided an opening, and an under-standing of their location in society and as autonomous individuals. However, as Dalit, rural neo-literate women, these journalists were at the periphery of structures of power – whether gender, caste or class. From this position, negotiating the public sphere of which they had limited experience and information, required considerable courage and self-confidence. Crucially, it also required knowledge of the injustice of gender conventions and the right to subvert these. Their new status and identities within the public sphere enabled a negotiation with their families that was not possible earlier – providing them with information and access to entitlements and institutions of power. (Shivmani talked about having had her father's crop restored, which had been claimed by a dominant family in the village, by going to the police station on her own and demanding justice.) These were not skills that could be imparted in a classroom: they were gained through increased mobility, engagement with the public sphere, and increasing knowledge of history, geography, politics and governance, democratic structures and processes. *Khabar Lahariya* provided for these women an experience and a space that was crucial for them to make visible and analyse power relations in the public domain. The fact that they were not coming into these roles in isolation, but had the opportunity to learn and share experiences with women who had been through similar journeys, facilitated a space for collective analysis of the social contexts that they lived in, and their own positions within these.

The lives and journeys of Kavita, Shivdevi and Shivmani indicate that empowerment is not a clearly defined label or a final outcome they have carried from the MSK to their present roles as journalists. The specific context of an educational programme like the MSK, as well as the contexts of their lives after they left it, to a large extent determined the ways in which they have negotiated their lives. In certain phases and with specific opportunities, they have been able to come into decision-making roles, have increased mobility and confronted oppressive relationships or violence with a political understanding of the situation as well as agency. Exposure to new places and people, new technologies, engaging with institutions of power such as politics, government departments, local administration – these were all ways in which these women increased their confidence and self-esteem, enabling them to imagine themselves anew. Entering broader domains of knowledge through the process of becoming journalists triggered a long-term process. It brought about greater realisation of their rights as citizens, it enabled them to forge new relationships and networks beyond the family and home. It is clear, however, that the presence of sustained networks for women to tap into after they have been through a short-term learning process, and the opportunity for continued learning in an unconventional arena such as journalism, has enabled the continuation of empowering processes in their lives. *Khabar Lahariya* provides a specific context in which to map empowerment and illustrates that transformative interventions require intensive investment and are lifelong processes. To have a broader impact, they cannot be limited to engaging with individual women, but must engage with larger structures within which women exist, and make possible and support their presence there.

Conclusion

Earlier this year, we undertook a small study to map the lives of a set of 50 women who had participated in the MSK between 1995 and 2000. As practitioners who had been closely involved in initiating and evolving the MSK intervention in Chitrakoot, we felt the need to take stock of the long-term impact of this kind of intervention. Issues such as women's literacy occupy a marginal place in state policy, and the value and outcomes of programmes such as the MSK are often questioned. We therefore used this study to revisit the usefulness of an empowerment framework in educational interventions.[6] Some of the findings of the survey provide a broader perspective in which to view our analysis of the educational interventions described above.

For all the respondents in the study, coming to the MSK had been a 'life-changing experience', irrespective of what they had or had not been able to do with the education they received. Greater self-confidence, enhanced self-esteem and awareness were reported as being the crucial outcomes. The fact that this continues to be such an important outcome of educational programmes reaffirms the fact that women access education not only to learn skills but also for the transformative potential, which for them is not just symbolic but real.

When discussing what they valued about the MSK, women overwhelmingly spoke of the process of learning. The pedagogy, including methods such as role plays, model-making, films and letter-writing, had great recall value. 'I remember the role plays we performed. There was one on child marriage, which gave us the courage to speak about the practice in our own families' recalled Maina. They said they learnt because they did not fear learning and were not treated like children, even though some of the topics they learnt they found in children's text books.

More than half the respondents enrolled in formal schools (usually fifth or sixth grades) once they graduated from the MSK, but less than half of those were able to reach the eighth grade. The testimonies showed that women questioned and challenged, and expressed strong desires to continue their education, but patriarchal structures (and lack of financial resources) have deep roots, making it extremely difficult for young women to challenge them.

The study showed that the women's access to information after they left the MSK was very low, even though this was a desirable outcome of the educational intervention. In cases where the women had had continued opportunities to access and produce information, their levels of confidence, agency and mobility were very high.

Another area where the limits of the educational experience were evident was in being able to address the issue of violence to women and in decision-making in relation to violence. During the workshops, a large number of women spoke of the violence, both physical and mental, that they had faced in their lives. The discussions revealed that women understood the violence was structural, that unequal power relations were at its core, and that women were not themselves responsible for violent behaviour towards them. However, they had not always been able to stop the violence nor had they been able to take decisions to leave violent situations. From a feminist perspective, this would be the desirable outcome of such an educational input.

While attempts to measure empowerment often try to map behavioural change or expect that education will actually lead to 'permanent' change, the fact that women have the critical consciousness to question and challenge, and try to negotiate such issues, counts as an important outcome. However, while we work with this understanding of power and empowerment, we still work within and negotiate more outcome-oriented approaches to women's education. In the design of our study of MSK participants, therefore, we tried to make a traditional assessment of the impact of education. We also established that outcomes of education cannot be mapped without an understanding of the rootedness of structures within which we live, and the long-term processes of negotiation and change that are part of transformative learning.

Clearly, a pedagogically innovative intervention, while showing an impact in terms of individual women's perspective and ability to understand structures of power, cannot be presumed to change oppressive structures of power themselves – either in the public or private domain. The process of negotiation of these oppressive structures needs to be seen as a measure of the empowering potential of education. This process and ability is not one that emerges out of a one-time dose of gender-informed curriculum. Building women's abilities to negotiate power in their everyday lives, within and outside the home, requires continued support and access to opportunities to pursue their learning, and broaden domains of experience and information. Women's educational programmes must take on this awareness of the inexorability of social structures, and the need for a more lasting engagement with the everyday, material conditions of women's lives if they are to have empowering or transformative outcomes.

Notes

[1] Nirantar is a feminist organisation that has been working on gender and education in India since 1993.

[2] Mahila Samakhya (MS), a national programme for women's education, initiated in 1988, occupies an important place in the evolution of discourses on women's literacy and education in India, especially in the context of state programmes. Unlike most other programmes, it defines education very broadly. It brings empowerment strongly within the purview of educational programmes, especially in the context of education for socially and economically disadvantaged groups (see Mahila Samakhya, 2007). MS presently covers ten states and 113 underdeveloped districts (www.education.nic.in/ms/). See also Bhog and Ghose (forthcoming), which talks about MS's conceptualisation of literacy as an important part of processes of women's empowerment.

[3] This paper discusses experiences of the MSK from the period that Nirantar worked on it (1994–97). The MSK curriculum has gone through considerable change in the years since Nirantar's involvement ceased. More recent reviews of the programme exist (see, for example, Purushothaman, 2010).

[4] Similar debates and dilemmas about the hierarchies of knowledge systems happened in sessions when the concept of 'living' and 'non-living'

161

things was discussed. Rivers came into serious contestation as living things (see Ghose, 2001).

5 A village-level teacher, part of the MS programme structure.

6 As part of the methodology of the study, we used group discussions, questionnaires and women's narratives (through long interviews) to try to understand the relevance of the experience of the MSK and how it has had a continued impact in different contexts of women's lives. We layered this broad exploration by identifying some critical areas for more specific exploration. These included mobility, decision-making and negotiation of relationships of power within the private domain, access to information and governance institutions, ability to catalyse change, access to further opportunities and employment – all of which are traditionally believed to be the outcomes of empowering education programmes.

References

Batliwala, S. (1994) 'The meaning of women's empowerment: new concepts from action' in *Population Policies Reconsidered: Health, Empowerment and Rights*, (eds) Sen, G., Germain, A. and Chen, L. C., pp. 127–38. Cambridge, MA: Harvard University Press.

Bhog, D. and Ghose, M. (forthcoming) 'Women's literacy in the Mahila Samakhya Programme' (provisional title) in *Cartographies of Empowerment: Tracing the Journey of Mahila Samakhya 1998–2008*, (eds) Ramachandran, V. *et al.* New Delhi: Zubaan.

Ghose, M. (2001) 'Women and empowerment through literacy' in *The Making of Literate Societies*, (eds) Olson, D. R. and Torrance, N. Blackwell Publishers.

Jenkins, H., Purushotma, R., Clinton, K., Weigel, M. and Robison, A. (2009), *Confronting the Challenges of Participatory Culture: Media Education for the 21st Century*, Macarthur Foundation. [Online] http://newmedialiteracies.org/files/working/NMLWhitePaper.pdf [Accessed 26 December 2011].

Joshi, Shalini and Ghose, Malini (forthcoming) 'Literacy and Women's Empowerment: A Tracer Study, in *The Power of Literacy: Women's Journeys in India, Indonesia, Philippines and Papua New Guinea. Philippines: Asia South Pacific Association for Basic and Adult Education.*

Maher, F. A. and Tetreault, M. K. T. (2001) *The Feminist Classroom:*

Dynamics of Gender, Race and Privilege. Maryland, USA and Oxford, UK: Rowman and Littlefield Publishers (2nd edition).

Mahila Samakhya (2007), Eleventh Plan Document, Ministry of Human Resource Development, New Delhi: Government of India

Nagar, R. and Sangtin Writers Collective (2006) *Playing with Fire: Feminist Thought and Activism Through Seven Lives in India*. Minneapolis: University of Minnesota Press.

Sen, G. and Grown, C. (1987) *Development, Crises and Alternative Visions: Third World Women's Perspectives*. New York: Monthly Review Press.

Page, N. and Czuba, C. E. (1999) 'Empowerment: what is it?' *Journal of Extension*, Vol. 37 No 5. [Online] Available from http://www.joe.org/joe/1999october/comm1.php [Accessed 26 December 2011].

Purushothaman, S. (2010) (ed.) *Innovations towards Education for Empowerment: Grassroots Women's Movement*. Best Practices Foundation.

Sakshar Bharat (2010) National Literacy Mission Authority, Department of School Education and Literacy, Ministry of Human Resources Development, New Delhi: Government of India.

Sharma, A. (2008) *Logics of Empowerment: Development, Gender, and Governance in Neoliberal India*. Minnesota: University Of Minnesota.

Stromquist, N. (2009) 'Literacy and empowerment: evidence of the link and its implications for action, *Occasional Papers in Education and Lifelong Learning: An International Journal*, Vol. 4 No 1–2, pp. 63–81.

CHAPTER TEN

Transnational migrants in the workplace: Agency and opportunity[1]

JUDY HUNTER

Introduction

Dr. John Cook[2] had introduced you to me for enrolment the class, but unfortunately I didn't have much time to see you yesterday, so I am sending email to you and try to explain what is going on. I'll attcht my information. I hope you can handle it.

Issues of transnational migration and employment have become a political and social flashpoint in this era of globalisation (Bedford, 2002; Li, 2007). Aotearoa/New Zealand, like many other developed nations, faces growing diversity and a migrant population that is frequently skilled and educated, but marginalised, underemployed and unemployed. Concerns about migrants' 'ability to communicate in English' are frequently cited by employers as obstacles to successful job recruitment. The government responds with increased gate-keeping through standardised testing and mandated employment-related language and literacy programmes.

The email excerpt quoted above was written by a young Japanese woman, Hiroko, who was part of a research project I conducted in New Zealand workplaces. I job-shadowed her over a four-month period at the engineering consulting firm where she worked. She had been a structural engineer in Japan and was now working as an autoCAD technician. The email was part of the correspondence as she applied to enrol in a structural engineering course at the local university in order to improve her understanding of the local concepts and discourse of structural engineering and improve her status in the workplace. On the surface, her email may be seen to affirm national concerns about English language and literacy, for it contains numerous formal language 'errors' of vocabulary, spelling and grammar. Some lexical items ('what is going on' and 'you can handle it') index a situation of possible foreboding rather than an application for a single undergraduate course for which she would not receive official credit toward a degree. But a different understanding of the email calls for a closer look at the complex facets of the issue. For this study, I would like to focus on workplaces themselves as sites that both afford and constrain migrants' agency, participation and learning.

Framing the issues

The process of dislocation that migrants experience as they enter new countries, cultures, neighbourhoods, schools and workplaces has profound impacts on their lives (Baynham and de Fina, 2005). Not only are their communicative repertoires and ways of being in the world differently interpreted and valued, they are often on their own in making sense of new norms and values. That means that the new culture and the new workplace can create steep learning demands. Billet's work (2001, 2006, 2010; Billet, Barker, and Hernon-Tinning, 2004) on the constellation of forces that enable and constrain participation, engagement and learning in the workplace provides a lens to investigate migrant workplace learning. Billet's approach is compatible with social practice views of situated literacies, which will be the frame for interpreting the case studies in this chapter (see Barton, Hamilton and Ivanič, 2000).

In line with other learning theorists (for example, Lave, 1996; Lave and Wenger, 1991; Rogoff, 1990), Billet sees learning as occurring through participation with others who can model, coach and guide new people and facilitate access to work activities. In Billet's words, 'learning through participating in work can be understood in terms of how the workplace supports or inhibits individuals' engagement in work activities and access to ... guidance' (2001, p. 210). Billet sees opportunities to participate in workplace activities as affordances that derive from employers' and others' judgements of a worker's competence, race, employment and work status, as well as from interpersonal relations at work. Billet invokes the notion of agency, which Hunter and Cooke define as the 'capacity to act with initiative and effect' (2007, p. 81). Billet states:

> *Individuals' agency ... shapes how they engage with what is afforded them in the workplace. Agentic action is guided by the learners' identities and subjectivities, which are themselves socially-derived through personal histories.* (Billet *et al.*, 2004, p. 237)

Moreover, as they engage in workplace activities and learning, individuals refine and remake vocational practice, so that what they do is never simply an exact copy of existing practices (Billet, 2006, p. 59). The interdependence between workplace affordances and individual agency is a key concept in Billet's approach to workplace learning.

The migrant workplace study

In this discussion I focus on two case studies within a larger qualitative, interpretive study. For the case studies, I approached employers who regularly hired migrants to ask if I could job-shadow migrant employees who had English as an additional language (EAL). In return, I offered to tutor them after the data collection. Consequently, I visited two young Asian women working in jobs requiring specialised skills in computer literacy. I saw each of them for one morning a week over approximately four months. I sat beside them at their work stations, observed their work and talked intermittently with them as they worked. I audio-recorded our time together, made field notes and collected work documents as permitted.

In the larger project, I looked at perceptions of communication demands and challenges among skilled EAL employees and among employers of immigrants. The study consisted of open-ended interviews with employers and skilled EAL employees in interpreting, accounting, IT, engineering, supervisory positions and teaching. Employees were from a variety of Asian countries, East Africa and the Middle East. Results from the larger study are included when relevant at a later point in this chapter.

Job-shadowing Hiroko
Hiroko worked for an Australasian engineering consulting firm in a major New Zealand city. She was well regarded for her highly specialised literacy skill with autoCAD, a complex software program for two- and three-dimensional drawing, used by engineers and architects. However, if she had not entered the country on a work/tourist visa, she would not have been accepted because she did not meet the International English

Language Testing System (IELTS) immigration requirements of 6.5 (very good user). As it happened, she had started work as a summer 'student assistant', but when the company saw her IT skills, they offered her a permanent position as a draughtsperson. With her employment status in an area of skills shortages, an engineering degree from Japan and experience there as a structural engineer, she applied for and was quickly granted permanent residency. Yet after a year on the job, at our first meeting she expressed a lack of confidence about her English language competence. Hiroko told me that what bothered her most about her English was that she could not make friends, laugh, talk and joke the way she could in Japanese. Later she confided that her job was boring; she wanted to do more structural calculations and direct client work. Both these interests presented obstacles for her.

The physical layout of the work site constrained interpersonal interaction. Hiroko's workspace was a corner computer station in a partitioned cubicle that she shared with one other employee. They sat at opposite corners of the cubicle, so that their backs were to each other, allowing some work privacy without completely isolating them at their desks. However, when Hiroko needed to consult with a co-worker other than her 'office' mate, she had to find her way through a warren of partitioned walkways. In other words, there was no ready access to co-workers for quick collaboration or opportunities to interact. What is more, people ate lunch and took tea breaks when their work permitted it, at their desks or in the lunchroom, which also meant irregular access to interaction.

When I began visiting her, Hiroko had a new supervisor, Carl, who spoke to her little. He insisted on being her sole contact regarding assignments from individual engineers in order to manage the draughting work closely. But he also commented to me:

> *She has a little trouble with that and I think that comes out of the fact that she's an engineer and I'm just a draughtsperson. I have encountered that before with other cultures; she has to accept that I am her boss … If I say something, if I say 'don't do that but do that job first', it is how it's going to get done.*

He felt – as did several other employers in the larger study I conducted – that migrants who had held high-level positions in their home country tended to expect their former status to carry over to New Zealand as well. This expectation was generally attributed to the hierarchical cultures that migrants came from. In contrast, employers tended to characterise New Zealand workplaces as flattened hierarchies or places where people had to earn their status.

Hiroko expressed a different rationale for talking directly to engineers: 'Sometimes I need to talk to [engineers] directly because I can't understand it [the drawing]. Somebody talk to Carl and Carl explaining this one, but sometimes different story.' Despite the directive from Carl, Hiroko persisted in speaking to them, possibly partly for interpersonal contact. She did ask engineers who approached her if they had talked to Carl first, but conflicts with him continued. Ultimately, he found a note from an engineer on her desk, told her he was 'sick' of her, and stopped speaking to her. She went to the department head, but found the situation extremely distressing and was certain she would be fired. At one point, clearly upset, she said to me: 'I'm going to redundant here, I'll let you know.' After some difficult days, when she told me she cried in the ladies' room and had several talks with the department head, with the three of them and with her co-workers, the situation appeared to ease. She believed that the department head was aware of Carl's reputation as 'grumpy'. She also sensed that the department head had closed the discussion when he told her that since Carl was her supervisor she needed to try to get along with him and follow his direction.

Shortly before I left, Hiroko took advantage of the company's education subsidy and began a course in structural engineering at the local university as another avenue towards greater workplace challenge and participation in the New Zealand engineering world. Despite the language errors evident in her email, she managed the application and enrolment process successfully.

Regardless of the ongoing difficulties with Carl, Hiroko found ways to participate socially at work. She joined the company soccer team where she said she could join in without having to talk much. She took team photos, circulating them on the company intranet, with brief informal email text, such as the following from a later event:

> hi all, Thank you for last night. I keep BBQ's photos in my Folder
> XXX. There are lots of cool photos☺ Please have a look, if you like.
> But nobody is allowed to delete photos! Hehe Thanks, Hiroko

Two young New Zealander co-workers approached her to teach them how to cook Japanese food. They shopped for supplies and prepared

the dinner at someone's home. More outings followed with other co-
workers to a family farm and a popular snorkelling spot. Hiroko became
more active in company social events, continuing to distribute photos
and gradually engaging more socially. During the months I visited her,
she also moved from her flat with other Japanese migrants to one with
migrants and students where English was the lingua franca. Thus the un-
demanding English-speaking social interaction at work was augmented
by English use at home. She reported that her friends from work and
home supported her during the difficult time with Carl.

Job-shadowing Jane

Jane left China with a new teaching qualification but realised quickly
that she would have difficulty teaching in English in New Zealand, so she
enrolled on a commerce degree programme at a New Zealand university.
After graduation she worked briefly as a receptionist for a small Chinese
firm in the city, but then became an accounts manager for LC Logistics,
a medium-sized company with branches in New Zealand and Australia.
Three years of tertiary education in an English-speaking environment
meant that Jane spoke more fluently and accurately than Hiroko, but
she was still dissatisfied with her English language skills. Her manager
reported having some difficulty understanding her spoken English.

Jane managed the merchandise accounts trajectories of several clients. Her manager told her she was responsible for the clients that he
assigned to her and gave her some autonomy in dealing with them. If
she had difficulties with clients, she felt she was able to count on him to
support her. However, she found that the scope of her work was somewhat limited. She organised the communication between the clients and
the company warehouse to track incoming goods for warehouse storage
and outgoing orders for delivery to clients' customers or retail outlets. In
addition, she was responsible for trouble-shooting when any discrepancy
arose between orders and actual goods in the warehouse. Jane sat at a partitioned workstation like Hiroko's, but it was at the edge of a large open
office space, with others visible and placed around the sides. Directly opposite her station were managers' offices, nearly always with open doors.
Thus her everyday work was less isolating than Hiroko's.

Like Hiroko, Jane found her job boring. Early on, when I commented on the language demands in managing and negotiating complex procedures, she replied, 'Actually it's just the basic English.' For the
most part, she prepared formulaic data sheets, such as 'picking slips' and

invoices, which had been pre-programmed to automatically complete prices, item names and warehouse locations when she entered product codes. Every morning she processed incoming emails from clients that specified lists of merchandise to be moved from the warehouse to retail outlets or purchasers, or incoming merchandise to receive, catalogue and store in the warehouse. She then printed out the picking slips and hand-delivered them to the warehouse supervisor on the lower floor. When they had been processed, ticked off and initialled, they were returned to her, to complete the data sheet and 'release' the order. She printed out the released orders and dropped them in the accountant's inbox. Besides generating orders, she followed up with her clients' counterparts by email. Many of them were also EAL employees, and they communicated effectively in English that differed slightly from the norm, as in the typical exchange below:

> Hi Sandy, I received order 55503 and we will send it as soon as we can. Did you send another 25 orders to me yesterday? I cannot read these orders as there are no attachment.

> Jane, Please do not send this order, actually put it in the bin, I will resend it after I talk to them, they have moved address. I have thrown it.

Jane had also written one report at LC Logistics when her manager asked her to give him some feedback about the company in an informal document. An excerpt follows:

> Secondly, we talk about management in [the company] ... People know little about company's strategy, goal and object. Therefore, there is no clear guide for people who work here. People do not know if there performance is satisfactory and achieved the required aim. Only when staff has clear guide and goal, they can act towards that goal.

The strong impersonal stance of her text is reminiscent of undergraduate business writing textbooks, with a focus on form and format, but not positioning and context. I asked Jane if she had proofread it and she replied that it was just an informal report and proofreading was not necessary. I also asked about her manager's response to the report and its highly negative tone. She reported that he had not commented. Overall, her job did not include opportunities to engage in report-writing.

When merchandise on a picking slip was misplaced, one of the women from the warehouse contacted Jane to solve the problem. On one occasion, a particular size of screw could not be found and Jane interrupted her other work to search among the shelves of screws with similar product numbers. She found them and reshelved them. Later, in response to my query, she told me that occasionally similar product numbers got mixed up and it was 'just a guess' that this was again the case. She said her past experience was that simple order problems could grow if she did not solve them quickly, so she always hastened to take care of them herself. What struck me about this apparently simple problem-solving task was that she based her success on knowledge and experience with past work problems. In other words, her problem-solving skills were highly situated, not generic.

Altogether, Jane's job was highly routine. From my observations and Jane's reports to me, the two examples above largely comprised the non-routine work she did. Despite spending the bulk of her time on repetitive computer work, Jane's job required company knowledge, commitment, consistent attention to detailed procedures, and an ability to recognise and act on potential problems. Also, the workload could be frenzied at times and slow at other times, which she had to adjust to. Her manager told me that he valued her highly for all the qualities listed above. But out of concern for her English language, he encouraged her to 'talk with the other girls in the office', which she did: during my visits, she joined in small talk at lunch and tea breaks. Despite his support for her, he voiced discomfort with the Asian style of interaction, viewing it as too deferential and attributing it to their culture. Hiroko's managers also made this point. Jane's manager said his experience suggested that many Asians were not motivated to learn English well.

Jane was ambitious to obtain more challenging, interesting work. With only a small number of office and administrative staff in the company, though, there appeared to be little opportunity for her to advance. Shortly after I arrived, she asked about logistics programmes at my university. When I brought her some print material, she pointed out that they were only pre-degree diploma programmes and would not take her anywhere. She had also asked friends about other logistics courses, which again seemed only to be low level. Toward the end of my visits with her, she told me that she and her husband had partnered with a New Zealander to buy a franchise in a plastic goods retail outlet in a major shopping mall. The New Zealand partner would help them negotiate local ways of doing business, and she and her husband would have more independence and control over their work. She did not intend to leave LC Logistics immediately, but the knowledge she gained there could carry over to the new enterprise.

Hiroko and Jane and the larger study

Like Hiroko's and Jane's managers, employers who were interviewed about migrant employees reflected the essentialising[3] typical in popular discourses, but they also framed migrants in terms of desirable workplace roles. As Waldinger and Lichter note in arguing for a more nuanced view of workplace prejudice than social equality and respect, 'the relationship between manager and employee is inherently unequal, which means that when hiring, the employer has a specific question in mind: 'Who's the best underling?' (2003, p. 144). In other words, employers look for employees who will fit into their hierarchical work practices. In this sense, these employers saw migrants favourably as having a strong work ethic and dedication to the job. Paradoxically, they also saw New Zealand work-places as flattened hierarchies. For instance, they often complained that migrant employees were not forthcoming enough when asked for their professional opinions and were reticent to engage in building workplace relationships. They attributed these behaviours to cultural differences. At the same time, they tended to see migrants as unknowns, as an employment risk. They essentialised migrant cultures based on experience with previous employees and adopted dominant deficit views of language and literacy in the face of workplace problems. In summary, all these factors contributed in different ways to the agency they exercised as employers of migrants, which was most visible in the case studies.

Meanwhile, the national government's establishment of explicit language requirements for entry and for work permits implied to migrant employees that qualified immigrants should be employable and able to function adequately in the workplace once these standards were met. Yet nearly every employee interviewed, including Jane and Hiroko, told stories of great frustration in finding work in their field. Like Hiroko and Jane, several considered or enrolled in local tertiaries to upskill or retrain. Although they found work above entry level, mostly related to their professions, their work status in New Zealand was largely below that of their home countries.

Workplace agency and opportunity

The discussion above illustrates Billet's notion of the interplay between agency and affordances for participation and learning in workplaces. On a global scale, the economic competition among developed countries for skilled migrant workers (Li, 2007) has afforded new employment opportunities for migrants such as Hiroko and Jane. Both found work that comprised digital literacy practices, ubiquitous in the globalised economy (Farrell, 2009). In contrast to the well-documented tensions between regulatory functions of digital record-keeping and work production (for example, Belfiore *et al.*, 2004), digital documentation was the main responsibility of these two women, and their value at work depended on their competence in these specialised literacies – that is, tracking logistics accounts for Jane and producing autoCAD drawings for Hiroko.

Both women, however, found their work unchallenging. What is more, their opportunities to learn new work practices and new repertoires of language and literacy were constrained by workplace practices, the nature of their responsibilities and the spatial organisation of their workplaces.

It is important to recognise that employers have considerable power to shape workplace practices, and this was evident in comparing Jane's and Hiroko's opportunities for workplace agency. On one hand, Jane was encouraged to work independently, make decisions and control her work agenda, albeit with limited choices. On the other, Hiroko was closely monitored and expressly forbidden to consult others in the course of her work. New Zealand employers have had little experience with non-Commonwealth, non-European migrants in professional and skilled positions, because New Zealand has only relatively recently begun to compete for transnational, skilled and qualified migrants (Bedford, 2002; Bedford *et al.*, 2005). All this has meant that employers may see migrants as unknowns and tend to essentialise them, as with Hiroko and Jane. For both women, these factors may have figured in their employers' willingness to hire them, and also in any reservations they may have had about them. For Hiroko, the supervisor's inexperience and stereotyping of migrants may well have contributed to negative attitudes and the way he treated her.

Jane and Hiroko were also constrained by the nature of their work and the physical configuration of their workspace. Both spent their workdays engaged with data generation at computer stations. In fact, their very jobs were circumscribed by the digital outputs they produced. Although individual jobs varied somewhat, the routine was relatively fixed for both of them, and they had clearly mastered it. With Jane's workspace bordering an open area, there was easy opportunity to consult co-workers and make small talk, which Jane took advantage of. Hiroko's workspace opened onto a maze of inhospitable walkways bordering other partitioned workstations so that interpersonal interaction required some effort.

For the employees interviewed and for Hiroko and Jane, agency was contingent on the affordances of these contexts. As Billet *et al.* (2004, p. 237) contend, agency depended on workers' interpretation of and engagement in workplace practices, guided by their 'identities and subjectivities'. In Jane's case, when further education seemed not to be a good choice, she took another direction. Operating a retail business was a path frequently followed by Chinese migrants who could not find employment and one that was readily available. Hiroko's devalued Japanese professional and linguistic competencies needed to be reconfigured for the New Zealand context. But taking up affordances also meant more than interpreting opportunities: it also depended on the visibility of those opportunities. For a while, face-to-face interactions with engineers were the only avenue Hiroko saw to participate in local ways of being, thinking and talking like an engineer. Certainly, similar issues arise for aspiring workers who are not migrants, but they are unlikely to be facing resettlement in foreign environments as well. In summary, despite Jane's autonomy of decision-making, her job afforded little opportunity for engagement in further learning, and her agency led her outside her job. Hiroko exercised her agency in seizing opportunities to interact socially and to take advantage of formal education.

What are the implications for language and literacy education? National policies serve the dominant business and government views that high scores on standardised language and literacy skills assessments are the key to employment in a competitive, globalised job market. However, Kramsch objects to the packaging of communicative competence as predefined skills applied to 'predetermined tasks' that are measureable under accountability schemes. Instead, she argues that in modern multicultural, multilingual contexts:

> *not all communicative situations are amenable to straightforward talk*
> *in a brief, concise, and sincere manner, and negotiation of meaning*

> *often flounders not because of a lack of linguistic comprehension, but because of a lack of understanding and trust of interlocutors' intentions. What often needs to be negotiated nowadays is not how to achieve the task, but the nature and the purpose of the task itself.*
> (Kramsch, 2005, p. 250)

She further claims that communicative competence is necessary but not sufficient for EAL migrants in the workplace; they must be able to 'position themselves in the world'.

The texts and workplace interactions in the case studies illustrate Kramsch's point that communicative competence is not as straightforward as it is traditionally depicted to language and literacy educators. The issues go beyond language interactions and linguistic abilities to the settings and environments in which they are situated. Perhaps somewhat luckily, Hiroko's email helped her successfully enrol in a university course. On the other hand, the presence of an engineer's note found on her desk provoked her supervisor's anger. In contrast, Jane's somewhat inappropriate report to her manager appeared not to have negative effects. It may be that the situated practices, purposes and relationships around these texts had more influence on the ways they were received than the language itself. In Hiroko's case, it could be assumed that the university welcomed fee-paying students, prompting one kind of response. But in her workplace, Hiroko had a conflictual relationship with her supervisor, prompting a quite different type of reaction. Jane's manager was trusting and supportive, and they therefore enjoyed a good working relationship. Jane's and Hiroko's cases show the value for migrants and workplace language educators of developing a framework for analysing and interpreting the nature of workplace practices and the ways that meanings, opportunities and constraints can vary in relation to changing relationships and practices.

The research shows that these two women were able to thrive to some extent in their workplace not just because of their individual agency and autonomy, but also because of their situations. It is important, therefore, to look at the constraints and affordances in the labour market and in the workplace that shaped their opportunities to participate in the language and literacy practices of their host country. When I visited Hiroko and Jane, their working lives were caught in a web of somewhat conflicting global and local forces. On the one hand, globalised economic competition among Western nations to fill skills shortages resulted in job opportunities for their specialised digital literacy skills. But on the other, on the local scale, Hiroko and Jane, like other migrants, faced discriminatory practices in the workplace, frustration at working below their capacity, and narrow opportunities to move ahead.

Notes

[1] The funding for this research was provided by the Massey University Research Fund. I would also like to acknowledge the support of Auckland Regional Migrant Services and the EEO Trust in recruiting participants.

[2] All proper names from the research are fictional.

[3] Gutiérrez and Rogoff (2003) refer to essentialising as ascribing over-generalised monolithic definitions to cultural groups.

References

Barton, D., Hamilton, M. and Ivanič, R. (eds) (2000) *Situated Literacies: Reading and Writing in Context*. New York: Routledge.

Baynham, M. and De Fina, A. (eds) (2005) *Dislocations/Relocations: Narratives of Displacement*. St. Jerome.

Bedford, R. (2002) 'International migration in New Zealand: context, components and policy issues', *Journal of Population Research*, pp. 39–66.

Bedford, R., Ho, E. and Lidgard, J. (2005) 'From targets to outcomes: immigration policy in New Zealand, 1996–2003' in *New Zealand and International Migration: A Digest and Bibliography*, No 4, (eds) Trlin, A., Spoonley, P. and Watts, N., pp. 1–43. Palmerston North, NZ: Massey University.

Belfiore, M., Defoe, T., Folinsbee, S., Hunter, J. and Jackson, N. (eds) (2004) *Reading Work: Literacies in the New Workplace*. Mahwah, NJ: Lawrence Erlbaum Associates.

Billet, S. (2001) 'Learning through work: workplace affordances and individual engagement', *Journal of Workplace Learning*, Vol. 13 No 5, pp. 209–14.

Billet, S. (2006) 'Relational interdependence between social and individual agency in work and working life', *Mind, Culture, and Activity*, Vol. 13 No 1, pp. 53–69.

Billet, S. (ed.) (2010) *Learning Through Practice: Models, Traditions, Orientations and Approaches*. Dordrecht: Springer.

Billet, S., Barker, M. and Hernon-Tinning, B. (2004) 'Participatory practices at work', *Pedagogy, Culture and Society*, Vol. 12 No 2, pp. 233–58.

Farrell, L. (2009) 'Texting the future: work, literacies, and economies' in *The Future of Literacy Studies*, (eds) Baynham, M. and Prinsloo, M., pp. 181–98. Palgrave Macmillan.

Gutiérrez, K. and Rogoff, B. (2003) 'Cultural ways of learning: individual traits or repertoires of practice', *Educational Researcher*, Vol. 32 No 5, pp. 19–25.

Hunter, J. and Cooke, D. (2007) 'Through autonomy to agency: giving power to language learners', *Prospect*, Vol. 22 No 2, pp. 72–88.

Kramsch, C. (2006) 'Communicative competence to symbolic competence', *The Modern Language Journal*, Vol. 90 No 2, pp. 249–52.

Lave, J. (1996) 'Teaching, as learning, in practice', *Mind, Culture, and Activity*, Vol. 3 No 3, pp. 149–64.

Lave, J. and Wenger, E. (1991) *Situated Learning: Legitimate Peripheral Participation*. Cambridge University Press.

Li, P. (2007/08) 'World migration in the age of globalization: policy implications and challenges', *New Zealand Population Review*, Vol. 33 and 34, pp. 1–22.

Rogoff, B. (1990) *Apprenticeship in Thinking: Cognitive Development in Social Context*. New York: Oxford University Press.

Waldinger, R. and Lichter, M. (2003) *How the Other Half Works: Immigration and the Social Organization of Labor*. Berkeley, CA: University of California Press.

CHAPTER ELEVEN

The Glory and Dismay Football Literacy Programme

JOHN PLAYER

Introduction

The Glory and Dismay Football Literacy Programme (GDFLP) is an open adult literacy class based in football stadiums in Edinburgh, Scotland. It has recruited 100 learners over a period of seven years, with 20 adults on average attending classes at any one time. Classes take place in Edinburgh at Heart of Midlothian Football Stadium at Tynecastle; Hibernian Football Club at Easter Road; and at Spartans Football Academy at Ainslie Park. GDFLP has attracted more learners than any other literacy group in the city and has continued to develop an identity, warmth, exuberance and dynamism.

From the outset of this programme, it was apparent that each learner had amassed considerable knowledge about football. Our job, as literacy educators, was to encourage participants to use this knowledge as a re-source and context for their literacy learning. I was keen to explore more formally the impact of the programme on 'hard-to-reach' adult learners and to look at ways of describing their experiences of the GDFLP. That is what this chapter is about.

This commentary attends to the social practice approach of the Scottish Government in adult literacy learning and draws upon the work of Paulo Freire but also acknowledges the important critiques of Freire's approach. These criticisms require a more situated theory of oppression and subjectiv-ity and call for the need to consider the contradictions inherent in Freire's universal claims of truth or process (Weiler, 1995; Bartlett, 2009).

The Adult Learning Project (ALP)

After completing my Adult Basic Education (ABE) training, I secured a post at the Adult Learning Project (ALP) in Edinburgh in 2002. ALP is, according to Galloway (1999, p. 226), a unique attempt to translate Freire's pedagogy to the context of a Scottish inner city area. He points out that:

> *Since its inception [in 1979], ALP's work has been influenced by the principles and practice of Paulo Freire, with a commitment to politicise the curriculum, construct learning programmes grounded in the struggle for cultural equality, develop the use of dialogical learning methods, and build an authentic relationship between learning and cultural action.* (Galloway, 1999, p. 226)

I was intrigued by the continual references in adult literacy education to Freirian concepts such as 'decodification',[1] 'dialogical methodology ' and 'praxis'. The use of decodification in the ALP was written up by Kirkwood and Kirkwood (1989), who referred to its experiences of trying out such methods within adult literacy work. However, the fusion of a skills-based literacy education and decodification of oppressive structures was not evident to me in mainstream ABE. Moreover, I was aware that in other literacy groups I helped to organise for the City of Edinburgh Council (CEC), much of the pedagogic practice was well meaning but appeared de-contextualised and individuated. This chapter begins to articulate and synthesise my prior community development experience using a critical literacy perspective. I wanted to explore how a programme such as the GDFLP might be contributing to critical as well as functional literacy development.

The idea of cracking the code of language in order to encode the world through an 'unveiling education', which was inherent in the ALP praxis, ensnared me. In particular, this meant cracking the code of *langue* and the 'deeper structure' of ideology through an engagement with *parole* or the vernacular of urban Scots. Through my observation of ALP's educational practice, I became aware that the decoding process enlivened adult students; through observations in literacy groups, I was convinced of its merits. This led to the GDFLP.

Background

Before coordinating the GDFLP, I had known of the existence of two football-based educational programmes and that these had had a positive impact on adults' and children's literacy acquisition. The first was a literacies programme with adults carried out by Platform Adult Learning Centre, Wester Hailes, Edinburgh in the 1990s. The second was through a study visit organised by ALP to Newcastle in early 2004, which included a visit to the Stadium of Light, the home ground of Sunderland Football Club. While at the stadium, we visited a learning centre that doubled up as a bar for visiting players and commentators at the weekend. The learning centre's focus was on schoolchildren who were either excluded or truanting from school. The 'razzmatazz' of the stadium and the buzz of football ensured that students turned up to the centre for lessons.

When we got back to Edinburgh, I took this idea, though slightly changed to incorporate an adult learning perspective, to Alan White, Community Coach at Heart of Midlothian Football Club, which was just a few streets away from the ALP office. He said he was very interested and offered us their function room, the Willie Bauld Suite, in the stadium. We then applied to the City, Literacy and Numeracy Project (CLAN) for a Challenge Fund[2] grant.

The original idea of the GDFLP initiative was to attract hard-to-reach male working-class learners who were keen to improve their reading and writing skills. Since its inception, however, the programme has expanded to draw in a significant cohort of working-class females. The GDFLP uses a learner-centred approach (for example, Gebre et al., 2009) which builds on a social practice model of literacy: that is, teaching builds upon learners' strengths. In this case, it particularly builds on their detailed knowledge of the 'beautiful game', football (see Figure 1.1).

Policy context

The GDFLP is in part a response to the Scottish Executive (renamed Scottish Government from 2007) Adult Literacy and Numeracy in Scotland (ALNIS) report (Scottish Executive, 2001, p. 1), which highlights the need to target priority groups. The evidence, the report suggests, is that a high proportion of those with low levels of literacy and numeracy are to be found among people who live in disadvantaged areas, workers in low-skill jobs, people on low incomes and people with health problems

Figure 1.1: GDFLP discuss the beautiful game (comic art entry in GDFLP Fanzine)

Source: Scottish Book Trust, 2009

and disabilities. The GDFLP learners are all from occupational social class 5, reinforcing the argument underpinning the ALNIS report that social class is a key determinant of literacy acquisition in Scotland. To operationalise the report's findings, CLAN was set up in Edinburgh to pump prime innovative literacy initiatives, such as the GDFLP, financially.

The ALNIS report (Scottish Executive, 2001, p. 12) suggests that attracting learners from the priority groups means making use of an understanding about which strategies are most successful. Given the importance of football to a large number of the priority group, the GDFLP advocates its use as a potential 'carrot'.

At the same time, both the ALNIS and HM Inspectorate of Education (HMIE, 2005, p. 10) reports insist that we recognise and accredit individual progress and that projects such as the GDFLP measure sufficiently those literacy and numeracy skills required for learners to attain their desired learning outcomes. The GDFLP does this through a certification and award ceremony, which is characteristic of the celebratory approach of learning inherent in ALP. It endeavours to apply rigour to learners' self-assessment processes and explores more appropriate forms of appraisal. This stress upon rigour is partly derived from Freire and Shore's influence. While highly critical of the 'standard transfer curriculum' and the 'banking' concept of education, they were emphatic about the need for rigour in education, stating:

> *We have, in doing so, to demonstrate that rigour is not synonymous with authoritarianism, that 'rigour' does not mean 'rigidity'. Rigour lives with freedom, needs freedom. I cannot understand how it is possible to be rigorous without being creative.* (Freire and Shor, 1987, p. 78)

Another aim of the GDFLP is to problematise the issues of Scottish football from the generative themes and issues that arise from a dialogical educational approach. I am using 'generative themes' (Freire, 1972, p. 69) to refer to cultural or political topics of concern or importance to adult learners in the GDFLP. One generative theme that has clearly arisen is that of 'winning football back to the people' (Stanistreet, 2005) and this is reflected in some of the discussions that take place in the GDFLP, which are illustrated later in this chapter.

Freire's concept of praxis is vital both for ALP, which remains the umbrella organisation for GDFLP, and, perhaps, for the Scottish Executive's contemporary use of a social practice account of literacy and

183

numeracy. The Scottish Executive (2005, p. 13) suggests that 'Reading and writing are complex cognitive activities that also depend on a great deal of contextual (i.e. social) knowledge and intention.'

This emphasis on literacy's purposes, rather than on discrete goals, strongly mirrors the policy options advocated by Fingeret and Drennon (1997, p. 108). The social practice approach advocated by the Scottish Government demands praxis in order to decode and unveil the 'deeper structure' of social relations (Freire, 1970, p. 31) and is part of the wider context of the GDFLP. I would suggest that the discourse analysis method, which permeates Freire's work, might help us grasp the logic and construction of mass football culture in the present age, its significance to adults and their potential for learning to deconstruct it.

However, this emphasis on the social practice perspective, of which critical literacy is an inherent component, is being undermined through the reassertion of functionality apparent in *Adult Literacies in Scotland 2020: A Strategic Approach* (Scottish Government, 2011). This retreat is evident in the stress made by this policy document on the use of literacy in connection with notions of 'employability and work'. Prioritising functionality over criticality represents a retreat from the ALNIS report (Scottish Executive, 2001) and a reassertion of literacy as predominantly a tool for employability, skills and financial capability. Practitioners' experience at the GDFLP and experience of the learners' lives would indicate a greater need for retention of the critical perspective.

Curriculum issues

Learners are asked every term to bring cuttings of newspaper articles about football teams, football celebrities and stars, match reports and analysis of football matches. This is to draw on learners' passion for football at the same time as reinforcing the critical literacy approach adopted by the programme. This approach is best described by McLaren:

> *Critical literacy, refers to an emancipatory process in which one reads not only the 'word' but also the 'world' (Freire and Macedo, 1987), a process whereby a person becomes empowered to be able to unveil and decode 'the ideological dimensions of texts, institutions, social practices and cultural forms such as television and film, in order to reveal their selective interests'.* (McLaren, 1994, p. 7)

The learners are then encouraged to engage in a form of 'critical discourse analysis' (CDA) (Fairclough, 1992, p. 169). Students are asked to compare and contrast language; to look at the verbs in order to see, for example, if they are colloquial or standard; to examine the words used to describe people in order to identify key words that might reinforce the celebrity status of football players; to look at what people are presented as doing in the text; and to consider why ideas and people are being presented as they are.

The GDFLP aims to use CDA to enable adult learners to explore how football fans and learners are represented and how their position is constructed through language, pictures and codes.

Illustration of a learner's use of CDA and critical literacy

The 'spectacle' of professional football is maintained through texts and football or, more pertinently, through the culture that surrounds it since it is as much a discursive process or formation as a physical sport. This notion of the spectacle has been introduced to ALP by Colin Kirkwood in his contribution to the ALP co-investigation in 2002 where he remarked:

> In the 1960s there was an intellectual movement called Situationism. One of its key concepts was 'the spectacle'. As a result of the antics of the Baader-Meinhof gang, the Red Brigades, and other ultra left wing phenomena, a moderate and sensible analysis of the development of the spectacle as a means of population management did not develop as it might have done. Arguably we need to return to the concept of the spectacle as a powerfully explanatory idea and develop around it not merely an analysis of society.

Our concern at ALP is the effect of texts and the spectacle in inculcating and sustaining or changing ideologies.

An example of CDA practice is derived from the following semi-structured interview with one of the long-term learners, 'AMJ'.

The interview began with a discussion in January 2008 about AMJ's educational and footballing background. I was keen to find out whether the GDFLP had enhanced his critical literacy. When I asked him 'Are we at war with Islam? Are we at war with Hibernian?' he laughed loudly. I asked 'Are we at war with Celtic? Do you feel we are at war with anybody?' 'There is only one war just now with Iraq. And I feel for people that are out there; innocent people that are getting killed for no reason at all. These troops should be brought home. Now!' AMJ thus articulated an anti-Iraq war stance.

Then I said, 'AMJ, … I'm going to ask you to read this … it's just an editorial from *The Sun* in December.' AMJ reads the editorial (see Appendix). 'Well, I think it's about time that people like this … eh … they should nae be allowed into Britain cause it's takin way jobs from people here and we're actually payin them when we could be payin x amount of money fur medical or even schools here.'

I said, 'So what you're saying is *The Sun* is critical of the government for not getting tough enough on asylum seekers?' 'Yes!' he asserts. 'That's a view you would kinda support?' 'Yes! Yes! Very much so!' 'And you would be concerned that they are free to resume drug dealing, burglary, and …'. 'Yes!' 'and that kind of thing?' 'Yes!' 'And you would agree with the line that Gordon Brown should deliver his promise a bit quicker?' 'Yes, very much so!' 'Making sure we got rid of illegal asylum seekers?' 'Not only that … in this country the punishment does not fit the crime!' 'So for this editorial you don't think the punishment is strong enough?' 'No! No! … ' 'For asylum seekers?' 'No! No! It should be the same fur everybody … doesn't matter who it is!'

I said, 'And the line from *The Sun*, is that similar to the *Daily Record*? Has the *Daily Record* got the same kinda tough line on asylum seekers?' 'I wouldn't say so!' 'Not tough enough for you?' 'Naw! I feel that the asylum seekers that come here are only after the money and then go away back to their own place where they've came fae.'

I was taken aback at AMJ's response to *The Sun* editorial because he had struck me as a compassionate individual and I had thought that he would display greater empathy with asylum seekers. AMJ joined the GDFLP in 2007 and when I had asked him how he felt the programme had benefited him, he replied, 'It has helped by meeting people from different cultures.'

In a class just over a year later at Heart of Midlothian FC, the group was exploring *The Sun* headlines from the Hillsborough disaster that blamed fans for stealing from and urinating on the dead. In response to the first question as to why *The Sun* put forward headlines like these, AMJ said, 'It was like the *Daily Sport* and *Sunday Sport* in that they will do anything to sell newspapers.' AMJ said *The Sun* had been 'out of order; they could get away with it years ago because unlike now people couldn't produce evidence from their mobile phone cameras to contradict the police evidence.' AMJ said he would go to the library to get a copy of *The Sun* from 1989 and see what it said beyond the headlines. He said he would like to 'substantiate' the evidence. He introduced this new word, saying he had heard it on police programmes on the television.

AMJ was beginning to 'decode the ideological dimensions of... cultural forms such as television and film, in order to reveal their selective interests' (Mayo, 1995, p. 363). He was critiquing the legitimacy of *The Sun's* 'unsubstantiated' claims about the Liverpool fans. These claims have subsequently been discredited, provoking hostility towards the newspaper. The GDFLP seems to have provided for AMJ a safe, critical reflective space where some views shift with critical reflection, others do not. There is thus evidence of AMJ gaining greater critical awareness in some areas but not in others.

Process, 'conscientization' and curriculum: 'Where I get my inspiration is in the Glory and Dismay.'

Heaney (1995) argues that 'Conscientization is an ongoing process by which a learner moves toward critical consciousness'. Heaney further argues that:

> *Conscientization means breaking through prevailing mythologies to reach new levels of awareness – in particular, awareness of oppression, being an 'object' in a world where only 'subjects' have power. The process of conscientization involves identifying contradictions in experience through dialogue and becoming a 'subject' with other oppressed subjects – that is, becoming part of the process of changing the world.*

The curriculum of GDFLP, which gives rise to such a process, has been acknowledged by Crowther and Tett (2011) when they suggest that:

> *The broad aim of 'the Glory and Dismay' is to link people's passion for football with Freirean 'conscientization' (i.e. critical awareness and action) as a basis for stimulating literacy skills.*

They go on to maintain that:

> *As students 'say their word' the tutors adeptly question, tease out and propose links to generative themes which helps deepen discussion*

187

and potentially 'name' the oppressor – globalization, ownership and control of the game by wealthy elites, inequality in society, cultures of racism and violence in football grounds and so on.

This process was epitomised for me at a GDFLP class in the Heart of Midlothian Executive Suite on 19 March 2009. There were 19 participants in the class, three workers, one volunteer and the keynote speaker, Tom Purdie[3]. One of the learners quickly went through the ground rules as many of the learners were 'bletherin and gabbin'. 'One singer, one song', 'Nae swearin unless it's in a text' and 'Switch yer mobys aff or put them on silent!' At appropriate points, Steven James (SJ), GDFLP learner, stood up with strips[4] that were autographed by Bert McCann, Jimmy Greaves, Denis Law and other great football players. SJ talked at length about how the hairs stood up on the back of his neck when he spoke to Denis Law. Tom then showed pictures of the (now defunct) third Lanark side. In the picture, fans were driving into the ground on motorcycles.

SJ linked his passion for football with Freirean 'conscientization', I felt, when he said that football was a tool used to manage people because after feelings of intense solidarity on the Saturday, when 147,000 fans would turn up for an international game, they would all have to go 'Back to the same grind on the Monday'. 'A form of population control', he argued.

The class that evening responded very strongly to SJ's contribution. James Gilfillin (GDFLP tutor) talked about the time when supporters all passed each other at the half-time changeover whereas now they remain segregated, and about his memories of disability vehicles inside football grounds. Agnes Rawls (AR) talked about the idea of 'football, bookies and boozers', and what Colin (GDFLP literacy tutor) described as the social fabric surrounding football. AR said she closely identified with SJ's description of his father coming home drunk and the fear and trepidation felt by the family. AR said that sort of behaviour was so widespread that 'it's just what you know'. Karen remembered her family coming home from watching the 1978 World Cup in the pub and that they were 'absolutely pished'. She remembered as a seven-year-old pouring a bottle of whisky down the toilet to stop them getting drunker. AR said that her brother played for Partick Thistle and that football was 'part of your identity'.

The class provided an educational experience that involved the collective deconstruction of the culture of football, which, in SJ's and Tom Purdie's view, provides an insight into 'social history'. Moreover, SJ recognised and articulated that evening the notion of football as a 'form of population control'.

In this session, GDFLP learners, such as SJ, were developing their critical literacy skills by decoding the discourse of football as social history and linking it to an oral tradition that represents the silenced voice of the Scottish working class. The GDFLP, I would argue, facilitates what Ana Maria Araujo Freire (Freire, 1997, p. 205) describes as 'an atmosphere of hope and confidence' to such an extent that SJ declared, 'Where I get my inspiration is in the Glory and Dismay.'

Conclusion

The project tries to reject any idea of 'deficit' amongst literacy learners. It attempts to build upon learners' and football fans' desire to learn and their knowledge of the game. Importantly, it builds upon their creativity, as well as the humour that surrounds the 'beautiful game' in Scotland. ALP's Freirian practice does not patronise learners but stretches them, through use of critical literacy, to consider how they are positioned as 'subjects' of the spectacle of modern football culture. However, the example of AMJ suggests that the results were, certainly from a Freirian perspective, contradictory. Freire (1985, p. 102) argued that 'there is no truly neutral education' and to claim neutrality is to deceive adult learners. Freire (1972, 1985) maintained throughout his career that it would be naive to expect the dominant classes to develop a type of education that would enable subordinate classes to perceive social injustices critically. Importantly, however, the AMJ example is that learners' consent to dominant discourses is always partial.

The engagement with AMJ highlights the contention that football presents us with a rich curricular code with which to unveil the 'logic of late capitalism', and, as importantly, to assist learners to 'write their word and change the world' (Freire and Macedo, 1987, p. 44).

Transformative learning is always social. This view is, indeed, one of the key aspects underpinning Paulo Freire's pedagogical method. His insights regarding the social nature of learning are emphasised by the stress upon learners 'speaking their word' (Freire, 1985) as the first step to becoming literate. This is supported by research (in particular, Sticht, 2005) and by the GDFLP experience.

As football is culturally central to many Scots' lives, it represents a channel through which discourses, both dominant and marginal, are constructed, reproduced and internalised. Hegemony, therefore, is partly transmitted through the medium of football. However, hegemony is always capable of being challenged. As Malicky (1997) points out, there is always a degree of consent to such discourses. As shown in the section about AMJ as a learner, it is achieved partially through a sedimentation effect, whereby the language of a particular discourse permeates, filters and settles within both an individual and collective consciousness.

The role of the adult educator, I would argue, is to study, alongside learners, the extent of such consent, whilst providing the space to examine alternative, counter-hegemonic, forms of discourse. The main mechanism for examining both consent and dissent has been CDA to deconstruct the tabloid press' intertextual linkages between the language of football and other ideological aims such as the exclusion and demonisation of the 'other'.

This chapter highlights an investigation of learners from the working class. This entails discovering what can be said through providing a critical and, hopefully, emancipatory voice for adult learners. 'Fitba' provides such a 'voice' for Scottish working-class men, and some women, as well as providing pride, the earthy humour of local discourse and popular aspiration. The programme succeeds because it draws upon the celebratory power of football, creates a dynamic subject and setting for literacy learning and reaffirms particular forms of cultural identity rooted in the 'voice' of suppressed Scots language.

Notes

[1] Decodification refers to a process of description and ideological interpretation, whether of printed words, pictures or other 'codifications'. As such, decodification and decodifying are distinct from the process of decoding, or word recognition. (Freire, 1970, p. 31)

[2] This CLAN funding, established in 2002, was for partnership work which contributed to increasing and improving adult literacies provision in Edinburgh.

[3] Tom Purdie wrote *Scottish Football: The Golden Years – from the Jim Rogers Collection* (Purdie, 2007)

[4] Football strip: shirt worn by football players that is uniform for their team.

References

Bartlett, L. (2009) *The Word and the World: The Cultural Politics of Literacy in Brazil*. Cresskill, NY: Hampton Press.

Crowther, J. and Tett, L. (2011) 'Critical and social literacy practices from the Scottish adult literacy experience: resisting deficit approaches to learning', *Literacy*, Vol. 45 No 3, pp. 126–31.

Fairclough, N. (1992) *Discourse and Social Change*. Polity Press.

Fingeret, H. A. and Drennon, C. (1997) *Literacy for Life: Adult Learners, New Practices*. New York: Teachers College Press.

Freire, P. (1970) *Cultural Action for Freedom*. Penguin.

Freire, P. (1972) *Pedagogy of the Oppressed*. Penguin.

Freire, P. (1985) *The politics of education: culture, power, and liberation*. Bergin and Garvey.

Freire, P. (1997) *Pedagogy of Hope; Reliving Pedagogy of the Oppressed with notes by Ana Maria Araujo Freire*. New York: Continuum.

Freire, P. and Macedo, D. (1987) *Literacy: Reading the Word and the World*. Routledge and Kegan Paul Ltd.

Freire, P. and Shor, I. (1987) *A Pedagogy for Liberation: Dialogues on Transforming Education*. Macmillan.

Galloway, V. (1999) 'Building a pedagogy of hope: the experience of the adult learning project' in *Popular Education and Social Movements in Scotland Today*, (eds) Crowther, J., Martin, I. and Shaw, M. NIACE.

Gebre, A. H., Rogers, A., Street, B. and Openjuru, G. (2009) *Everyday Literacies in Africa; Ethnographic Studies of Literacy and Numeracy Practices in Ethiopia*. Kampala, Uganda: Fountain Publishers.

Heaney, T. (1995) *Issues in Freirean Pedagogy*. Chicago: University of Chicago.

HMIE (2005) *Changing Lives: Adult Literacy and Numeracy in Scotland. A Report by HM Inspectorate of Education*.

Kirkwood, G. and Kirkwood, C. (1989) *Living Adult Education: Freire in Scotland*. Open University Press.

Malicky, G., Katz, H., Norton, M. and Norman, C. (1997) 'Literacy learning in a community-based program', *Adult Basic Education*, Vol. 7 No 2, pp. 84–103.

Mayo, P. (1995) 'Critical literacy and emancipatory politics: the work of Paulo Freire', *International Journal of Educational Development*, Vol. 15 No 4, pp. 363–79.

Purdie, T. (2007) *Scottish Football: The Golden Years – from the Jim Rogers Collection.* Tempus Publishing.

Scottish Book Trust (2009) *Glory and Dismay: Our Story of Football, Learning Connections and the Scottish Government.* Wm Culross and Son.

Scottish Executive (2001) *Adult Literacy and Numeracy in Scotland (ALNIS).*

Scottish Executive (2005) *An Adult Literacy and Numeracy Curriculum Framework for Scotland.* Stationery Office.

Scottish Government (2011) *Adult Literacies in Scotland 2020: A Strategic Approach.*

Stanistreet, P. (2005) 'Winning back the people's game', *Adults Learning,* Vol. 17 No 3, pp. 4–5.

Sticht, T. (2005) *Synthetic Phonics and the Shift from Oracy to Literacy: Lessons from Adult Literacy Research* [Online] www.literacytrust.org.uk/Database/Primary/phonicsSticht.html [Accessed 15 March 2011].

Weiler, K. (1995) 'Freire and a feminist pedagogy of difference' in *The Politics of Liberation: Paths from Freire,* (eds) McLaren, P. and Lankshear, C. Routledge.

Appendix: *The Sun* editorial, 'Eviction time'

CHAPTER TWELVE

ESOL learners online: New media as a site of identity negotiation

JAMES SIMPSON AND RICHARD GRESSWELL

Introduction

This chapter examines how young adult refugees learning English in further education colleges in England can challenge the identity positions offered to them by the discourses and policies that affect their lives and learning. We explore how such challenges might be made in the course of their engagement with digital literacy practices that are not only supported by their teachers but also align closely with the typical literacy practices of many young people in contemporary Britain.

We begin by outlining our contention that, in policy and practice, the field of English for speakers of other languages (ESOL) offers students limited and deficit subject positions (identities), primarily as immigrants, skills trainees and prospective employees in low-paid work. We go on to explain how – when using new technology at the scale of their classroom literacy practices – young adult ESOL students can be afforded opportunities to negotiate identity positions that challenge those offered to them, or even imposed upon them, at the level of policy. ESOL classrooms are prime sites of identity work: ESOL learners undergoing the migration process have lost many of the familiar social, cultural and linguistic resources that enable the construction of identity. To make sense of who they are, and to remake themselves in their new environment, they have to use new linguistic and other semiotic resources. An appropriately broad range of pedagogic experiences – including engagement with digital technologies in class – can provide them with access to such resources. We discuss examples from two different ESOL classrooms of the way young adult migrants use new literacy technologies in classroom settings to claim particular identity positions that extend beyond the limited ones offered to them by policy and institutions. Both examples focus on new literacy practices in which written and oral language, as well as visual and multimedia resources, can be deployed in ways that afford the repositioning of the self and the renegotiation of identity.

The central contention of this chapter is that when a broad range of practices is available to students, their identity options are extended. However, this is not simply something to be celebrated and we end the chapter by problematising the issue. The out-of-class literacy practices of these young ESOL students contrast with more traditional, established and dominant 'schooled literacy' practices. The chapter describes aspects of an ESOL pedagogy that correspond with the everyday practices that students employ outside classrooms. We conclude by highlighting the tension between these everyday practices and the types of literacy practices that they might need to engage in – and the literacies that they might need to access – if they are to succeed in a traditional sense (for example, by gaining qualifications or moving to higher education).

Identity and migration

In order to discuss the identity positions offered to young adult ESOL students, and the identities claimed, negotiated and indeed rejected by them, we appeal to a dynamic, broadly constructivist understanding of identity. In this account, the use of semiotic resources – linguistic or otherwise – is the very *doing* of identity. As Blommaert (2005, pp. 203–4) summarises: 'Identity is semiotic through and through, and every act of semiosis is an act of identity in which we "give off" information about ourselves'. In the doing of identity, for example, when someone takes a turn in spoken interaction, they also position themselves in certain ways, enabling interpretations to be drawn: they allow their interlocutors to invoke 'social norms, roles, identities' (Blommaert, 2005, p. 252).

It is important to note that positioning is not unidirectional. In their paper on positioning in interaction, Davies and Harré (1990, p. 48) define it as 'the discursive process whereby selves are located in conversations as observably and subjectively coherent participants in jointly produced storylines'. This suggests that acts of semiosis, including the things a person does and says, not only relate to the way they position themselves. Positioning is dialogic: one positions oneself and is positioned by others. Notwithstanding this, power relations in interaction are rarely symmetrical. Positioning by policy or an institution can be challenging for an individual to counter or resist.

The students we discuss below are English language learners who are migrants to English-dominant countries. In migration contexts, identity construction happens in a new culture and a new language. David Block says of migration:

> *It is in this context, more than other contexts, that one's identity and sense of self are put on the line, not least because most factors that are familiar to the individual — sociohistorically, socioculturally, sociolinguistically and linguistically — have disappeared and been replaced by new ones. In this situation individuals must reconstruct and redefine themselves if they are to adapt to their new circumstances.* (Block, 2007, p. 5)

Some of the reconstruction and redefinition that Block talks about takes place in learning contexts. As the branch of English language teaching (ELT) that deals with adult language learning in migration contexts, ESOL is distinctive because of its tight connection with government policy on employment and employability, citizenship and social cohesion. ESOL, and English language use by migrants, is frequently cited in bigger debates on immigration, 'Britishness', social cohesion and the economy, among others. The way ESOL is implicated in these discourses (Foucault, 1970) results in a certain positioning of ESOL as a field of study — and the particular positioning of ESOL students themselves.

Identities offered

ESOL students come from a hugely diverse range of geographical, social and economic backgrounds. They include asylum seekers and refugees, people from more settled communities, so-called economic migrants escaping poverty in their home countries, people joining their spouses and family members, and — in the UK and Eire — EU nationals, especially from countries that joined the EU more recently (Cooke and Simpson, 2008). They find themselves positioned institutionally and in policy in certain ways. Predominantly, the identity positions offered to students are as:

- a learner of 'skills'
- a potential employee
- an immigrant and potential 'citizen'.

We discuss each in turn, before turning to identity and new literacies, and examining two examples of how ESOL students challenge these limited identity positions.

ESOL student as skills learner

A review of basic skills published in 1999 (DfEE, 1999) recommended implementing a national strategy called Skills for Life, which aimed to meet the learning needs of adults with low levels of basic skills, including ESOL learners.

Though funding for ESOL under the Skills for Life policy is now a thing of the past, adult migrant learners of English continue to be positioned as 'skills training' students. This positioning can exclude them from other areas of the adult education curriculum that have trajectories more likely to lead to 'the mainstream' and to higher education.

Elsa Auerbach, writing about the marginalisation of adult ESL (English as a second language) educators in the US, claimed that at the root of the peripheral status of the field of ESL was its status in policy as being in service to other areas and disciplines, rather than a bona fide subject of study in its own right. She said:

> The official rationalization for our marginal status is that ESL is a skill, not a discipline; we're preparing students to do something other than learn English, and it is that other something that counts ... As such, our work is defined more as training than educating; language is seen as a neutral tool, a set of decontextualized skills ... (Auerbach, 1991, p. 1)

There are echoes of this situation in ESOL in England today. The 'something other' that students are prepared for is quite clearly employment, and menial employment at that. ESOL students are being educated in the 'skill' of English so they can play a service role in the socio-economic structure, as we discuss below. Positioning ESOL as a 'skill' also enabled the government to take a close interest in its management. Skills for Life brought with it the creation of a statutory core curriculum for ESOL, teacher-training and inspection regimes, and qualifications mapped against national standards. Hence, successive governments have been able to dictate the nature of the English language education to which migrants can gain access, through the curriculum and through restriction to certain types of syllabus.

ESOL student as potential employee

In policy circles worldwide, there is a tight connection between English language provision and a discourse of 'employability', with ESOL students finding themselves positioned as potential employees with a responsibility for rendering themselves 'employable'. In England, the employability agenda has run like a thread through much contemporary political rhetoric, including that which impacts on ESOL, since the early twenty-first century (e.g. HM Treasury, 2006).

Under the Coalition Government (formed in 2010), much of the funding of ESOL provision in England is channelled via the Department for Work and Pensions (DWP) and its 'work programme'. ESOL courses that are part of the work programme are expected to 'pay by results' (see Simpson et al., 2011), meaning that the funding for ESOL classes depends on whether students move from the ESOL course into paid employment. In summary, at policy level ESOL students are viewed in terms of how they can become more economically productive. Predictably, with ESOL students positioned as migrant workers needing English to contribute to the economy, ESOL provision increasingly orients towards short, modular, employability-focused courses.

The implication for pedagogy is that what counts as knowledge, what is legitimised at policy and institutional level, becomes limited to progressing on these courses and into work. Many – but not all – students will indeed be concerned with finding work and with doing a job. All students, of course, also have other reasons for learning English beyond employment. But a dominant understanding of ESOL as a skill in service to employability leads to a pedagogy that offers students a narrow set of identity options, and consequently limited scope for both language and identity development.

ESOL student as immigrant and potential 'citizen'

The citizenship and social cohesion agenda first appeared in English government discourse around 2001, after street disturbances between Asian and white youths and the police in several northern English towns. Reports published after those events talked of people living 'parallel lives' and there were warnings from prominent public figures about 'sleep-walking into segregation'. Behind the focus on English towns and cities are larger debates over multiculturalism, the meaning of Britishness, the so-called war on terror and the links in public and media discourse between immigration and security. Threading through these ways of speaking are the themes of 'social cohesion', 'shared values', (standard) English as the common language of Britain, and the implication that multilingualism is a cause of fragmentation and segregation of communities (Blackledge, 2006).

Social cohesion was central to the policy of the previous UK government. Yet the concept of cohesion remained ill defined: in much government discourse, 'cohesion' seems to be a by-word for 'good behaviour'. Despite the contested nature of cohesion, the ESOL sector has been part of this agenda from the start, and at no point more clearly than with the introduction of the language and citizenship test in 2002. An alternative to the computer-based test for lower level ESOL students is an ESOL and citizenship class. The materials developed for teaching ESOL and citizenship are generally well received by teachers and students (Taylor, 2007), who enjoy the content of their classes. Yet students are indignant about the link between language classes and nationality, especially given that simply finding a place on a course has been a huge hurdle for many of them (Cooke and Simpson, 2009). Far from fostering a sense of integration and inclusive citizenship, the result of bringing together ESOL pedagogy and the citizenship agenda has been to promote a feeling of *exclusion*: some migrants, such as those from EU countries who are not subject to language and citizenship legislation, are seen as belonging more in the UK than others.

Identities rejected, challenged, claimed

In this section we present two analytical vignettes, both drawing on the experiences of young migrant English language learners in a city in the north of England. These illustrate how – through the use of new technologies and with the support of their teachers – students can be afforded opportunities to negotiate identity positions from which they can challenge the limited set of identities imposed upon them by policy and institutionally.

Literacy practices involving new technology afford extended options for identity construction. These might be written practices such as email, text chat, mobile phone messaging and use of Twitter. Increasingly they involve the use of other modes: photo and video production and file-sharing, audio blogging, visual communication in virtual spaces such as Second Life and online role-play games. Each of these offers the opportunity to develop and emphasise different aspects of identity with new sorts of texts, and in new, multimodal, multimedia, multilingual and globally-spread social spaces. The first example we present here involves blogging; the second, the production by students of a music video.

Blogs

Electronic communication of all kinds can enable students to do identity work, playing a part in enabling migrant students to reconstruct and re-define themselves. By now, most people with access to new technology and an Internet connection are familiar with blogging and the nature of blogs. A blog (web log) is a frequently modified web page containing individual entries displayed in reverse chronological order (Herring, et al., 2004). Blogs are recreational, are used in business, and are popular with journalists and citizen journalists. Blogs are also employed in language learning and teaching. Bloch notes that, for language teachers, 'blogging would seem a potentially useful tool for creating a space to discuss issues that may not be the focus of the traditional classroom' (2007, p. 129). A consensus in pedagogic descriptions of blogs is that they lend themselves to easily accessible publication and dissemination of student writing, to information-sharing, to the collaborative construction of meaning, and, significantly, to learner control. With increased bandwidth and ease of use of new technology, blogs are likely to incorporate visuals and audio, as well as links to videos, pictures and content using other media and posted on sites such as YouTube and Flickr.

Video

The creation and sharing of Web 2.0 media such as video is an accessible means of exploring issues, voicing concerns or simply being creative and telling stories. Furthermore, it is an effective way of making connections within and between communities, building relations and claiming identities. Given the growing familiarity of younger ESOL learners with digital technologies, the use of video media in and around classroom settings presents new and exciting opportunities in language and literacy education. This is particularly the case in relation to the affordances of video and related digital media in connecting the ESOL classroom to the lives of the learners. While the *sharing* of video clips outside classroom spaces by learners is common practice, particularly through mobile devices, the *making* of video is not yet so widespread. However, the literacy practices that video creation draws on – for instance, Internet searching for images and music, embedding code, tagging, titling, sequencing images – are already everyday social practices for many younger ESOL students. With the continuing evolution of the Internet, we are presently witnessing a shift towards video media dislodging written text online as a means of sharing information and knowledge. While print remains central to education, video and other digital media – still peripheral in this sphere – seem set on an upward trajectory in coming years.

Vignette 1: Claiming an identity in a blog

Frehiwet, an 18-year-old ESOL learner, arrived unaccompanied in the UK three years ago. Her formal schooling as a child was interrupted and intermittent: she moved between several countries in a life of migration, with limited access to education in each place. Now she finds herself living in unfamiliar surroundings, under the care of the Asylum Seeker and Refugee Team of her new city's social services department.

Frehiwet is in an Entry 2 ESOL class – that is to say she is on the second to lowest tier of the five-level curriculum ladder around which ESOL is organised. She has ambitions to gain access to further or higher education and perhaps work in a profession where she can make the most of her developing digital skills. Outside the classroom she has many friends, mainly through her participation in the community and events of her local church. Furthermore, she spends much of her free time online in virtual social networking spaces such as Facebook. In the classroom, although very conscientious and hard-working, she is somewhat marginalised. This marginalisation is partly social: most of her friends are in other classes. It also relates to her limited access to the practices of ESOL pedagogy. Because of her interrupted schooling, Frehiwet is unable to participate fully in the classroom practices that are on the whole mediated by traditional print literacies of tests, books and worksheets. Here we juxtapose descriptions of two classroom activities in which Frehiwet participated. The first activity took place in a lesson about the geography of the UK, using the ESOL and citizenship materials mentioned earlier, while the second relates to a 'photo-diary' class blogging project a few weeks later.

The first activity was a 'warmer' for a listening comprehension activity about cities in the UK. Working with a partner, Frehiwet was asked to place pieces of card labelled with city names onto a map of the UK. The students read the city names and then discussed together where on the map they should place them. After much deliberation, the two learners made a final decision as to the location of the cities, then checked with the teacher whether they were right. Out of the ten city names on the map, none were correctly placed, including the city where they lived. Frehiwet and her partner seemed demotivated by the task.

In the second activity, Frehiwet and the other students in her class were loaned digital cameras to record aspects of their lives. This project was part of wider work which involved the creation of a class blog over the academic year and as part of an additional course leading to a certificate awarded by the college (rather than externally verified). In one part of the activity, Frehiwet was selecting photos, firstly to upload to Flickr, a photo-sharing website, and then to choose some of those to add to the class blog to share with the class. While Frehiwet was finding and choosing pictures, she talked about them to the teacher and another student at the computer. She spoke at length about her friends in the pictures who had come from all over the UK to attend a special service at her church. 'These are my friends from Birmingham, Newcastle and Sheffield' she said, carefully emphasising the place names. She talked of the trips she had made to those cities to see her friends and the experiences she had had there.

Although Frehiwet has a great deal experience of people and places in the UK, in the first activity she was unable to represent this personal knowledge through a map: she has little experience of maps. In formal educational spaces, an understanding of the world through maps is often equated to a good knowledge of geography. Consequently, in this exercise Frehiwet appears unknowledgeable and even ignorant: there are few positive identity options here for her. This presents a dilemma for Frehiwet because in this case a 'knowledge of maps' is the 'powerful literacy' – it is the privileged academic one and her access to such literacies will impact on her progression through ESOL, education, employment and citizenship.

The map activity contrasts with the photo–diary task and the identity options available to her. Here she comes across as knowledgeable and sociable. What is more, she is able to reaffirm her Christian identity, which she did on many further occasions with her work on the class blog, through the sharing of images and video clips. However, the same dilemma arises: while she is able to negotiate a more positive identity position, she does so through image media that do not have high status institutionally or in policy. In terms of assessment and ultimately progression, she is able to make little use of her digital skills, her spoken language and her personal knowledge of the world.

Vignette 2: Challenging identities with digital music
The second example examines the ways a group of young migrant English language students present their shifting identities in relation to the world through the use of online digital media. The students are from around the world. Like Frehiwet, many have had little or no formal schooling, disrupted as it was by the upheavals that brought them to the UK. And like Frehiwet, some of these students find it difficult to participate in print literacy-mediated ESOL classroom practices. With their teacher's support and encouragement, the students have formed a rap group that they call GlobalEyes. Working with their teacher and others from community-based arts and educational organisations, they have learned how to make digital music. They have produced a video of one of their songs, 'Open your eyes' (which can be viewed online or downloaded at http://www.esoluk.co.uk/esol/creativity.html).

The song alternates between a chanted chorus and individual verses which are delivered as rap. The chorus goes:

> Who on Earth do you think you are
> judging people doesn't get you far
> setting styles and our cultures free
> Immigrant isn't my identity

In the video, the group perform their song in the foreground, with their image superimposed upon images that successively index globalisation and global movement of people (maps and flags); life in their city (photos and video footage of the inner-city areas where they live); the law and immigration legislation (a judge with a wig and gown); and, accompanying the final line of the chorus, a British passport (see Figure 1). The text of the chorus appears written at the top of the screen, a line at a time, as the chorus is sung.

From a language learning perspective, it seems that digital technologies have a great deal to offer the students in the class. The work involved meaningful (and 'authentic') writing practice in the writing of the song, meaningful (and 'authentic') discussion in English for the planning of

Figure 1: 'Open your eyes' by GlobalEyes

the video, collaborative endeavour (peer and teacher scaffolding) in the writing of the song, and fluency development in the practising and performing of the song. Learning via new technology has surely also helped students develop their technical digital literacy skills. In collaboration with their teacher and others in the local community, they have learned how to use an array of new technologies to record the song and the video, and how to upload it onto the Internet. Students and their teacher have found opportunities to exploit the students' digital capital. Some of these young adults might appear to be 'low-level literate' in relation to traditional classroom work but this is not necessarily reproduced in their digital work. This is not surprising, given their access to technology in the form of the Internet, their smart-phones and so on.

Most obvious in the video is the students' explicit rejection of their positioning in policy as 'immigrant' – 'immigrant isn't our identity'. But what of the identities that they are claiming? In rejecting the immigrant label, they are reconceptualising or remaking themselves, drawing upon the affordances of new technology to do so. By producing a rap song, they are claiming identities as young people who are part of global youth culture. In aligning with rap, they are invoking an international, transnational use of English. In his paper on hip-hop and authenticity, Pennycook quotes Canagarajah when discussing how a particular community of young foreign migrant language learners, in our case – 'appropriates English to dynamically negotiate meaning, identity and status in contextually suitable and socially strategic ways' (Canagarajah, 1999 in Pennycook, 2007, p. 102). The GlobalEyes students are using an English that is valued outside the class in their everyday lives, though not necessarily within institutional educational contexts.

Bringing the outside in: Some tensions

Connecting classroom practices with students' lives 'outside' has been described as 'bringing the outside in' (Baynham *et al.*, 2007; papers in Lytra and Møller, 2011). Digital technologies can offer bridges that afford such linkages. From our vignettes it certainly seems that new literacy technologies can enable students to challenge established, institutionally ratified identity positions. However, the literacies that Frehiwet and the GlobalEyes group are engaging with are quite distant from the types of literacies that are privileged institutionally and by some strata of society. Frehiwet establishes an identity position through the use and discussion of photographs on a blog. GlobalEyes reject the 'immigrant' label, using rap music and multimedia. The semiotic resources deployed seem to be of a different order from those that are valued in formal learning contexts – massively multimodal, collaborative and audience oriented (Hull, 2010) as they are.

Yet while it is clear that policy and practice position ESOL students as exam-takers, potential employees and citizens, students too might position themselves in this way. That is to say, they want to pass exams (whatever the currency of these might be), find jobs and make secure their immigration status. This being the case, how significant is their use of Web 2.0 media for identity? Is it peripheral, while the more dominant and more highly valued literacies are more central?

In the first edition of this book, Kathy Kell talked about two domains of literacy (Domain 1 and Domain 2), in her case in the context of post-apartheid South Africa. In Domain 1, 'schooled' or 'book' literacy is presented as a generic skill and is associated with incremental progression along vertical learning pathways – going up a level (cf. Baynham and Simpson, 2010). In Domain 2:

> ... *new communicative modalities are being thrown up ... oral, gestural, visual channels of communication jostle with the printed word,*

and the cell-phone ... such practices seem to show up staged and sequenced literacy pedagogics as outdated. (Kell, 2001, p. 105)

The passing of exams and citizenship tests, and the process of applying for jobs, lie in Domain 1. The practices engaged in by Frehiwet and Global-Eyes are the literacy practices of Domain 2. A central tension for pedagogy is located in the space or gap between the two. How might this tension be resolved? On the one hand teachers might start thinking about how classroom practices can utilise a range of media to enable better access to dominant and hegemonic literacies. Ultimately, though, in a digital world with which youngsters such as Frehiwet and GlobalEyes are at ease, institutional practices (and, most significantly, assessment) must start to develop a greater awareness of the role that media such as video, images and blogs can play in the education of young adult learners of ESOL.

Conclusion

We have argued that policy and institutional discourses limit students' identity options. Our examples have shown that when students are enabled through the use of new technology to claim a broader range of identity positions, their scope for language development, and identity making and remaking, likewise extends. We maintain that there is a space in pedagogy for literacy practices that can emerge at the intersection of new technology, language learning and global culture.

In summary, we hope this chapter has contributed to a growing understanding of the profoundly democratic literacy technologies associated with new media. It has pointed to a tension between identity options available to students and the emergent aspect of identity work: how identity is brought about in new literacy practices. We have problematised this by posing questions about the extent to which traditional dominant literacies will accommodate novel everyday practices.

References

Auerbach, E. (1991) 'Politics, pedagogy, and professionalism: challenging marginalization in ESL', *College ESL*, Vol. 1 No 1, pp. 1–9.

Baynham, M. and Simpson, J. (2010) 'Onwards and upwards: space, placement and liminality in adult ESOL classes', *TESOL Quarterly*, Vol. 44 No 3, pp. 420–40.

Baynham, M., Roberts, C., Cooke, M., Simpson, J. and Ananiadou, K. (2007) *Effective Teaching and Learning ESOL*. NRDC.

Blackledge, A. (2006) 'The racialization of language in British political discourse', *Critical Discourse Studies*, Vol. 3 No 1, pp. 61–79.

Bloch, J. (2007) 'Abdullah's blogging: a generation 1.5 student enters the blogosphere', *Language Learning and Technology*, Vol. 1 No 1/2, pp. 128–41 [Online] http://llt.msu.edu/vol11num2/bloch/default.html

Block, D. (2007) *Second Language Identities*. Continuum.

Blommaert, J. (2005) *Discourse*. Cambridge University Press.

Cooke, M. and Simpson, J. (2008) *ESOL: A Critical Guide*. Oxford University Press.

Cooke, M. and Simpson, J. (2009) 'Challenging agendas in ESOL: skills, employability and social cohesion, *Language Issues*, Vol. 20 No 1, pp. 19–30.

Davies, B. and Harré, R. (1990) 'Positioning: the discursive production of selves', *Journal for the Theory of Social Behaviour*, Vol. 20 No 1, pp. 43–63.

DfEE (1999) *A Fresh Start: Improving Literacy and Numeracy* (The Moser report). Department for Education and Employment, Basic Skills Agency.

Foucault, M. (1970) *The Order of Things: An Archaeology of the Human Sciences*. Tavistock.

HM Treasury (2006) *Leitch Review of Skills: Prosperity for All in the Global Economy – World Class Skills*.

Herring, S., Kouper, I., Scheidt, L. A. and Wright, E. L. (2004) 'Women and children last: the discursive construction of weblogs' in *Into the Blogosphere: Rhetoric, Community and Culture of Weblogs*, (eds) Gurak, L. J., Antonijevic, S., Ratliff, C. and Reyman, J. [Online] http://blog.lib.umn.edu/blogosphere/

Hull, G. A. (2010) 'Literate arts in a global world: reframing social networking as cosmopolitan practice', *Journal of Adolescent and Adult Literacy*, Vol. 54 No 2, pp. 85–97.

Kell, C. (2001) 'Literacy, literacies and ABET in South Africa: on the knife-edge, new cutting edge or thin end of the wedge?' in *Powerful Literacies* (first edition), (eds) Crowther, J., Hamilton, M. and Tett, L., pp. 94–107.

Lytra, V. and Møller, J. (2011) (eds), 'Bringing the outside in', *Linguistics and Education*, Special Issue, Vol. 22 No 1.

Pennycook, A. (2007) 'Language, localization, and the real: hip-hop and the global spread of authenticity', *Journal of Language, Identity and Education*, Vol. 6 No 2, pp. 101–15.

Simpson, J., Cooke, M., Callaghan, J., Hepworth, M., Homer, M., Baynham, M., Allen, T., Grant, R. and Sisimayi, S. (2011) *ESOL Neighbourhood Audit Pilot (Harehills)*. Leeds City Council/University of Leeds.

Taylor, C. (2007) *ESOL and Citizenship: A Teacher's Guide*. NIACE.

CHAPTER THIRTEEN

Using Scots[1] literacy in family literacy work

ALAN F. P. ADDISON

Introduction

In Scotland, the idea of 'voice' is of paramount importance if Scotland's citizens are to break free from the democratic deficit experienced between the life of people in communities and the policies and programmes of the state (see Martin, 1999). Scots literacy can be part of a move to develop a voice to talk back to the institutions that for so long have used a 'dominant form of literacy at the expense of those from non-mainstream cultures' (Tett and Crowther, 1998, p. 449). It is an attempt to further a spirit of dialogue between the dominant discourse and silenced voices.

Family literacy work in Edinburgh 'respects, strengthens and extends literacy practices as a powerful force for change' (Auerbach in Heywood, 2000, p. 6) and this chapter argues for the further acceptance of vernacular literacy practice as a legitimate resource and opportunity for learning. Scots literacy credits the vernacular as a force that stems from people's everyday lives (Barton and Hamilton, 1998, p. 247), from the world as it actually is, and then seeks to build on the diversity of literacy as a social practice – that is, literacy as it is embedded and used in everyday living. Its aim is to lead to the destigmatising of local literacy practices and the creation of a democratic culture in which local knowledge and experience is seen as a legitimate tool for learning.

By creating collective opportunities for families to use the vernacular legitimately, Scots literacy aims to enhance the culture within which these expressions take shape and create a space for vernacular literacy practices to be developed as positive educational resources. Scots literacy makes no attempt at silencing minority voices but celebrates the pluralistic nature of working-class communities, democratising literacy work so that the idea of 'dominant' is replaced by the idea of 'egalite' in a process that encourages the voice of marginalised groups. By so doing, Scots literacy focuses on the diversity of thought, language and world view that reflects the actual lives and experiences of children, families and community members rather than a reproduction of a constructed and imposed ideal (Tett and Crowther, 1998, p. 452).

The context

Scots literacy is part of the family literacy work developed by Edinburgh's Community Education Service. The intellectual base of the work is founded on the 'socio-contextual approach' of Auerbach (1989) which is critical of deficit and pathologising views of families that seek to develop literacy through the 'transmission of school practices' into the community. Auerbach argues instead that neglected aspects of family literacy practice include the following: parents working independently on reading and writing; using literacy to address family and community problems; parents addressing child-rearing concerns; supporting the development of a community's own language and culture; interacting with the school system (1989, p. 178). The project discussed here refers particularly to work relating to the issue of home language and culture, and its interaction with the school system. As Heywood (2000) points out, the aim of Scots literacy in Edinburgh has been to:

- encourage parents to value their own language and not subsume it to Standard English
- highlight the importance of oral language in terms of literacy and personal development
- look at aspects of oral language (e.g. storytelling, nursery rhymes, word games) and relate these to learning how to read and write (p. 28).

These aspirations have informed our attempts to develop the use of Scots literacy as a learning resource, and the following account examines aspects of this work to date. By helping people to compare and contrast their own vernacular literacies with school literacy practices, it is hoped that this can lead to a valuing and recognition of the cultural resources embedded in literacy as a social practice.

The work takes place mostly within nine primary schools in an urban working-class community, designated as an area of disadvantage. The positive aspects of this work were highlighted in an evaluation, which said 'The project has undertaken a good deal of work to generate a responsive and negotiated curriculum which builds on the literacy practices of parents' (Crowther and Tett, 1996, p. 17) but went on to say that regarding 'Scottish context and culture ... the project has some way to go' in that it failed to recognise the cultural significance of vernacular Scots. However, bearing in mind that the work takes place mostly within primary schools, institutions where the literacies of working-class communities are marginalised, and where most of our adult students learned that their language was an inferior or slang version of Standard English (McClure 1980, pp. 13–15), how could the project find the space to value vernacular Scots legitimately?

To raise awareness and sensitivity to local literacies, the project began student-led investigations that have focused on identifying literacy practices in the home and community. In an informal piece of research which asked the question: 'Dae ye speak Scots or slang?' to adult students in existing literacy groups, the repeated answer we received was, 'Ah speak slang'. These negative self-images (60–70 per cent of the 70 people questioned) became a major concern for the project. If a community perceives its means of communication and self-expression to be inferior, then how does that reflect on self-image and confidence?

The practice of family literacy in Edinburgh is committed to developing a curriculum that is built through a democratic process, sensitive to the voice of local communities. Nevertheless, we were forced to ask ourselves how we could be sure that we were negotiating democratically if the students' voices taking part in negotiations have suffered years of unconstrained, institutional delegitimisation. Surely a voice that has been subjected to constant delegitimisation cannot participate equally, particularly when faced with a common-sense view that its own 'mither tongue' (Kay, 1986) is inherently inferior.

The power of Standard English as the only legitimate language in Scottish education has been slowly diminishing in the last decade as part of a general revival and democratisation of Scottish culture. The Scottish Office Education and Industry Department (SOEID) stance has eased and provided a basis for developing Scots in the classroom (Robertson, 1996, p. 12). The suggestion in the *English Language 5–14 Guidelines* that 'Children's earliest language is acquired in the home ... and schools will build on that foundation' (SOEID, 1991, p. 3) has encouraged the production of literary devices such as *The Kist*, an anthology of literature in both Scots and Gaelic for use in schools (SCCC, 1996).

However, this acknowledgement of a diverse cultural context for language and literacy is not uniform, and Standard English is still the only means used for measuring ability, both orally and textually:

> *Language is at the centre of pupils' learning. It is through language that they gain much of their knowledge and many of their skills. High priority is, therefore, given to developing pupils' ability to use **English language** effectively [SOIED's emphasis].* (SOEID, 1994, p. 8)

On the one hand, community histories and concerns 'fostering a sense of personal and national identity' are taken account of in policy (SOEID, 1991, p. 7) and, on the other, this can often mean reducing the actual language of participants to a tartan gesture, identifying with things past, brought out to celebrate the birthday of the national bard, Robert Burns. Most modern urban dwellers would find his eighteenth-century Scots all but impossible to understand. Where Scots is acknowledged and accorded legitimacy, it is often in terms of an obsolete tradition, something past rather than present. As one primary school teacher remarked after one of our Scots sessions in her class: 'It's such a pity the real language has died away and all we're left with is slang.' Our aim is to demonstrate the relevance and the living and evolving nature of this tradition as a resource *for the present.*

As a living language, Scots is mainly absent from the curriculum of most classrooms. There are virtually no children's books for phonetic teaching of Scots in schools. The child has no formal comparisons to make when told the phoneme blend 'oo' in 'hoose' is actually 'ou' as in 'house'. Yet, according to Giegerich:

> *Scots is a group of dialects (or, it has been argued, a language) in its own right, with many lexical, syntactic, morphological and phonological features that distinguish it from Standard English.* (Giegerich, 1992, p. 46)

Scots is a language and a literacy that deserves to be named as such. According to Harris, 'Naming languages explicitly is vital' as not being specific automatically excludes and problematises speakers of British urban dialects (Harris, 1995, p 140). These non-standard voices are effectively marginalised by the cultural power of Standard English and 'the teaching of literacy can be seen, in Foucault's terms, as a process of disciplinary power in which literacies other than Standard English are delegitimated; they are accorded the status of subjugated knowledges which are partial and inadequate' (Crowther and Tett, 1997, p. 129).

By rejecting the language and literacy of the home, this disciplinary knowledge delegitimises language acquisition prior to school. Harris (1995, p. 121) believes 'these groups of learners are adversely affected by a pedagogy which ignores the linguistic properties of their natural varieties of language'. This in turn leads to what Niven and Jackson (1998, p. 57) term the 'Scottish cringe' in that the delegitimisation of the indigenous language has led Scots to wear a 'tartan chador', a veil that acts as a barrier and screen to the outside world. Bearing in mind family literacy's formal links with the dominant curriculum, the dialectic between dominant and vernacular literacies is the context for this work.

Scots literacy and the school

It can hardly be denied that school literacy embodies the language of power; a language which disadvantages working class and other excluded communities. (Tett and Crowther, 1998, p. 456)

The Scots literacy programme is co-investigating with parents, family literacy workers and schools the acceptance of Scots literacy in the school classroom. Our experience is that many classroom teachers, if they use Scots in literary terms, do so in a way that is confined to the past and is unrecognisable for people living in modern urban communities. This reproduction of 'things Scottish', however, ignores the present use of Scots by the school population. There are efforts by some teachers to link their lessons, albeit at famous anniversaries, to issues of culture and identity. However, this can often amount to tokenism unless modern-day usage of Scots is more systematically addressed and valued across the curriculum. Our own attempt to inject discussion of the use of Scots, its value and limitations, is outlined below.

The following examples are based on work carried out with adult literacy groups in the primary schools specified in the project's remit. This remit is concerned with enabling parents/carers of school pupils to be 'partners' in their child's education. Our means of doing this is to explore the relevance of Scots for both adults and pupils learning literacy.

Play production

Our first major attempt at a project was the writing and production of a school play *Everyday's a School Day* by our adult students/parents (Malcolm *et al.*, 1997). This production took six months to complete. The title represents the fact that school or learning opportunities do not merely exist within the confines of a school building between Monday and Friday. The purpose was to explore the use and implications of literacy, past and present, in school.

The structure of the play followed a simple format of a dialogue between teachers and a class of children. The teachers' scripts were written in Standard English, while the pupils in the play spoke Scots. The issue of language difference is the focus of the play.

Act 1 Scene 2

Pupil 1: We're daen one oan global warmin'.
Horace: Eh?
Pupil 1: We've got tae look efter the earth.
Horace: Does it not look efter itsel like?
Pupil 1: Naw. It's polluted.
Pupil 2: (*speaks from another group*) We're daen one aboot the moon.
Horace: (*moving to new group*) The moon's made o' cheese. (*Class laugh*)
Teacher: You must be the new boy?
Horace: (*Looking around*) Mmmm?

In the 1950s, the teacher tells the pupils to 'Speak English', while in the present the slightly more relaxed approach of the curriculum is reflected in the teacher response, 'Oh I do wish you would speak English.' In both cases, however, the results are the same and the class becomes silent. Horace, a character in the play, turns to the audience at the end and says, 'Aye ... some things huvnae changed. Ah'm no stayin here any longer'. The idea of a silent class, as an analogy with the silenced voice of the Scottish working class, was not missed by the parents involved in the production. During the writing of the play, the adult students had to address issues surrounding the use of language, its selection and significance. Vernacular literacy practices were used in the text and a comparison of Scots with Standard English took place as, for the first time, the parents came to terms with transcribing their own pattern of speaking. Both the head and other teachers of the school agreed that it was a work of some standard and could be used as a literacy learning aid as well as a dramatic entertainment for the whole school, including parents.

The Scots literacy tackled in the play is based more on oral language than on school texts. Most of the learning achieved by the parents stemmed from their own knowledge. The parents had tackled the issue of literacy, comparing and contrasting Standard English with Scots. By contextualising their arguments within the curriculum, the parents had used their knowledge to start a debate between dominant and vernacular literacies.

Magazine production

> I wis brought up an atheist. Neither Ma or Dad, sisters or brothers went tae church. So ah went oan tae grow up withoot any faith ither than whit ah saw in front o' me in ma day tae day life. No that many years ago ma family wir involved in a drastic accident an' ma youngest son wis left at death's door in the Sick Kids fir months. I kent what prayers wir then! An' a' these folk wir comin' tae see us. A' these religious folk whae ah'd always thought wir oan anither planet. An' they prayed wie us night an' day ... ('Becoming a Christian', in Family Allsorts, Ahmed et al., 1999)

Following on from the success of the play, parents in another primary school decided to produce an educational magazine for their community. This was an opportunity not only to highlight their own vernacular knowledge but also to widen the debate surrounding the question of language legitimacy – that is, should their knowledge be transcribed in Scots or should the medium be Standard English?

Some very complex issues soon arose for the project, however, in that not all the participants in this group were Scots: there were Bangladeshi, Punjabi, Chinese and English people, and only three (myself included) who were Scots speakers. Standard English was the literacy medium shared by us all. The composition of the group meant that vernacular literacy practices were diverse and Scots could not assume a priority in a pluralistic and more open idea of identities. The 'new' Scotland is a multicultural one and the magazine would have to reflect that diversity. To reach as many folk as possible, the magazine group chose to draw upon the diverse knowledge of the different members of the group and the wider community. Different languages were used in the text, with translations, but the common denominator of Standard English was also included.

During production of the magazine, *Family Allsorts* (Ahmed *et al.*, 1999), all the languages of the group were discussed, compared, recorded and 'named'. The different phonetic symbols, grammatical structures and meaning representations were compared and contrasted, shifting the literacy awareness of all of us to a more global perspective, while the eventual content of *Allsorts* reflected a diversity of knowledge. By choosing *not* to write mainly in Scots, the group had shown a willingness to engage with all expressions of language equally. Dominant value structures, associated with literacy teaching, were overshadowed by that willingness to engage with all forms of knowledge in a meaningful, egalitarian way.

The second edition of *Allsorts* will focus more closely on the diversity of literacy and language that exists in the community. More textual space will be given to Scots and other languages, with Standard English used more for translation purposes within the extended glossary. The radical nature of this work, continually engaging with the cultural dialectic between dominant and vernacular literacy, has led to a wish to link with other marginalised cultures to begin a process of sharing experience. For this reason we shall be exploring the possibilities of going online with the magazine.

Poetry recital programme

This programme involves parents and family literacy tutors writing and reciting poetry to primary school children within their curriculum, as part of a dramatic dialogue. We have done this in five schools across all age groups of pupils. The main focus of the programme is to legitimise present-day vernacular Scots language amongst school children or, more hopefully, to get them to think and question why their own natural ways of speaking are not overtly addressed in the curriculum. After we have performed the recitals, we ask the pupils if they could write for us. When asked if they would write in their own way, they are told not to be 'feert tae stick in a bit o' French if you like', as a means of democratising literacy awareness.

> ### Scots in space
> *Come in Earthling!*
> *we are from the planet Mars,*
> *Travelling from the universe*
> *In search of distant stars*

Away an bile yer heid!
Wir too busy fir a blether
Tourin the earth at speed
Tae get away fae wir awfie weather

Our on-board spell check is searching
To decipher your language ... so strange
It keeps coming up NOT KNOWN
This language is not in its range

(Poetry Recital Programme 1)

To open the literacy debate in the classroom, the stanzas above involve two 'voices' which have characters using vernacular Scots and Standard English. This eventually results in a breakdown of communication. After the readings, the children are asked about the cause of the communication problems and what they think should be done. Thus, the school classroom has become the centre of a cultural debate, focused on the legitimacy of language dominance and on the problems this creates. Teachers are asked to fill in an evaluation form after the sessions and so far most responses have been positive.

Having aimed our programme directly at the school curriculum, we then invited the parents of the children to discuss the topic. This is a very delicate situation indeed. Centuries of language oppression have led to a great many people believing their language to be educationally irrelevant, if not barbaric (Beveridge and Turnbull, 1989, p. 6). Many see Standard English as the only language in which to couch their aspirations.

The parents' sessions are structured into a question and answer format as to whether Scots literacy is legitimate or not. The majority at the start believe it to be irrelevant. What is promising, nonetheless, is that parents do come along to the sessions and are interested in what is going on in the curriculum. After questions and answers, Scots literacy students and tutors give a short session on the history of Scots, using language maps, *The Kist* and *A Glasgow Bible* (Stuart, 1997) as examples of Scots texts. The *Chambers Scots Dictionary* (Warrack, 1993) and the *Scoor-oot: Dictionary of Scots Words and Phrases in Current Use* (Stevenson, 1989) are on hand to legitimise the language as lexicographical. On completion of this history, we then ask how people feel about the legitimacy of Scots, now that it has been given a context. Many people are genuinely surprised that their language has a history at all, 'Ah thoucht Ah'd find the

217

bit in history where we started turnin English intae slang', as one parent put it. However, as another ironically stated, 'Whit's the point when we're tryin tae git them tae stoap speakin like that?' As we have discovered through our research, the inferiorisms experienced by the community are deep rooted and must be approached tactfully. More importantly, our programme does not seek 'to advance the position that people be denied access to dominant literacies or that their own vernacular literacy is somehow privileged' (Crowther and Tett, 1998, p. 456).

The important gain made by the above sessions is not that pupils or parents suddenly feel liberated to use their vernacular Scots more openly, but that more people are becoming involved in thinking critically about literacy and their own educational experiences of learning it. Ideas of bilingualism – that is, Scots/Standard English, as opposed to slang/Standard English – have entered the debate and are indicative of a shift in thinking. Participants are willing to compare and contrast their language with that of other cultures. One parent, when asked whether they would come to another session, replied 'Aye,' reflected for a second then added, 'It's a'right fir me tae say that eh!' This is perhaps one of the most important aspects of Scots literacy in that it can encourage a re-reading of the student's words which, in turn, can contribute to a re-reading of their world (Freire and Macedo, 1987). Language that has recently been taken as inferior and inadequate may become accepted as a language of learning and an educational resource rather than a cultural embarrassment.

Conclusion

No doubt, Standard English will continue to be the main focus of the curriculum in schools and the language of aspiration for many in Scotland and, no doubt, working-class communities will continually be made to feel inferior. However, because we cannot change everything does not mean that we cannot contribute to changing some things and our aim is to continue to argue for a pedagogy that engages with the powerful values embedded in the dominant form of literacy teaching.

From a perspective of working with the grain of cultural experience rather than against it, as seems to happen in much of schooling, our programme on Scots literacy historicises (realistically) present-day vernacular Scots and seeks to legitimise voices that have been ridiculed and silenced. Scots literacy is one attempt to free student voices from stigma so that more democratic curriculum negotiations can take place between adult students and educators. In Gramsci's terms, it is anti-hegemonic in that it refuses to accept the dominant value system as the only way of making sense of the world (Hoare and Smith, 1998, p. 12). Using Scots literacy is also part of the new powerful literacies debate which engages with real experiences of literacies in use and which recognises that there are many forms literacy can take, not just one. It argues for the use of 'vernacular literacies' and highlights their importance as sources of knowledge – particularly if literacy is to be recognised as more than an ability to decode the alphabet. Scots literacy, from this perspective, serves to initiate, organise, justify and support action from voices normally unheard.

Note on Scots

[1] Scotland has two distinctive indigenous languages, Scots and Gaelic. Gaelic (Gaidhlig, pronounced 'Gallic') is the older of the two, a Q-Celtic language that came to Scotland with the arrival of the Irish people who set up the kingdom of Dalriada. From the fifth to the twelfth centuries, Gaelic was spoken across the whole of Scotland and only entered decline after the establishment of the Anglo-Norman feudal system.

Scots is a sister language of English that developed alongside the process of 'Normanisation' which spread English across the country as the language of law and court. During the period of independence from England, Scots developed different linguistic traits as the link with English language development was broken and more European influences developed. Heywood says that:

> Rural varieties of modern-day Scots are romanticised and often treated as the 'real thing'. Literary Scots, used in poetry and prose, is often also highly valued, although some linguists would argue its conventions are synthetically generated. The least valued variety of Scots is the language of the urban working class, which is frequently regarded as vulgar Scots ... We use the term Scots throughout ... to refer to all varieties of Scots, so that we avoid lending weight to educationally and socially divisive notions that treat the language of urban, working-class Scotland as vulgar Scots or even 'corrupt' English. (Heywood, 2000, p. 5)

There are now some 80,000 native Gaelic speakers in Scotland who have fought hard for the survival of the language. With Gaelic-medium education and broadcasting on the increase, there is hope that the language can grow and expand. There is a large percentage of the population that currently speak Scots, but there is continued debate about its validity as a language. New initiatives in schools and in writing have given the Scots language new vigour and the development of the Scots Language Development Centre bodes well for its future.

Thanks to

Ah wid like tae thank aw the folk, parents an carers, whae gie sae much o' their time tae help us tae develop oor praxis [theory and practice thegither]. In particular, Cathy Ahmed fir her idea o' *Allsorts*; Helen Cluness fir daen sae much o' the hard slog (an her faimily fir pittin up wie it); Susan Glancy fir keepin me right aboot China; an Vicky Poon fir keepin me right aboot anither China; Dalbir Singh fir her comparisons o' Scots wie Punjabi; Michael Sufoux fir bringin aw they leids fae Africa; Cass Malcolm – the 'light' o' *School Days*; Liz Young fir her braw East Lothian Scots; an Brian Robertson fir a much-needed community activist perspective. Ah wid also like tae thank Jimmy Donald an Michelle McDougall, family literacy tutors extraordinaire. Ma special thanks goes tae Dr John Mackie fir aw his correspondence oan oor Scots leid.

References

Ahmed, C., Cluness, H., Glancy, S. and Singh, D. (eds) (1999) *Family Allsorts: the magazine for all sort o' folk*. North Edinburgh: Community Publishing.

Auerbach, E. (1989) 'Towards a social contextual approach to family literacy', *Harvard Educational Review*, Vol. 59 No 2, pp. 165–87.

Barton, D. and Hamilton, M. (1998) *Local Literacies*. Routledge.

Beveridge, C. and Turnbull, R. (1989) *The Eclipse of Scottish Culture*. Polygon.

Crowther, J. and Tett, L. (1996) *Family Literacy: Evaluation of the Connect Project*. Moray House Institute, University of Edinburgh.

Crowther, J. and Tett, L. (1997) 'Inferiorism in Scotland: the politics of literacy north of the border' in *Crossing Borders, Breaking Boundaries*, (eds) Armstrong, P., Miller, N. and Zukas, M., 27th Annual SCUTREA Conference Proceedings, pp. 126–30.

Freire, P. and Macedo, D. (1987) *Literacy: Reading the Word and the World*. Routledge.

Giegerich, H. J. (1992) *English Phonology: An Introduction*. Cambridge University Press.

Harris, R. (1995) 'Disappearing language: fragments and fractures between speech and writing', in *Literacy Language and Community Publishing: Essays in Adult Education*, (ed.) Mace, J., pp. 118–44. Multilingual Matters.

Heywood, J. (ed.) (2000) *Involving Parents in Early Literacy*. City of Edinburgh, Education Department.

Hoare, Q. and Smith, G. N. (1998) *Antonio Gramsci: Selections from the Prison Notebooks*. Lawrence and Wishart.

Kay, B. (1986) *The Mither Tongue*. Mainstream Publishing.

McClure D. J. (1988) *Why Scots Matters*. Saltire Society.

Malcolm, C., Robertson, B. and Young, E. (1997) *Every Day's a School Day*. North Edinburgh: Community Publishing.

Martin, I. (1999) 'Introductory essay: popular education and social movements in Scotland today' in *Popular Education and Social Movements in Scotland Today*, (eds) Crowther, J., Martin, I. and Shaw, M., pp. 1–28. NIACE.

Mayo, P. (1999) *Gramsci, Freire & Adult Education: Possibilities for Transformative Action*. Zed Books.

Niven, L. and Jackson, R. (eds) (1998) *The Scots Language: Its Place in Education*. Watergaw.

SCCC (Scottish Consultative Council on the Curriculum) (1996) *The Kist, Teachers' Handbook*. Glasgow: Nelson Blackie.

SOEID (1991) 5–14 *English in the Curriculum*, Scottish Office Education and Industry Department. HMSO.

SOEID (1994) *Education 5–14: A Guide for Parents*. HMSO.

Stevenson, J. A. C. and Macleod, I. (1989) *Scoor-oot: A Dictionary of Scots Words and Phrases in Current Use*. Athlone Press.

Stuart, J. (1997) *A Glasgow Bible*. St. Andrew Press.

Tett, L. and Crowther, J. (1998) 'Families at a disadvantage: class, culture and literacies', *British Educational Research Journal*, Vol. 24 No 4, pp. 449–60.

Warrack, A. (1993) *Chambers Scots Dictionary*. Edinburgh: Chambers Harrap.

Contributors

Alan Addison
Graduated as a carpenter and, much later, in English Literature. He returned to work as a family literacy tutor in North Edinburgh, the place of his birth, cultural learning and setting for his chapter.

Tannis Atkinson
Worked as an adult literacy educator and plain language editor for many years before commencing doctoral studies at the Ontario Institute for Studies in Education of the University of Toronto. She is founding editor of *Literacies*, the Canadian journal published 2003–2009 that linked research and practice in adult basic education.

Amy Burgess
A research fellow in the Graduate School of Education, Exeter University. Her research and publications focus on adults learning literacies, both inside and outside educational settings. She is particularly interested in issues of writing and identity. She is currently Chair of RaPAL (Research and Practice in Adult Literacy).

Jim Crowther
A Senior Lecturer in Adult and Community Education at the University of Edinburgh. Prior to his academic post he was a tutor and organiser of adult literacy in Edinburgh. He currently researches and writes on adult literacy, popular education and the politics of policy. He is the editor of *Studies in the Education of Adults*.

Maggie Feeley

Has worked in adult literacy in Ireland since the 1980s and has a particular interest in innovation, advocacy and research. She teaches about education and equality in a number of third level institutions, and is a senior post-doctoral research fellow in the School of Social Justice, University College, Dublin.

Malini Ghose

A founder member of Nirantar, a resource centre for gender and education in New Delhi, India. She has worked in the fields of literacy, education and women's rights for over 20 years as a practitioner, researcher and advocate.

Richard Gresswell

An English language teaching consultant, research student and ESOL teacher. He is very interested in the use of digital media in language and literacy education, particularly in relation to the construction of learner and teacher identity in online spaces.

Mary Hamilton

A Professor of Adult Learning and Literacy in the Department of Educational Research at Lancaster University. She is a founder member of RaPAL. She researches and writes in the areas of literacy policy and governance, practitioner enquiry, and everyday literacy practices and change.

Judy Hunter

A senior lecturer and coordinator of the Adult Literacy and Numeracy Education Diploma programme at the University of Waikato, NZ. Her research focuses on language and literacy practices in workplace, educational and health settings. She is co-author of *Reading Work: Literacies in the New Workplace* with the In-Sites Research Group.

Jane Mace

Has been teaching, training and writing about literacy and adult life since the mid-1970s. She was a founder member of the Write First Time collective (which, for ten years, published adult literacy student writing) and of the still-lively RaPAL. Research for her most recent book *The Give and Take of Writing: Scribes, Literacy and Everyday Life*

(NIACE, 2002) led her to a current interest in Quaker uses of literacy and approaches to clerking business meetings in a religious setting.

Disha Mullick

Has worked as a project coordinator at Nirantar, a resource centre for gender and education in New Delhi, India, for the past five years. She has been primarily involved in training and support for the Khabar Lahariya project, and workshops on new media and in research work on gender and education.

John Player

Has been a community worker in urban Scotland for 30 years. He has been based with the Adult Learning Project (ALP) in Edinburgh for ten years, and has recently carried out research into the impact of the Glory and Dismay Football Literacy Programme (GDFLP) on hard-to-reach adult learners. He is currently researching how neo-liberalism plays out in concrete ways in Scotland, focusing on The Royal Bank of Scotland (RBS) and Glencore International plc.

James Simpson

A lecturer in the School of Education, University of Leeds. His interests include literacy studies and the teaching of English to speakers of other languages. He is the co-author, with Melanie Cook, of *ESOL: A Critical Guide* (OUP, 2008) and the editor of *The Routledge Handbook of Applied Linguistics* (Routledge, 2011).

Brian Street

An Emeritus Professor of Language in Education at King's College, London and Visiting Professor in the Graduate School of Education, University of Pennsylvania. He has a commitment to linking ethnographic-style research on the cultural dimension of language and literacy with contemporary practice in education and development. He has published 18 books and 120 scholarly papers.

Lyn Tett

A Professor of Community Education at the University of Huddersfield and Emeritus Professor at the University of Edinburgh. She has been involved in literacies work since 1978, initially as a practitioner, then as a policy implementer and now as a researcher. Her research in literacies focuses on its role in challenging the processes of social exclusion.

Karin Tusting
A lecturer in the Department of Linguistics and English Language, Lancaster University, where she is an active member of the Literacy Research Centre. She has published on literacy studies, linguistic ethnography and communities of practice, and has a particular interest in the role of paperwork in people's working practices.

Sandra Varey
A postgraduate research student in the Department of Educational Research, Lancaster University. Sandra has previously taught adult literacy, and her doctoral research focuses on two different representations of adult literacy learners: their biographical narratives, compiled from life history interview data, and their individual learning plan (ILP) paperwork.

Index

accountability requirements 2, 8, 50, 76
  see also statistics
accreditation frameworks 38, 47, 48, 49,
  105, 142
Addison, Alan 11, 209–21
Adult Learning Project, Edinburgh
  180–90
affective dimension of literacy 9, 131–46
  see also learning care
Atkinson, Tannis 7, 75–87
audit culture 2, 8, 33, 105, 115
Australia 52, 143
authorial selves 89, 92, 97–101
autonomous model of literacy 16, 18, 20

Basic Skills Agency (BSA) 37
Basic Skills Cymru 38
'basics' 26, 27
bell curve 78, 81
big society 120
blogging 199, 200–2
Bourdieu, Pierre 20, 21
Burgess, Amy 7–8, 89–103

Canada 7, 79–80, 82, 106, 143
citizenship 8, 117–28
  active 52, 121
  as ascribed status 120
  as asserted practice 120, 121, 125
  citizenship test 198
  civic education 119
  civil rights 119
  discourses of 119–23
  dominant policy discourses, contesting
  127
  duties 119, 122
  ESOL students 197–8
  political identity 120

political rights 119
social identity 120
social rights 119–20
  see also democracy
Coalition Government policies 45, 119,
  197
collaborative approach to learning 136,
  140, 141
communities of interest 9, 136
Community Learning Strategy
  Partnerships 40
community-based initiatives 34, 39, 43,
  45, 48, 52, 202
computer literacy 25
confidence, developing 91, 94, 100–1,
  158, 159
conscientisation 148, 187, 188
critical literacy 5, 20, 26, 125, 180, 184–7,
  188, 189
Crowther, Jim 8, 117–28
cultural identity 143, 190
cultural literacy 20, 25, 125, 209–21
cultural politics 11, 209–21

Davie, George 124
decodification 180, 190
deficit model of literacy 2–3, 5, 8, 9, 46,
  84, 92, 96, 118, 119, 189, 193, 211
delegitimisation of voices 211, 213, 218
democracy 8–9, 117–28
  democratisation of media 149, 154
  extending and deepening 118
  in the new work order 22–3
  political literacy education 123–6
  see also citizenship
democratic intellectualism 124
democratic literacy technologies 4, 205,
  209, 210, 218–19

227

Index